Mugletonian Celestial Harmonies and Divine Songs

Edited by Mike Pettit

Visit us online at www.muggletonianpress.com **and
view our entire range of Muggletonian Literature**

A Muggletonian Press Book

Copyright © Mike Pettit 2010

All rights reserved. No portion of this publication may be reproduced, stored in a retrieval system, or transmitted in any form or by any means, electronic, mechanical, photocopy, recording or otherwise, without prior written permission of the copyright owner. While many of the original texts which form the basis of this publication are to be found in the public domain the texts found herein have been typographically modernised and reformatted at great expense. Please respect the resulting copyright that such work has created.

ISBN 978-1-907466-03-8

Cover Image: J. Kennerley engraving commissioned by Joseph & Isaac Frost that was attached to the 1829 edition of "Divine Songs of the Muggletonians"

Published by:
Muggletonian Press
129 Hebdon Road
London SW17 7NL
England

I would like to make it clear that in editing and publishing this volume I am not seeking to advocate any element of *Muggletonian* theology. I fully subscribe to historic orthodox Christianity as expressed in the Reformed Confessions of Faith and would plead with all the readers of this work to consider the claims of the triune God.

From the Heidelberg Catechism

Question 6. Did God then create man so wicked and perverse?

Answer: By no means; but God created man good, and after his own image, in true righteousness and holiness, that he might rightly know God his Creator, heartily love him and live with him in eternal happiness to glorify and praise him.

Question 7. Whence then proceeds this depravity of human nature?

Answer: From the fall and disobedience of our first parents, Adam and Eve, in Paradise; hence our nature is become so corrupt, that we are all conceived and born in sin.

Question 8. Are we then so corrupt that we are wholly incapable of doing any good, and inclined to all wickedness?

Answer: Indeed we are; except we are regenerated by the Spirit of God.

Mike Pettit

CONTENTS

	Page
Introduction.	5
Celestial Harmony, or Songs of Grateful Praise.	7
Divine Songs of the Muggletonians.	59

INTRODUCTION

One thing that is certain is that the Muggletonians loved their hymns, whenever a Muggletonian meeting is documented there is usually a mention of hymn singing. When they met up in ale houses they did so at least partly to sing together, often renting special cupboards in the ale houses in which to store their hymn books and other paraphanalia.

In his 1869 paper Alexander Gordon, entitled "Ancient and Modern Muggletonians", recorded the his views on this subject as follows:

> "It will not do to forget, in this connection, the collection of Divine Songs, or Songbook, as it is familiarly called, which supplies to them the place of a collection of hymns, and indeed is the only approach to a devotional manual. For while prayer is by them eschewed, songs of gratitude and thanksgiving are deemed lawful, though by no means incumbent upon any believer who may think them savouring too much of the exploded idea of worship. Collections of these Songs were circulated in manuscript from the earliest days of the sect, many of them having been written by the immediate followers of Muggleton. A great number of these manuscript collections are still preserved by the body; several of them being in the autograph of the composers. The first mention of a printed Songbook in the records of the body, is on the 16th February, 1794; many entries of the sale of the volume are to be met with up to 14th August, 1796. No copy of this book has fallen in the present writer's way; it seems, from a letter of James Frost, 29th March, 1812, that it was not executed at the expense of the body, but "made a present of to the church by a printer." The church, however, compiled in 1829 the collection at present in use. It consists of two hundred and twenty-eight Songs, all by Muggletonian authors, and a good number of them expressly written for the collection. The largest contributor is Boyer Glover, a London watch-and-clockmaker, who may be deemed the poet of the Muggletonians. His name first occurs in their records in 1771. He contributes forty-nine Songs. James Miller (who wrote between 1730 and 1750), follows with twenty-seven. There are one or two by John Nicholls, a musician, who

"played on the Lord Mayor's Day and in the waits," who died, old and helpless, about 1745, and through whom the only fragment that exists in John Reeve's autograph came into the possession of the body. The earliest Song-writers seem to be Thomas Turner, John Ladd, William Wood, Elizabeth Goodwin, and Elizabeth Henn. Thomas Tomkinson also tried his hand at verse composition."

This volume combines the texts of the very rare 1794 "Songs of Grateful Praise" with the larger but slightly more common 1829 "Divine Songs of the Muggletonians".

The Muggletonians used these hymns to express their unique theology, for example verse 4 of the twelfth hymn in "Songs of Grateful Praise" contains expositions of the two seeds doctrine the immediate notice doctrine and the physical nature of God doctrine

> "The Devils of us do complain,
> We know they are the Sons of Cain;
> And all their Prayers are in vain,
> For their God cannot hear them;
> He has no Ears how should be hear,
> His formless Ghost cannot appear;
> For this strange God they must pay dear,
> Therefore let us not fear them."

These hymns filled the void left by the Muggletonian rejection of prayer and worship, and as such they represent the theology of the common members of the Church.

CELESTIAL HARMONY,

OR

Songs of grateful Praise,

TO THE

EVER BLESSED GLORIOUS

KING or SAINTS,

AND

MERCIFUL IMMORTAL GOD,

our

LORD JESUS CHRIST.

Then let all Saints in Raptures join.
With joyful Souls to snake a Choir;
To praise the GOD of our Salvation,
Who did first your Souls inspire.

William Wood, of Braintree

M,DCC,XCIV,

CONTENTS.

In sixteen Hundred, fifty and one	9
Happy Muggletonians who only	11
O Christ our Saviour	14
Ye brave Sons of Adam	15
How happy is every Believer	16
Love with unconfined Wings	18
Come all you thirsty Souls that's dry	20
Ask me not whence all this Joy	23
Once a Captive in Egypt I was	25
O Christ eternal God alone	28
Hail! Hail! two Prophets great	32
Now will I rejoice and sing	35
When I view my God's Creation	37
When first the Truth I heard	39
Now no more may Monsters boast	40
An uncreated Essence	42
Come raptur'd Souls rejoyce and sing	44
Curst Serpents often bruis'd	45
O Come my Friends and join with me	48
Why should I make Freedom a Slave	50
Who comes here	52
O God of all Gods and Prince of all Peace	54
Eternal Life it is to me	57

SONGS

Of Grateful Praise to the

EVER BLESSED, GLORIOUS KING of SAINTS

And MERCIFUL IMMORTAL GOD,

Our LORD JESUS CHRIST,

(Tune, *De'el take the Wars*)

I.

In Sixteen hundred fifty and one,
This Morning GOD did Freedom proclaim,
CHRIST did declare, himself GOD ALONE;
Unto his Ambassador John Reeve by Name:
Lodowick Muggleton was also included,
Wisdom to the Elect to make known,
Shewing how Reason, is utterly excluded,
From the eternal JEHOVAH's Throne;
True, Saints now Milk and Honey,
Can purchase without Money,
GOD's Blood the Cordial good,
Doth cleanse them pure within
They are the Friends of GOD,
Saved in this last Record,
Which is a fenced Wall,
Protecting from all Thrall;
And such as it environs are free from Sin.

II.

Christal Streams transparent swift proceeding,
Front the Rock in mount Zion Laid,
Giving a brightness reason far exceeding;
Into his chosen this Day was conveyed:

The upper Springs of rapid inspiration,
Like Golden Oil most Sweetly did glide
Filling the nether Springs with deep Revelation;
Which well in the Valley will ever abide.
Darkness swiftly Flying
Light its room Supplying,
His mind was refined above the rest of Man;
What Moses veil concealed,
Was now to him revealed
This was a Glorious Day,
When faith bore all the sway,
And Heavens Gate was set open for Men.

III.

We are free from Task Masters rescued,
A Yoke which our fore Fathers Wore;
With Canaans Language we're greatly endned,
More than SAINTS who lived here to fore;
Our Souls sore distressed by the Streams of Bable.
Sat Weeping while Darkness did us surround,
To gain Relief none on this Earth was able,
Til the third Record we found:
Here grace true Light free offered,
And hearing likewise profered;
Free Grace did release us from the bond of Woe,
What we deserved to Feel.
Was bruised in CHRIST's Heel,
Even Jeshanun's mighty GOD,
Who left divine abode.
To Die for poor Sinners his seed below.

IV.

Behold O ye faithful how your GOD tremendous,
For you exerted his infinite Power,
When Dying freely from ruin to rend us;
Did all Power of death devour.
Then did he enter O death thy dark pavilion.
And by a Power superior Far,
He conquered the Keys of thy vast Dominion,
Which proved him the mighty Man of War.
This the Freedom founded,

In which our Souls are grounded.
His Life atoned our strife to Death's all conquering Law
In Concert joyn your lays,
On these three happy Days,
And Joyfull let us be,
Since great Eternity;
Did dye for his seed when condemned by Law.

V.

Then Hallalujah Glory be to JESUS,
Hosanna Sing to our crucified GOD,
The great deliverer from Death did release us;
And from the Serpent's devouring Rod.
All he requires is only Love each other,
Those that offend rebuke in Love,
Faiths Life depends on Love to its Brother,
Love is the nature of GOD above,
His last great authorised,
Of his coming us apprised.
The signs of the times declare him at the door,
Then rest my Soul in peace.
Waiting the grand release
For you are sure to Sing,
To CHRIST your glorious King.
In sweet Hallelujahs when times no more.

J. PEAT.

Second SONG.

I.

Happy Muggletonians who only,
True faith have to receive,
Revelation ever new;
Gave to great Muggleton and Reeve.
Which makes us to CHRIST our King,
Sweet Hallelujahs ever Sing.

II.

No more now we seek for rest,
Or wander up and down in strife,
Faith gives Peace and peace possest;
Assures of eternal Life,
Which makes us to CHRIST our King,
Sweet Hallelujah s ever Sing.

III.

The bread of Life, the very GOD,
By faith we now can plainly see,
Which does sweet content afford;
And fills us with satiety.
Which makes us to CHRIST our King,
Sweet Hallelujahs ever Sing.

IV.

The living Water too we've found.
Which does our thirsty souls suffice,
Faith the balm has cured our wounds;
The spring from whence all Joys arise.
Which makes us to CHRIST our King.
Sweet Hallelujahs ever Sing.

V.

His free grace we will adore,
Each sitting under his own Vine,
Praises giving ever more;
Since we shall share in Joys divine.
And to CHRIST our gracious King.
Sweet Hallelujahs ever Sing.

VI.

How shall we enough declare,
O GOD thy vast unbounded Love,
When thou didst in CHRIST appear;
And left Mankind thy GOD above,
Wee'l to thee most gracious King,

Sweet Hallelujahs, ever Sing.

VII.

This mystery the World cannot know,
Nor we it fully comprehend,
What GOD in Man did undergo,
O CHRIST our Saviour, GOD and Friend.
Wee'l to thee most gracious King.
Sweet Hallelujahs ever Sing.

VIII.

No other GOD wee'l ever own,
No other Majesty adore,
Thou art the self existing one,
GOD Man, Man GOD for ever more.
Wee'l to thee most gracious King,
Sweet Hallelujahs ever Sing.

IX.

O Father Son and Holy Ghost,
Triune in Titles, never three,
Lord Jesus CHRIST denyed by most;
Is this hid sacred mystery
God and Everlasting King,
To whom wee'l Hallelujahs sing.

X.

This is the Muggletonians Faith,
This is the GOD which we believe,
None salvation knowledge hath;
But those of Muggleton and Reeve.
CHRIST is the Muggletonians King.
With whom eternally they'l sing.

James Miller.

Third SONG.

I.

O CHRIST our Saviour.
Tis our endeavour,
In time and ever.
Thee to adore.
What but Faith can behold,
Those glorious crowns of Gold
Which GOD will unfold,
When times no more.

II.

See the skys rending,
And Faiths ascending,
Angels attending
In Clouds above
While reason here below,
Opens their Eyes in woe,
Torments to undergo,
And never move.

III.

While faith with faith will rise,
Above the falling Skys,
Entering to endless Joys.
Which nee'r will cease.
In Odes of endless Love,
As we to Heaven move,
Which GOD shall sing above,
In perfect Peace.

James Miller

Fourth SONG.

Made on William Ringer, Robert Ingram and Edmund Toulman receiving the Truth,

(Tune *The Lillies of France,*)

I.

Ye brave Sons of Adam your Voices now raise,
  To our great Creator the Theme of our Praise;
For the joyfull Tydings which we have receiv'd,
  By the Third Commission in which we believe,
Then let us all join in Chorus that only believe,
  In the Declaration of Muggleton and Reeve.

II.

In seventeen hundred and ninety the Year,
  This glorious Truth unto us did appear;
On the Twenty eighth of March was the Day,
  That in our poor Hearts did these Glories display,
Which makes us join in Chorus and truly believe,
  In the Declaration of Muggleton and Reeve.

III.

We long Time in Bondage was held but thro' Fear,
  Our Hearts they were kept quite from utter dispair.
And when the glad Tidings to us it did come
  With inward Rejoicings we spy'd out our Doom,
Of eternal Salvation we freely believe,
  Through the Declaration of Muggleton and Reeve.

IV.

No Mortals on Earth, are so happy as we,
  Our Pardon is seal'd our Salvation we see.
Through the Blood of our God which we freely drink
  And those that dispise shall eternally sink,
Who through strong Opposition do quite disbelieve
  In the Declaration of Muggleton and Reeve.

V.

The Mystery of God is to us now reveal'd,
  Which to Prophets and Apostles in part lay conceal'd
Till the seventh Angel by which we have found,
  In John's Revelation began for to sound;
Then came forth the glad Tidings to us that believe,
  In the Declaration of Muggleton and Reeve.

VI.

With Patience we wait till the Time it do come,
  When Jesus our God he will bid us come home,
The new Kingdom to enter which he has prepar'd.
  Which he by his Prophets have often declared,
And for us that in the third Commission believe,
  In the Declaration of Muggleton and Reeve.

Robert Ingram

Fifth SONG.

(Tune The Tars for all Weathers)

How happy is every Believer
  Under this Third and last Record,
No priestcraft nor fleshly Deceiver,
  Who cries out aloud from the Word
Can knock down that Peace which we carry,
  Whilst we thro' this Wilderness pass;
Can frighten our Spirits or hurry.
  Our Souls for to feed on the Dross,
Chorus. So with Praises we'l sing to JEHOVAH,
  Who did REEVE and MUGGLETON send
  His Mystery on Earth for to finish,
  Our SHEPHERD, our BRIDEGROOM and FRIEND,
  Our SHEPHERD, our BRIDEGROOM and FRIEND

II.

The Men of the world they do wonder,
  That we our Number so small,
They with one another do ponder,
  Because we their Spirits do gall.
Shoul'd be possessed with the great Mystery,
  That none but ELECT People know,
And understand the sacred History,
  They grudge our true peace here below.
    Cho. So with Praises, &c.

III.

Tho Reason in man, do imagine,
  That we in Delusions are led,
We know that JEHOVAH in that Line,
  Where he has his last Prophets fed,
In Record the third we rejoice in,
  Because there our GOD we have found,
Through Faith our Salvation we do win,
  While we live on this earthly Ground.
    Cho. So with Praises, &c.

IV.

Altho' the dry dust must us inclose,
  When Death shall our Lives take away,
Our Bodies and Souls they will there dose,
  Till Morn of the eternal Day,
When Adam and all his dear Children,
  Will rise in a glorified state,
To Joys that no Saint could ever pen,
  We know it is our happy Fate.
    Cho. So with Praises, &c.

ROBERT INGRAM.

Sixth SONG.

I.

Love with unconfined Wings,
  Hovers within my Breast;
And by divine revelation brings,
  My Soul true Peace and rest,
As I was musing by my Faith,
  On pure Eternity,
I Find no Monarch on this Earth,
  Enjoys Such Liberty.

II.

By Faith I now have truly found,
  The Worship God requires;
Obedience is the perfect Ground
  By which my Heart's inspired,
Rejoyce therefore my mortal Soul,
  That thou dost live to see
That no man living can controul,
  This perfect Liberty.

III.

There's many men hath riches store
  Yet are so worldly bent,
Though they have much they crave for more
  And never are content:
But I that am the poorest of all,
  From Worldly Cares are free,
Which makes me know they live in thrall,
  And I at Liberty,

IV.

'Tis neither Pardon from the Pope,
  Nor Prayers made to Saints,
That I do value no nor hope,
  Nor ever make Complaint,
Tis Christ above the Lord of Love,

That for true Saints did Die,
Tis only he has pardoned me
  And gave me Liberty.

V.

By Faith and Patience now my Guide,
  My Conscience is made clear;
And now the Lord is on my side
  I need no foes to fear,
I neither fear the Stroke of Death
  Nor Devils Tyranny,
But Freely can resign my Breath
  For perfect Liberty.

VI.

Patience that Virtue is so pure
  It waiteth for the Change,
It makes true Faith for to endure
  And never more to range,
It settles all the State of Man,
  In true content to be
No other Worship ever can,
  Have perfect Liberty.

VII.

Should Persecution flow amain
  I do value it as dirt,
True Faith it is I now retain
  And never fear the hurt,
Before I would from this Commission turn
  In Fiery Flames I would fry,
Tho' Soul and Body to Ashes burn
  I shall have Liberty.

VIII.

You firm Believers every one
  With Hearts loving and true,
These Lines of mine to muse upon

I dedicate to you.
Let Faith and Patience be your Guide
  And shortly you shall see,
CHRIST JESUS will for you provide
  A perfect Liberty,

WILLIAM WOOD, Joiner

Seventh SONG.

I.

Come all you Thirsty Souls that's dry,
  To JACOB'S WELL repair,
And drink your thirst to satisfy
  For Jacobs God is there;
This Well will free your Souls from hell
  If in your Souls it flow,
For all that drink at Jacobs Well
  They Jacobs God do know.

II.

In Egypt's Land I often fell,
  For I'd lost both my Eyes,
But when I drank at JACOB'S WELL
  My Soul was filled with Joys:
I held God fast until he blest
  And would not let him go,
Says he go rest now you are blest,
  I am Jacob's God you know.

III.

I see my self at Liberty,
  Which made me God adore
I see Gods Soul had dyed for me,
  When Blood from Christ did pour;
I drank and drank and had my fill
  And wash'd me o'er and o'er
For all that drank at JACOB'S WELL
  Can never thirst e'er more.

IV.

From Strength to Strength my Soul did rises
  To Sion's holy Hill
No Reason can my Joy Surprise,
  Nor none my Peace Can kill
For when I at that Well do knock,
  With Joys my Soul did flow,
For all the Sheep that are God's Flock,
  Are washt as white as Snow.

V.

This Water like the Widow's Oil,
  It never can me fail;
Nor Neither will it ever Spoil,
  It never can grow stale;
Great Euphrates and Jordan,
  When Time does end will Fly,
But I'll pass Hell to Jacob's Well,
  For that can ne'er be dry.

VI.

That Hell it is the Grave of Death,
  Wherein my Soul must dye,
And When I have immortal Breath,
  To Jacob's Well I'll fly;
That Well is God's Spirit pure,
  Which for me here did dye,
And then I'll think new Wine secure,
  With God Eternally.

VII.

The Flesh of Devil's great and small,
  I with my God shall eat,
And all the cursed Priests of Baal,
  We'll trample under Feet;
And when Justice does them attend,

We'll turn from the our Eyes,
And with our Glorious God ascend,
Into eternal Joys.

VIII.

Come Death and Hell give up your Dead,
  Our Glorious God will cry,
Go cursed Serpents take your Bed,
  Of burning Sand so dry;
And you my Saints whom I once blest,
  When for you I did dye,
Ascend with me and take your Rest,
  In blest Eternity.

IX.

Great Babylon now tumble,
  Our glorious God will cry,
For now your Saints I'll humble,
  In blood eternally;
And when our God has spoke the Word,
  All Peace from them will fly,
And drown'd the Whore in her own Blood,
  To all Eternity.

X.

Unjust Unjust the Devils cry,
  When I give than their Doom,
'Tis you that ought not I to die,
  And Misery assume;
But I need not for to fear them,
  They can't my Peace-destroy,
For every Devil I condemn,
  It floweth forth new Joy.

XI.

For when my God calls me from Death,
  To him I'll swiftly fly,
And leave curst Devils here to weep,
  In Pain eternally,

For like St. PAUL I'm freed from Sin,
  And am well satisfied,
'Tho nothing else to glory in,
  But Christ once Crucified.

                               Boyer Glover

Eighth SONG.

I.

Ask me not whence all this Joy,
Whence does Songs my Time employ,
Why I chaunt forth Praise divine;
Freedom, Freedom, Freedoms mine.
Why I chaunt forth Praise divine,
Freedom, Freedom, Freedoms mine.

II.

Darkness long kept me fast bound,
Sin and Death my Soul did wound,
Reason's Chains made me to groan;
Freedom, Freedom then unknown.
Reason's Chains, &c.

III

But when REEVE and MUGGLETON,
Shew'd three Titles in the Son;
Then assuredly I knew,
Freedom, Freedom, Freedom true.
Then assuredly, &c.

IV.

When I saw the Serpent's Head,
By Man bruis'd, my Sorrows fled;
Christ's Ascension from the Grave,
Freedom, Freedom, to me gave.
Christ's Ascension, &c.

V.

Freedom such as ne'er was known,
Till that God resum'd his Throne;
Long the Mys'try lay conceal'd.
Freedom, Freedom now reveal'd.
Long the Mys'try, &c.

VI.

Tell me not what Reason saith,
Reason has not Light of Faith;
Reason doom'd to endless Woe,
Freedom, Freedom cannot know.
Reason doom'd; &c.

VII.

Though he long has claim'd the Field,
The last Fight shall make him yield;
Adam's Sons shall then regain,
Freedom, Freedom lost through Cain
Adam Sons, &c.

VIII.

Till that Time all we can know,
Revelation does bestow;
By the Power of Faith therein,
Freedom, Freedom's plainly seen.
By the Power, &c.

IX.

Brethren now come join with me,
In Praises for your Liberty;
'Till we chaunt in heavenly Bowers,
Freedom, Freedom, Freedoms ours,
'Till we chaunt, &c.

George Hermitage.

Ninth SONG.

I.

Once a Captive in Egypt I was,
  A Stranger in a foreign Land;
There ruled by rigorous Laws,
  While under proud Pharoah's Command:
A Task there was set me to do,
  Too great for me to perform,
Which made my poor Soul for to rue
  A long Time Day and Night for to mourn,

II.

At Length Joyful News to me came,
  From my Father who is King of Kings;
His Ambassadors brought me the same,
  Who were Messengers of glad Tidings:
They shew'd me I was noble born,
  And a Captive no longer should be,
My Rags then I threw off with Scorn,
  For my Father had ransomed me.

III.

They shew'd me I was of royal Seed,
  Then my lineal Descent I could trace,
And noble born I was indeed,
  Inriched with pure spiritual Grace;
Altho I was lost I am found,
  And my Father me dearly, doth love,
With Joy my Soul did abound,
  When I found of me he did approve,

IV.

Now there is put upon the best Robe,
  And also a ring on my hand,
My Feet with truee Peacs now are shod,
  So I am able to walk and to stand;

The fatted Calf for me was killed,
  I have had a dainty rich Feast,
A Cup of rich Blessings was filled,
  I have drank and my joys are increased.

V.

This my Father for me did provide,
  I hunger and Thirst now no more.
For my Soul is well satisfied,
  And I have Treasure in store:
Now on Jacob's Pillow I rest,
  And there I can sweetly repose,
I know I am eternally bless'd,
  This the Prophets to me did disclose.

VI.

I am seal'd with the Seal of God's Love,
  And assured of a heavenly Crown,
Now Reason can't of me approve,
  How fain would they trample me down;
But I'm arm'd with my Sword and my Shield,
  And joyfully I sit and sing,
Sweet Truths royal Dainties doth yield,
  And Pleasures that's fit for a King.

VII.

My Raiment is curious indeed,
  'Tis of Needle-work that's rich and rare
From my God alone it doth proceed,
  He wrought it fit for me to wear;
The rich Jewels of Truth and of Faith,
  And sweet Revelation divine,
With such grace adorned me hath,
  As hath caused my faith for to shine.

VIII.

My Soul hath been washed from Sin,
  And is cloathed in Bridal Array,

The King's Daughter's all glorious within.
  And will shine in an eternal Day:
Then the Church of God will be complete,
  Like a glorious Bride she will shine,
The Bridegroom with Joy will her meet,
  And behold her bright Beauty divine,

IX.

My Heart it is cheared with Wine,
  And Oyl, makes my Face for to shine,
My God hath prepared me in Time,
  To meet him in Glory divine;
With Faith and with Patience I wait.
  Till my Soul takes a Sleep in the Clay,
To be rais'd then in a royal State,
  On my glorious Coronation Day.

X.

Oh then with the Wings of a Dove,
  Whose Feathers are of yellow Gold;
With Joy I Shall soar up above,
  My Bridegroom and King to behold;
He will honour me with a bright Crown,
  And give me a noble Repast,
In his Kingdom I then shalt sit down;
  And drink the best Wine at the last.

XI.

Then my Pleasures eternal will be,
  My Joy will never have end,
I shall live with God eternally,
  My Father, my Bridegroom and Friend;
My Tongue will then harp divine lays,
  I sweet Hallelujah shall sing,
My Voice will sound forth the praise,
  Of Sions most glorious KING.

Rebecca Bolt.

Tenth SONG.

I.

Oh Christ eternal God alone,
Who was eternally,
Self pre-existing Source of Love;
From all Eternity;
Before that Men or Angels were,
With Glory thou alone,
Or any Creature did appear,
Fill'd the emperial Throne.

II.

When the rude Chaos hudled lay,
With all Things there confin'd,
Death, Hell and Darkness did obey,
Thy powerful Word divine;
What ever should created be,
Thou fully didst discry,
Would unto all eternity,
Thy Glory Magnify.

III.

Thy Wisdom and Almighty Power,
Before this World took Date,
The Angels saw and did adore,
In their created State;
United all with new born Praise,
Did Hallelujahs sing,
To thee they tun'd their tunefull Lays,
Their great eternal King.

IV.

But one superior far was made,
Of the angelic Host,
Whom Reason's Quintessence display'd,
Should greater Wisdom boast;
His Person brighter than the rest,
He did the rest excell,
Twas he our Parents dispossest,
The Tree by which they fell.

V.

This glorious orbe which now you see,
So beauteous fair and fine,
The Almighty made by who's Decree,
'Twill stand as long as Time;
From senseless Dust he call'd it forth,
And Adam too also,
Eternal Ruler of the Earth,
And Lord of all below.

VI.

When from his high eternal Throne,
The Lord his Work surveyed,
And found his Image Man alone,
With no assisting Aid;
A deep and silent Sleep he sent,
Which did his Soul invade;
Untill that Power omnipotent,
A lovely Woman made.

VII.

Awakeing then he soon did rise,
As from a swooning Nod;
View'd the fair Product with Surprise,
Of his Almighty God;
Woman says he shall be thy Name,
For nothing can I see;
Throughout Creation's beauteous Frame,

So like Myself as Thee.

VIII.

Before She did a Being come,
She was by God design'd;
A Net to catch the Devil in,
And propagate Mankind;
The way by which the Holy Ghost,
O'er shadowing would come down;
That all that were in Adam lost,
In Christ should all be found.

IX.

The anointed Cherub now above,
From whom the Lord withdrew;
No longer joyn'd the Bands of Love,
Or paid Obedience due;
But his Creator looked on,
With luciferial Pride;
And whom he had his Being from,
He secretly defied,

X.

His damn'd Ambition was so great,
He rather chose to be;
Deprived of that happy State,
Then share Supremacy;
For which from Heaven was he hurl'd,
And sealed here below;
Left in the midst of this fair World,
The Harbinger of Woe.

XI.

With Envy he beheld the Pair,
The Lord had here placed;
Contriving how he might ensnare,
And bring them to Disgrace;
The great Jehovah did at length,
With-hold his helping Hand;

Left both to their created Strength,
The Devil to withstand.

XII.

The subtil Serpent soon did come;
The Woman to accost;
An Instrument prepared by whom,
He'd be for ever lost;
His comely Person and Address,
She did too much admire;
He courted her with such Success,
As to obtain Desire.

XIII.

O'ertoping of her present light,
For Faith then dormant lay;
Appear'd to her so seeming bright,
Her innocence betrayed;
To his unchast Embraces obey'd,
Where he was soon entomb'd
As swift as thought himself convey'd,
Into her silent Woomb.

XIV.

Dissolving there himself in seed,
Her soul polluted through;
And with unlawful Lust indeed,
Beguil'd poor Adam too;
Naked, disrob'd of Innocence,
Both did their Maker shun;
Conscious enough of their Offence,
Did from his Presence run.

XV.

The Curse I need not now relate.
Each was to undergo;
Adam's Posterity does share,

Enough while here below;
Come true Believers envy not,
What wicked Men attend:
For all their Treasure soon will rot,
Their Heaven will have an End.

XVI.

Since you'r enlightened from Above,
In Praises joyn with me;
Adoring God's elective Love,
To all Eternity;
Knowing when Christ our God does come,
To put an End to Time;
Reason will here with Reason burn,
While we in Glory shine.

J. Miller.

Eleventh SONG.

I.

Hail ! Hail ! two Prophets great,
Whose Message does relate;
To the State of Adam's Seed,
Them to free from Bondage;
  And to show,
   Joys that flow,
   Here below,
In us from God that Fountain,
Blessed are those Eyes that see;
God here died to set him free,
Says Reeve and Muggleton.

II.

Their Mission does record,
That God our mighty Lord;
That two Beings here gave Breath,
Dyed to redeem all,
  Adam's Seed,
  Who did need,

  To be freed,
From everlasting Bondage;
In his Agony below,
Sweat from God like Blood did flow,
Says Reeve and Muggleton.

III.

This Record it is clear,
A wounded Heart will chear;
If by Faith he here can see,
This great and secret Treasure;
  When Death's Sting,
  Down did bring,
  Heaven's King,
As low as mortal Creature;
All the Godhead Life did die;
God did languish, bleed and cry,
Says Reeve and Muggleton.

IV.

Look up lost Souls and see,
Your Maker on a Tree;
Dying here by Serpents Hands,
Who was void of Pity;
  For they cryed,
  When he dyed,
  Satisfied,
Now we have slain this Traitor;
But their Power was no more,
When they'd shed the purple Gore,
Says Reeve and Muggleton.

V.

For in Earth's silent Womb,
The faithful did entomb;
Heaven's God and senseless King,
'Till his appointed Hour;
  Then he Rose,
  To oppose,

Death and those,
Who here had brought him under;
And when he quicken'd from the Ground,
Death receiv'd that conquering Wound,
Says Reeve and Muggleton.

VI.

When he rose from the Grave,
He Power had to save;
All the Faithful in the Dust,
To live with him for ever;
  Ever sure,
  To endure,
  Quite secure,
In everlasting Pleasure;
Then we all in Love shall joyn,
For to praise the God divine;
Of Reeve and Muggleton.

VII.

These Prophets now a sleep,
Death long them cannot keep;
For God's Promise it is sure,
There's nothing can impede it;
  Death will fly,
  And will die,
  At the cry,
Surrender all to Judgement;
And now I'll reverence with my Pen,
The Memory of two pious Men;
John Reeve and Muggleton.

VIII.

I them no Worship pay,
Now the're in silent Clay;
For all Praises it does belong,
To our dear Redeemer.
  He is King,
  And I'll sing,
  To that Spring,

Which floweth Love for ever;
Though I them reverence with my Pen,
With God they were but mortal Men;
Nam'd Reeve and Muggleton.

IX.

Who did glad Tidings bring,
From Heaven's glorious King;
That the Streams of Life will run,
Through our Souls for ever;
     When we fly,
     Up on high,
     And do cry,
All Praise to Christ for ever;
Then through Death our course is run,
To surround that glorious Son;
With Reeve and Muggleton.

X.

When we rise from the Grave,
And glorious Bodys have;
Oh how swift we shall ascend,
Up to that glorious Fountain;
     Eor to drink,
     At that Brink,
     When we think,
What he suffered for us;
Death and Hell will fly away,
At the dawning of the Day;
Says Reeve and Muggleton.

                           B. Glover.

Twelsth SONG.

I.

Now will I rejoyce and sing,
To Christ Jesus my God and King;

Who joyful News to me did bring,
And to all true Belivers;
Thou formed the Earth and Heavens high,
And in a Virgin's Womb did lye;
And also thou did chuse to dye,
From Death to relieve us.

II.

All Glory and Honour be to the,
Who shewed such Mercy unto me;
Thy precious Blood by Faith I see,
Which makes my Election sure;
Who can but love such a God as this,
I believe in him I cannot miss;
Enjoying of eternal Bliss,
For Ever to endure.

III.

In Ignorance I have been led,
And could not find the living Bread;
But now with it I'm daily fed,
Through God's continual blessing;
He sent John Reeve and Muggleton,
Brought me from Sinai to Sion;
Which caused me to sing this Song,
With Joy beyond Expression.

IV.

The Devils of us do complain,
We know they are the Sons of Cain;
And all their Prayers are in vain,
For their God cannot hear them;
He has no Ears how should be hear,
His formless Ghost cannot appear;
For this strange God they must pay dear,
Therefore let us not fear them.

V.

Their nothing God I care not for,
Their false Worship I do abhor;
I know it often causes War,
And dayly breeds Confusion;
There is seven Churches fall of spite.
Each Church doth plead that they are right;
When they all more dark than Night,
Nothing but meer Delusion:

VI:

Therofore my Friends come joyn with me
In Praises to his Majesty;
Who from false Gods has set us free,
By this his last Commission;
Christ's holy Name let us adore,
He is our God we have no more;
He has for us great joys in store,
And without intermission.

Made by John Gates, once Clerk of Eggam in Berkshire.

Thirteenth SONG.

I.

When I view my God's Creation,
  Oh what Wonders great I see;
When I think of his Redemption,
  What a Sight it is to me;
      To see that none could die,
      Justice to satisfie,
      But the alone eternal God

II.

When he left his boundless Kingdom,
  Of immortal Glories bright,
And for us became a Creature,

How I wonder at the sight;
    To see that none could die.
    Justice to satisfy,
    But the alone eternal God.

III.

'Tho I see him here a creature,
  When in mortal Flesh below,
When he grew mature by nature,
  All Perfection he did shew.
    And When he here did die,
    Justice to satisfy
    Then dyed the whole Eternal God

IV.

On a Cross I see a dying,
  God's great Spirit which was pure
Cursed Devils him envying,
  Oh! what Pain he did endure;
    When he was crucified,
    The Blood flowed from the Side,
    Of the alone eternal God.

V.

Here the Devils' Power ended,
  They no more to him could do,
By the Power of his Spirit,
  He the chains of Death broke thro'
    And tho he here did die,
    Justice to satisfy,
    Now lives the alone eternal God.

Boyer Glover,

Fourteenth SONG.

I.

When first the Truth I heard,
  My Soul was dead with Sin,
To die I was afraid,
  Such horror I was in;
I knew not where to fly,
  Or where to find relief,
Afraid I was to die,
  This fill'd my Soul with Grief.

II.

The Scriptures I compared,
  As many more had done
And found that I was noble born
  Of God I was a Son;
The more my Soul did gaze,
  The more my Faith did see,
That I my God should praise,
  To all Eternity.

III.

This is a Treasure sure,
  Which none can take away
It ever will endure,
  My Night is turn'd to Day;
My Prayers are turn'd to Praise,
  My glorious God and King,
Who me from Death will raise,
  Redeeming Love to sing.

IV.

No envy can destroy,
  The Peace which I possess,
The Gift of God is Joy,
  And endless Blessedness;
Obedience to God

Surpasses Sacrifice,
Obey the Prophets Word,
　　And you to Bliss will rise.

V.

Then you'll wise Virgins be,
　　Your Lamps all fill'd with Oil,
The Bridegroom's Face you'll see,
　　None can the Marriage spoil;
And when your God you see,
　　In his burning Throne above,
Faith will that Oil then be,
　　Returning Praise for Love.

　　　　　　　　　　　　Boyer Glover.

Fifteenth SONG.

I.

Now no more may Monsters boast,
Nor Reason's God the Elect deceive;
Poor dispis'd ones throw down Mountains,
Whilst in Truth we do believe;
Grace and Truth hath long abounded,
And all Monsters are confounded.

II.

Then let each Soul that's here be glad,
Rejoicing now with faithful Zeal,
See the Conduit of Salvation,
Where we all have set our Seal;
Whilst the Mountains catch at small Things,
Still our Conduit floweth forth all Things.

III.

You great Sir, we greet in Love.
The Object Vipers would destroy,
Since your Company in Braintree,
Now once more the Saints enjoy;

By a Power that Divine is,
Makes our Water sweet as Wine is

IV.

Then let all Saints in Raptures join,
With joyful Souls to make a Choir;
To praise the God of our Salvation;
Which did first your Souls inspir;
And protected you so long too,
And with Armour made you strong too.

V.

Perils great have you endured,
Because you charge the World with Sin;
You are the mark of all their Malice,
Shot against by every Fiend;
But your Armour is your Defence Sir,
Until Death release you hence Sir.

VI.

Then in dust a silent sleep,
You take and bid the Saints adieu;
Till all Time be gone and ended,
Then our God makes all Things new;
Mountains then will shake and shiver,
Then we Saints are blest for ever.

VII.

See the Saints in Clouds ascending,
With Acclamations fill'd with Joy;
Persecutors then beholding,
Which did oft' the Saints annoy;
We attending you ascending,
Into Glories never ending.

VIII.

Sad and dismal will that be,
To Reason and his blind Desire;
Seeing the weakest are made strongest,
Adds more Fuel to their Fire,
Fears and Horrors whelm them under
Whilst they perish all with Wonder.

By William Wood, Painter.

Sixteenth SONG.

I.

An uncreated Essence,
From all Eternity;
Was the great Jehovah,
Which by Faith I see;
His Eyes like Flames of Fire,
His Feet like Brass do shine
How can you but admire,
A God that is so divine.

II.

His Voice like many Waters,
St. John he doth compare;
But sweeter is than Roses,
By exceeding far;
In him is no Desire,
His Spirits to confine
How can you but admire,
A God that is so divine.

III.

His Body clear as Chrystal,
More softer is than Down;
In him is all Perfection,
With an immortal Crown;
The Beams of his bright Glory,
The Sun it doth out shine;

How can you but admire,
A God that is so divine.

IV.

At his own Will and Pleasure,
More swifter is than Thought;
In a Kingdom without measure,
Which by Faith I am taught;
He is altogether lovely,
So glorious and so fine;
Forever let's admire,
A God that is so divine,

V.

Thousands of bright Angels,
Do in his Presence stand;
Beholding of his bright Glory,
And waiting his Command;
Delighting in his Service,
The readily do obey;
The Commands of their Creator,
Which he on them shall lay.

VI.

Then let us return our Praises,
And Thanks unto that King;
Which at his own Time appointed,
His Saints will likewise bring;
Into his blessed Mansions,
Full Union for to have;
In his everlasting Kingdom,
Who raised us from the Grave.

Robert Pickard.

Seventeenth SONG.

I.

Come raptur'd Souls rejoyce and sing,
  Your Dear Redeemer's Praises;
For he is our only God and King,
  The divine Rock of Ages,
Who from his glorious Throne above,
  Into this Earth descended;
Let us adore his matchless Love,
  Ne'er to be comprehended

II.

A Virgin's Womb did God contain,
  The very Lord of Glory,
Yet unconsumed, amazing strange,
  Seek not but still adore the
Jesus an Infant pure was born,
  In Bethleham oh! ponder;
How mean his Birth and how forlorn,
  Which made proud Reason wonder.

III.

Herod that mighty Prince of Hell,
  Sent forth his bloody Edict,
And many thousand Babe's there fell,
  But Christ was safe in Egypt
His great Vicegerents did him protect,
  And kept him from all Danger,
'Till freely he resign'd his Breath,
  When in the Hands of Strangers.

IV.

Here he obeyed his own Decree,
  Submitting to Death's Power,
Immortal God by Faith I see,
  Sin, Death and Hell devour;
Death was too weak for to detain,

A precious Life so pure,
The conquering Hero rose again,
  By which Death's Death is sure,

V.

Eternal Life he has regain'd.
  In a triumphant Manner,
Or we forever should have lain,
  Under pale Death's dark Banner;
Now God ascended far on high,
  Into those Realms of Pleasure.
Center of Bliss, Eternity,
  Believers only Treasure.

James Miller.

Eighteenth SONG.

I.

Curst Serpents often bruised,
The Seed of Adam's Heel;
When they false Gods refused
Their Reason did them kill.
But when that God came from above,
The Wine Press for to tread,
His Power did unite with Love,
To break the Serpents Head.

II.

Great Locusts God Surrounded,
Men mighty in Dispute;
But God them all confounded,
Their Reason could not root;
For there lay Boundless Purity
In his pure Flesh below,
No Reason could inherent
Where Purity did flow.

III.

Two Creatures God created
Out of the Dust below,
His Nature there be placed
Which in their Souls did flow,
Their Souls was always pure divine
When Faith in them did Flow,
But Reason came with a curst Design,
His Nature for to sow.

IV.

This Serpent he infused
His Reason into Eve,
His Council she refused
Till that she did receive;
Thus like a God did Reason rove
So powerful was he,
That Reason in her Soul did move
For to eat that cursed Tree.

V.

When that this cursed Serpent
In Eve had taken Root,
She overcame her husband
To eat that cursed Fruit,
But how their Souls they did repeat
To lose such Harmony,
Relenting Light made them repent
And they to God did cry.

VI.

Then did the great Creator
A glorious promise make,
To take on Human Nature
For his lost Image sake;
Says God I will fulfill my Word
To break the Serpent's Head,
I will tread out your Sins in Blood

Untill my Soul is dead.

VII.

My glorious Person you once see
In silent Death shall lie,
I will a Captive to Death be
That you may live on high.
My Body on a Cross shall bleed
My Justice to repay,
That you and, all your righteous Seed
May have eternal Day.

VIII.

You, Reason has subjected
Now to a mortal Death,
Because I you respected
I'll vail immortal Breath,
And then grim Death I'll overcome
In pure Mortality,
Then call you to my glorious Home
In the Boundless Heavens high.

IX.

I will pursue the enemy
Into a Virgin's Womb,
And there my Godhead Life shall die
Pure Flesh for to assume;
And in that Body I will smite,
Death Devil Hell and Grave,
My Soul in Mercy shall delight
You and your Seed to save.

X.

I will go up from Bosrah
With Garments dyed red,
And suffer cursed Serpents
For you my Blood to Shed,
And those that drink that Blood in Love

Shall Live with me on high,
But all that drink that Blood in Wrath,
Are damn'd eternally

XI.

Your righteous Seed they must relent
When Justice they offend,
When in their Blood they do repent
I will my prophets send,
Who shall declare to them my word,
When unto me they cry,
Ill give them Strength to drink my Blood
That they may never die.

XII.

I'll give to them a certain Sign,
That they may know the Seed,
That unto Mercy does resign
And who in Justice bleed;
He that can but stretch out his Hand
Shall touch me when on High,
But he that has the withered Hand
Is damn'd eternally.

Boyer Glover.

Nineteenth SONG.

I.

O come my Friends and join with me
In praises to Christ's Majesty,
Who freely did resign his Breath
And pour'd out his Soul even unto Death.
  Oh! my glorious God and redeeming King.

II.

And when he quicken'd from the dead,
O there he broke the Serpent's Head;
The Sons of Adam to set free,
That we may praise him eternally;
  Oh! my glorious God &c.

III.

O what a glorious Sight to see,
The Power of Death conquer'd by thee;
Royal Prerogative did thee compel,
To conquer the Enemies, Sin, Death and Hell;
  Oh! my glorious God &c.

IV.

And now he'as opened the Book of Life,
That in my Soul has banished all strife;
A new Name in the Book has wrought,
The Work of Redemption by Faith I'm taught;
  Oh! my glorious God &c.

V.

O Lord thou art the living Bread,
And is alive tho' you was dead;
That when thy glorious Face I see,
I shall live with thee eternally;
  Oh! my glorious God &c.

VI.

And leave behind the Seed of Cain,
Upon this Earth for to remain;
The Face of God ne'er to behold,
For Reason's curst tho' he is so hold;
  Oh! my glorious God &c.

VII.

God sent two Prophets great I see,
Those glorious Truths to shew to me;
And to all those that do truly believe,
The Decleration of great John Reeve;
  Oh! my glorious God &c.

VIII.

And great Muggleton by Faith I see,
Was chose by God's glorious Decree;
And those that great Muggleton disown,
Upon this Earth will be left to groan;
  Oh! my glorious God &c.

John Williams.

Twentieth SONG.

I.

Why should I make Freedom a Slave,
Although the world be unkind Sir;
Since my servant Reason I have,
Each critical Monster to mind Sir;
My Reason shall draw, make Brick and find Straw,
It shall have no Time to be idle;
It early shall rise each Knave to surprise,
And put on the Bit and the Bridle.

II.

The Children of this World are in Arms,
To kill and destroy for a Season;
Not one bewailing an other Mens' Harms,
Thus it is to be ridden by Reason;
Go on with Work, fight Devil, fight Turk,
Your Reason and you are accurst too;
Since Reason's your Lord & you rule by the Sword,
And suck up Mens' Blood 'till you burst too.

III.

Dust it's for which your do strive,
No Treasure like that they can savour;
Each Moment 'tis left for those that survive,
To take from the Dead as a Favor;
For still I perceive if they could but live,
Until this World's end were it longer;
They'd still it enjoy and kill and destroy,
The weaker must fall by the stronger.

IV.

Let Reason fight and plunder and kill,
And he'll continue fomenting;
Until with Blood they all have their fill,
Without the least Dram of repenting;
Let them fill their Cup up and drink e'ery Sup,
For Reason on Blood will be feeding;
My life shall stand in the promised Land,
While Mountains of Reason lye bleeding.

V.

Then let any Soul rejoice and be glad,
With Raptures of sweet Elevation;
What 'tho this World be drunken and mad,
It shall not stop my Revelation;
My Sword in my Mouth shall still defend Truth,
And make Reason's Children to wonder,
It early shall fly and soar to the Sky,
And sound in their Ears like Thunder.

VI.

Then since the Sword so ripe in Mankind,
And ushers the Soul to the Grave too,
I'll keep house at home in my mind,
And enjoy those Riches I have too;
I'll neither borrow nor lend, I cannot it spend,

It will be my portion tomorrow,
Whilst Devils that fight must bid all good Night,
And enter a Deluge of Sorrow.

VII.

And thus poor Cam will finish his Days,
And solace his Soul with delighting,
In sounding forth my God's divine Praise,
Whilst Monsters and Devils are fighting;
My Faith unto me a Castle shall be,
Of impregnable Strength and Defence Sir,
Each handler of Steel my Sentance shall feel,
Before that poor Cam goes hence Sir.

By William Wood, Painter.

Twenty-fifth SONG.

I.

Who comes here?
From Edom with dyed Garments
Our God so dear,
With Blood he was made red,
When the Wine Press he did tread
For his lost Elect,
Whom he lov'd so dear.

II.

For Sin we
Justly all deserve to die,
The Law makes it appear;
But God came down to die,
Justice to satisfy,
For his lost Elect
Whom be lov'd so dear.

III.

Look and See
The boundless Love of God,
When he suffer'd here;
He laid his Glory down
And of Thorns he wore a Crown,
For his lost Elect
Whom he lov'd so dear.

IV.

His Power and
Glory with him he brought down,
When he center'd here;
And naught he did divide,
For the God head whole died,
For his lost Elect
Whom he lov'd so dear.

V.

With Power on
High he left his regency
While he suffer'd here;
This Power bore such sway,
That they could not disobey
The Commands of their God,
And Creator dear.

VI.

Great Reeve and
Muggleton they do declare
That God suffered here;
And When Christ was crucified,
The eternal Father died,
For his lost Elect
Whom he lov'd so dear.

VII.

His Body nail'd
Upon a cursed Tree,
To the World it is clear;
But none are satisfied
What it was in him that dyed,
But his lost Elect
Whom he lov'd so dear.

VIII.

In Love now
Let us all together join,
While we are Mortals here;
In Praises for to sing,
To our dear redeeming King,
For his boundless Love
When he suffered here

B. Glover.

Twenty Second SONG.

I.

O God of all Gods, and Prince of all Peace,
To sing forth thy praises let the Saints never cease;
Who in thy divine Love makes Mortals thy Guests,
By kind Invitations to Peace and to Rest,
What Love can be greater can any one tell,
Than our God by his Death to redeem us from Hell?
Then let all that are alerted his Praises forth shew,
That had bowels of Love to poor Mortals below.

II.

For in the Beginning when Man was quite lost,
Out of Life into Death by the Enemy tost,
Oh sweet was thy promise thy own to redeem,
By promising Life out of pale Death again;

By Faith thy Babes saw it tho' not in their Days,
And lay down in peace to thine Eternal Praise.
     Then let all &c.

III.

A Tower of Water God built to Mens wonder.
To keep the Elect and the Rebels asunder,
It stood on twelve Pillars so bright and so clear.
The Sun was seen thro them all the whole Year;
The Pillars were faithful, beautiful and strong
To hold up the Tower tho' ever so long.
     Then let all &c.

IV.

The next was a Temple which God himself rais'd,
Froth the Womb of a Virgin his divine Name be prais'd
For himself to dwell in which had twelve Pillar's strong
And the Powers of Hell could do them no wrong,
This Temple by Serpents was trampled down plain,
And in three Days and Nights it was rear'd up again,
Oh Mistery of Misteries, and blessed is he,
That hath Faith to look into this great Mistery.

V.

When the Holy of Holies ascended on high,
And over grim Death he had got Victory,
The Pillars stood fast and like Stars they did shine;
Their Mouths breathed forth Revelation divine;
And now in the Dust Death doth them retain,
'Till Jehovah with Power will raise them again.
     Then let all &c.

VI.

In process of Time thick Darkness did grow.
That it compass'd about this whole Region below,
That Men went a groping to find out the way,
But all to no purpose in those darksome Days
'Till at length a bright Light froth Heaven did shine,

Which all that are elected can witness divine.
  Then let all &c.

VII.

In God's decreed Time in Fifty and one,
In the Month February from his heavenly Throne;
He made himself known unto all elect Men,
The third and last Time he shall ever come again;
He sent forth two Champsons his Truth to maintain,
And to shut up all Mouths that prattled in vain,
  Then let all &c.

IX.

And out of their Mouths proceeds spiritual Fire,
To burn up all those that against them conspire;
With the sword of the Spirit divine Truth to defend,
And to cut them all down that with Truth do contend
They have also the Keys of Heaven and Hell,
No Champions like those in this Region doth dwell.
  Then let all &c.

X.

These Champions have with them rare Gilead Balm,
Which in a great Earthquake will make a great Calm;
It cures all Wounds that are made by Deaths Sting,
It makes the Dumb speak & sing Praise to their King;
It makes the Blind see these glorious Days,
It makes the Lame walk and give God the Praise.
  Then let all, &c.

XI.

It makes the Deaf hear their divine Revelation,
Which expels all the Fears of eternal Damnation;
The Knowledge of God in them is inspired,
Which all the Elect have so long Time desired;
The Nature and Form of Angels they, know;
What Heaven is above and what Hell is below,
  Then let all &c.

XII.

And of the right Devil and rise of his Seed,
They have satisfied all true Men indeed;
The Soul it is mortal they truly do say,
Tho' Devils and Monsters of Men do say nay;
With many more Secrets they are fully replenish'd,
Their Work it is done and God's Mistery is finish'd.
    Then let all &c.

                                    W. Wood, Painter.

Twenty-third SONG.

I.

Eternal Life it is to me,
  Now I by Faith do know;
That God has died Upon a Tree,
  To save my Soul from Woe;
For Justice was wrath with sin,
  For which God did attone;
Or else in darkness I had been,
  And God should ne'er have known.

II.

The holy City was brought down,
  Which Jerusalem did tipefie;
This was when God he vail'd his Crown,
  And for to redeem us did die;
In the Sanctum Sanctorum of Love,
  Did the Holy of Holies dwell;
When God he came down from above,
  For to conquer Death and Hell.

III.

At Cana a Town of Galilee,
  A Miricle great was wrought;
Christ made the Water Wine I see,
  When the Water to him was brought;

This Miricle it did show,
  Those Souls which are divine;
When Revelation it did flow,
  That their Waters then were Wine

IV.

Christ unto his Apostles said,
  In Glory you did shine;
And when I am dead be not afraid,
  In my Kingdom above there is Wine;
And when by Faith they did know,
  They should in Glory shine;
Oh! how their Spirits then did glow,
  When they drank that spiritual Wine.

V.

When Moses he the Rock did smite,
  He made the Waters flow;
This did the Soul of Man delight,
Who Thirst did undego;
  The Water gush'd forth like a Flood,
To allay the thirst of Man;
  That Water tipified Christ's Blood,
When he was God and Man.

VI.

All that believe the third Record,
  They do drink of this spiritual Wine;
And have the Promise of the Lord,
  That they ever in Glory shall shine;
For by Faith in the Prophet's Word,
  Their Souls are made divine;
They live by drinking of God's Blood,
  And their Waters are turn'd to Wine.

Boyer Glover.

FINIS.

DIVINE SONGS
OF THE
𝕸𝖚𝖌𝖌𝖑𝖊𝖙𝖔𝖓𝖎𝖆𝖓𝖘,

IN GRATEFUL PRAISE TO THE *ONLY TRUE GOD*, THE LORD JESUS CHRIST.

'IN hymns and songs of old the prophets praised
One personal God, with elevation raised,
So now, in these last days, some few that know
The same true living God, do likewise so;
Those learn'd in poet's fictions, may outshine
In reason's art; know, these are all divine,
Made by those babes and sucklings, counted fools;
For why? They ne'er were taught in learned schools;
But let such know, that wisdom from above
Is innocent and harmless as a dove.'

JOHN NICHOLS.

PRINTED BY SUBSCRIPTION.

𝕷𝖔𝖓𝖉𝖔𝖓:
PRINTED BY

R. BROWN, 26, ST. JOHN-STREET, CLERKENWELL.

1829.

R. BROWN, Printer, 26, St John-street, Clerkenwell.

ADDRESS.

BELOVED BRETHREN,

WE, with the assistance of several friends, have selected these Songs, principally from the oldest manuscripts, and have taken the greatest care to give a correct copy. It has been, from the earliest period, the practice of the righteous fathers to rejoice, and sing praise to God; as Christ said, *'Abraham rejoiced to see my day, and he saw it, and was glad.'* John viii. 56. Those saints who lived previous to the coming of Christ, sang the song of Moses, that is, Christ would come, according to his promise; and those saints, since the coming of Christ, sing the new song, that is, Christ has come. These songs are the overflowings of spiritual faith in the hearts of the beloved of God, who are his chosen vessels, prepared in this world to meet him at the end thereof, and then to live with him forever. Thus do the saints pour out of the abundance of their hearts, the gladness of soul unto God, for his great mercy, in that he hath suffered death to redeem them from eternal death, and he hath sent his prophets, to assure them that it is so. In this assurance they rejoice with singing and great joy unto Jesus Christ, their Redeemer; unto whom let all nations, kindreds and tongues, rejoice and be exceeding glad, for by him doth salvation come; as it is written, *'There was none in heaven or in earth that could open the book of life, and loose the seals thereof but the Lion of the tribe of Judah, the root of David, who was that Lamb, as he was slain, he was able to open the book, and to loose the seals thereof.'* Revelations *'O, sing unto the Lord a new song, for he hath done marvellous things, his right hand and his holy arm hath gotten him the victory.'* Psalm xcviii. '*I will sing of mercy and judgment unto thee, O, Lord, will I sing.*' Psalm ci. Thus David magnified God in this his wonderful work.— Also Isaiah, the prophet, speaketh of Christ being the only God, where he saith, '*for unto us a Child is born, unto us a Son is given, and the government shall be upon his shoulder, and his name shall be called Wonderful, Counselor the mighty God, the everlasting Father, and Prince of peace.* Isaiah ix. 6. This prophecy was fulfilled, when God chose JOHN REEVE and LODOWICK MUGGLETON, to declare this secret unto man, that Christ is the only. God, and they were the last prophets that should ever speak or write, by commission from him, while the world doth last; then this same Jesus will descend from heaven, with his holy angels, to put an end to all time; and he will collect his jewels, by. gathering them from the grave, over which he hath gained the victory; then will he reap and gather his, harvest of wheat, and the tares he frill burn with unquenchable fire, because of their wickedness against him; then will the saints and elect of God rejoice in singing in an heavenly choir, the praise of his most glorious majesty, the King of heaven, with the fulness of joy; and they will sing with great joy the song of the Lamb, with all other heavenly delights, the elect will enjoy for ever, where the lion and the lamb lay down together in peace; then will all the prophets and apostles sit upon thrones in heaven, giving all honor, power, and glory unto God, for ever and ever. Amen.

JOSEPH & ISAAC FROST.

List of Subscribers

A.

AMOR, Mr. Thomas
Amor, Mrs.
Alvey, Ann

B.

Burton, Mrs. Rebecca
Berridge, Mr. John
Berridge, Mrs.
Brown, Mr. Thomas
Brown, Sarah
Brown, Mr. Joseph
Brown, Mr. George
Blackman, Mr. James
Bunton, Mr. David
Bunton, Mrs.

C.

Cates, Mr. William
Cates, Mrs.
Crundwell Mr. Thomas
Crundwell, Mrs.
Cruse, Mr. Christian
Cruse, Mrs.

D.

Dowsett, Mrs. Susannah
Drayton, Mrs.
Dickinson, Mr. George
Drummond, Mr. John
Drummond, Mrs.

F.

Fever, Mrs. Sarah
Frost, Mrs. Margaret
Frost, Mr. James
Frost, Mr. Joseph
Frost, Mrs.
Frost Mr. Isaac.
Frost, Mrs.
Frost, Mr. Samuel
Frost, Mr. Benjamin
Fleming, Mr. John
Fleming, Mrs.
Friend, a

G.

Gandar, Mrs. Sarah
Gandar, Mr. Joseph
Gandar, Mrs.
Glaskin, Mr.
Glaskin, Mrs.
Graham, Mr. William

Graham, Mrs.

H.

Holloway, Mr. John
Hovendon, Mr. Robert
Hewitt, Mr. Thomas
Hewitt, Mrs.
Hudson, Mr. Thomas
Hogg, Mrs. Theodosia
Hogg, Mr. Joseph
Hogg, Mr. Thomas
Hogg, Mr. Robert
Hunt, Mrs. Hannah
Hunt, Mr. Joseph
Hunt, Rosannah
Hunt, Mr. George
Hunt, Mrs.
Hunt, Mr. Samuel
Hunt, Ruth
Hunt, Elizabeth
Hall, Mr. Benjamin

L.

Law, Mrs. Ann
Law, Mr. Daniel
Lupton, Mrs.

N.

Norledge, Miss Sarah

R.

Rodes, Mrs. Ann
Robinson, Miss Sarah

S.

Smith, Mr. Richard
Spooner, Mr. Thomas
Smith, Mr. James Pierce
Smith, Mrs.
Simpson, Miss Hannah

U.

Upton, sen. Mr. Thomas

V.

Vincent, sen. Mr. William,
Vincent, Mrs.
Vincent, jun. Mr. William
Vincent, Mrs.

W.

Windsor, Mr. James
Wallis, Mr. Robert
White, Mr. William
White, Mrs.
Wilder, Mr. John Thomas
Wood, Mr. James
Wood, Mrs.

INDEX

A.

		Song.	Page
ALL saints that are present	William Wood.	22	113
Arise, my soul, arise	James Miller.	23	114
Ask me not, whence all	George Hermitage.	6	82
An uncreated essence	Robert Pickard.	14	99
All praise to my God	Mathew Hague.	30	125
All dominion and glory	John Nichols, sen.	31	126
As I was musing all alone	Boyer Glover.	32	128
All glory to my gracious God	Thomas Perry.	173	341
All hail to our redeeming king	Miller.	56	167
Arise, my soul, sweet songs	Rebecca Batt.	47	153
All glory unto God alone	Robert Dawson.	109	249
A glorious throne in the heavens	John Ladd.	24	115
A kingdom of love. Hail! my	T. Tomkinson.	165	324
Arise, 'Tis morn, my soul, arise	P. Lathorp	186	361

B.

Believers, now let us rejoice	W. Miller.	80	206
By faith I can see how my God	J. Peat.	57	168
Before I viewed this glorious	T. Scupholme.	33	129
Behold a wonder! two	E. Goodwin.	58	169
Behold our great God	J. Dale.	50	160

C.

Cease, vain world, for to declare	J. Miller.	81	208
Come, all select souls	J. Nichols.	82	208
Come, true believers, join with	R. Robinson.	83	209
Come saints, rejoice with	P. Pickersgill.	84	210
Curst devils, once with malice	B. Glover.	92	221
Come all you thirsty souls that's	B. Glover.	5	80
Christ my precious bleeding	A. S. Toone.	90	219
Come, raptur'd souls, rejoice and	J. Miller.	15	100
Curst serpents often bruised	B. Glover.	16	101
Cease, my soul, no more perplex	T. Perry.	39	88
Come all you that are dry	B. Glover.	34	132
Come reason, now let's reason	J. Miller.	59	170
Come, all true saints, who do	J. Miller.	62	176
Come, loving saints, with me	W. Miller.	64	182
Come, all true saints, who have	J. Miller.	65	184
Could the law give salvation	A. Weeks.	67	187
Christ, thou dear redeeming king	B. Glover.	69	188
Come, my friends, with me	J. Gandar	221	421

D.

		Song.	Page
Dear friends in truth, that in	R. Gregory.	135	282
Death thou mighty king of	B. Glover.	60	173

E.

Eternal Jesus, source of love	B. Glover.	96	228
Eternal life it is to me	B. Glover.	21	111

F.

For to look on the works of	W. Sedgwick.	99	232
From Jericho to Jerusalem	B. Glover.	101	235
Faith, like a sovereign balsam	W. Miller.	71	191
Faith is a glorious crown for	W. Tomkinson.	77	199
Fare ye well, ye dark Egyptians	E. Kitchen.	108	247
Faith's the balsam like the olive	W. Miller.	79	202
Faith, hope and charity	Mr. Hatter.	25	117

G.

Glide swiftly, ye streams	B. Glover.	104	239
Great Muggleton and Reeve	R. Smith.	105	240
God's prophets now at rest	B. Glover.	107	243
Great Reeve and. Muggleton	B. Glover.	119	262
God of glory, great Redeemer	J. Miller.	121	264
Great God, thy people always	M. Jenkins.	150	304
God in bright burning glory	B. Glover.	137	286
Great Jesus, our Saviour and	T. Tomkinson.	139	289

H.

Hark! hark! I hear the Almighty's	J. Ladd.	29	121
Happy mortals, filled with praises	B. Glover.	123	266
Hark, hark, ye sons of faith	W. Wood.	126	270
How sweet and pleasant are	T. Mudford.	129	275
How blest and how happy am I	R. Batt.	40	141
How blest and how happy am	A. S. Toone.	138	287
Happy Muggletonians who only	J. Miller.	2	75
Hail! Hail! two prophets great	B. Glover.	9	90
Happy ye above all mankind	T. Cook.	130	276
How blest is that soul who from	T. Perry.	37	138
Hail! hail! this new day	J. Miller.	86	214
How shall we, bounded here	J. Miller.	88	218
How happy is that soul that sees	B. Glover.	61	174
Hark, hark, the trumpet sounds	E. Kitchen.	110	250
How blest are the saints when	A. Weeks.	89	218
How happy the soul that's	R. Batt.	181	354
Hail! blessed dawn, all hail! We	Miller.	35	134
Honor'd Sir, to whom honor doth	T. Ladd.	141	290

Divine Songs

		Song.	Page
Hark! hark! I hear the trumpet	C. Peers.	53	164
How happy's that mortal who	W. Curtoyse.	175	347
How happy is Britain's fair isle	W. Miller.	143	293
How blest is my time now	J. Dale.	212	402

I.

I do believe in God alone	M. Carter	133	279
In Sixteen hundred, fifty and one	J. Peat	1	73
In the days of my ignorance	B. Glover	134	280
It is by my faith I'm dictated to	M. Hague	91	220
In one thousand six hundred	R. Wynne	112	252
In darkness I wander'd about	B. Glover	114	255
In Christ in whom we do	M. Outridge	68	187
Israel's great God, he	R. Pickersgill	111	251
In the year fifty-one, in the	R. Tyrer	153	307
In a virgin, God entombed	Boyer Glover	36	136
In the first of St. John, it is very	W. Cates	52	163
I know by the third, which is the	E. Clay	149	303
In celestial regions, eternal	E. S. White	207	392
I AM did unto Moses make	J. Berridge	222	422
In vain do anti-christ (an acrostic)	T. Terry	205	391

J.

Jehovah, that infinite God	B. Glover	136	284
John Reeve is God's prophet	I. Frost	94	225
Jehovah three different modes	W. Mathews	63	179

L.

Love, what art thou that art	T. Tomkinson	142	292
Love with unconfined wings	W. Wood	4	78
Love! love! sons of our only God	J. & I. Frost	228	433
Let my soul soar up on high	B. Glover	93	224
Laugh, and at reason's God	R. Wynne	54	165
Life's but a journey to the grave	W. Miller	113	253
Let's lift up our souls and rejoice	W. Wood	95	227
Let us with lifted voices sing	P. Lathorp	70	190

M.

My swelling heart now leaps	T. Perry	144	294
My soul doth glorious scenes	R. Batt	72	193
My heart is as light as a bird in	B. Glover	42	145
My brethern in Christ	T. Luther	97	230
Muggletonians rejoice	H. Pickersgill	66	185
My father me a portion gave	B. Glover	155	309
My heart doth rejoice and I live	F. Cates	227	432
My soul glides on God's holy stream	I. Frost	216	411

N.

		Song.	Page
Now will I rejoice and sing	J. Gates.	10	93
Now to the scriptures I my mind	W. Cates.	215	410
Now sing unto the Lord on	W. Tomkinson.	206	392
Now no more may monsters boast	W. Wood	13	97
Now the world are affrighted	B. Glover	140	289
No more of your canting and	H. Bonel	55	166
No more I despair - adieu to all	A. Ward	226	431

O.

		Song.	Page
Oh! cease, vain man, for to declare	J. Miller	172	337
O wondrous great, amazing!	W. Sedgwick	146	298
Oh! what a glorious sight it is	W. Sedgwick	147	300
Oh! God how wondrous are thy	J. Ladd	148	301
Once reason and folly strong hold	A. Ward	152	306
Oh! wondrous great, amazing	B. Glover	158	314
Once more this day of great joy	J. Peat	169	331
Oh! think on my state, now	G. Robinson	171	337
Oh! liberty, where shall I find	B. Glover	174	344
Oh! how happy are we	J. Nichols, sen.	178	350
O Christ our Saviour	J. Miller	3	77
Once a captive in Egypt I was	R. Batt	7	84
Oh, Christ, eternal God alone	J. Miller	8	87
One great Eternal God (a sun dial,)	J. Miller	27	119
O come, my friends, and join	J. Williams	17	104
O God of all Gods, and prince	W. Wood	20	109
Oh! God, how shall I all my joys	J. Dale	26	118
One thousand, six hundred and	A. Delamain	98	230
Oh! Christ my God and king	J. Miller	100	234
Oh! how happy's my condition	J. Straght	128	273
Oh! death, what is thy bitter	M. Thomas	102	237
Oh! how my soul does ponder	B. Glover	49	159
Oh! what great and glorious	B. Glover	103	237
Oh! glorious Jesus, our eternal God	R. Batt	106	241
Oh! Lord, my God and king	T. Luther	131	277
Oh! happy elect, ye elect	R. Batt	132	278
O death, where is thy dreadful sting	B. Glover	38	139
O, happy's the man that has got	M. Hague	154	308
Oh! praise the Lord my raptur'd	T. Perry	45	151
O glorious day which once more	J. Miller	41	143
Once I was with darkness blinded	J. Miller	145	296
Oh! Lucifer, of you I'm going to	S. Fever	115	256
Oh! what a sight it is to see	J. Peat	73	194
Oh! God, the true centre of life	W. Wood	156	311
Oh! what joy my soul will see	B. Glover	157	312
Oh! how my soul does soar above	B. Glover	159	316
Oh! how happy is that man	T. Walton	116	258
Oh! what joys there doth arise	C. Peers	182	355
Oh! now, blessed saints, by divine	W. Wood	218	415
Oh! how my soul it doth rejoice	C. Frost	225	430

P.

		Song.	Page
Proud reason does pretend for to	W. Sedgwick	180	352
Praises to my Maker's glory	G. Hermitage	44	150

R.

Rouse, rouse up, awake, my	R. Pickard	188	363
Rejoice, all my friends, while to	J. Frost	118	260
Rejoice, ye saints of God above	J. Miller	117	259
Reeve and Muggleton who led	W. Cates	28	120

S.

Swift on the wings of faith let's	B. Glover	185	359
Since I am enlighten'd once more	J. Miller	192	370
Sweet is the love to those that	J. Nichols	160	317
Saints, behold your great Creator	M. Miller	161	318
See this happy day, which with	J. Miller	162	319
See, see, our Creator, Redeemer	B. Glover	183	355
Saints, join with me to praise the	J. Dale	210	398

T.

To praise, to praise the glorious	A. S. Toone	194	374
Though reason prates of mighty	B. Glover	51	162
Too mean's this world with all its	E. Henn	196	376
Tis by the third commission	B. Glover	198	380
The uncreated body of Christ our	J. Miller	200	384
True saints, come rejoice	J. Miller	163	319
The first created blessed pair	W. Miller	164	322
This day great Muggleton and	W. Miller	166	326
To God, our creator, redeemer and	E. Henn	168	328
'Tis true I can't worship now as	R. Batt	170	333
Though I a captive slave have	J. Cullam	177	349
The truth in all its splendour	M. Frost	120	263
The Lord is God, none else can be	E. Fever	74	195
Though we live among devils	M. Miller	75	196
This is the day God's holy	M. Jenkins	223	426
To thee, my God, gratitude I owe	J. Frost	224	427

W.

When Jesus our God had descended	J. Miller	151	305
When Christ he here was crucified	B. Glover	203	387
When heaven's great God	J. Miller	208	395
When Reeve at first by God's	J. Frost	209	396
When first the third record I heard	B. Glover	211	401
While thro' this wicked world	J. Miller	213	404

		Song.	Page
When darkness in her sable dress	W. Wood	214	408
When I view my God's creation	B. Glover	11	95
When first the truth I heard	B. Glover	12	96
When first I saw how God came	J. Peat	219	419
When God had left Jacob he	B. Glover	220	420
Why should I make freedom	W. Wood	18	106
Who comes here	B. Glover	19	107
When I saw my great Creator	B. Glover	179	351
While my treasures I'm surveying	B. Glover	187	362
When God he descended	B. Glover	189	366
When shall I see that happy	Mrs. Thomas	190	368
What dreadful horror I did see	B. Glover	191	369
Welcome day of great joyful news	J. Miller	193	371
Welcome, are those happy days	W. Miller	195	375
When men of learning leave	T. Turner	46	153
When into silent sleep from all	E. Henn	197	378
Welcome, welcome mighty Jesus	J. Peat	199	382
When my soul it doth ponder	R. Batt	201	385
WHAT glorious truths these are to	E. Glover	202	386
When that in Babel I did dwell	M. Hague	204	389
While the herdsmen swine are	J. Miller	43	147
What love, O God, can equal thine?	J. Miller	122	265
When to false worship I did go	B. Glover	76	197
When my sins did accuse me	B. Glover	124	267
When I praise the God of Jacob	R. Burton	125	269
When first the truth I came to	T. Pickershill	167	327
Whilst I by faith can soar above	M. Thomas	78	200
Whene'er my faith it soars above	R. Wayne	176	348
What Wonders great, my soul doth	R. Batt	85	212
When my faith soars up on high	C. Peers	184	357

Y.

Ye faithful Muggletonians all	W. Miller	217	412
You men quite void of fear	B. Glover	48	157
You faithfull Muggletonians, who	J. Frost	127	272
You saints and servants of the	Gaskcoyne.	87	216

SONGS
OF GRATEFUL PRAISE
TO THE
EVER-Blessed Glorious King Of Saints,
AND
MERCIFUL IMMORTAL GOD.
OUR LORD JESUS CHRIST.

FIRST SONG.

(TUNE; 'De'el take the wars.')

IN Sixteen hundred, fifty and one,
This morning God did freedom proclaim,
CHRIST did declare himself God, ALONE,
Unto *his Ambassador, John Reeve by* name;
Lodowick Muggleton was also included,
Wisdom to the elect to make known,
Shewing how reason is utterly excluded
From the eternal JEHOVAH'S throne;
True saints now milk and honey
Can purchase without money;
God's blood, the cordial good,
Doth cleanse them pure within;
They are the friends of GOD,
Saved in this last record,
Which is a fenced wall,
Protecting from all thrall;
And such as it environs are free from sin.
      Which is, &c.

2.

Chrystal streams transparent swift proceeding,
From the Rock in mount Zion laid,
Giving a brightness reason far exceeding;
Into his chosen this day was convey'd:
The upper springs of rapid inspiration
Like golden oil most sweetly did glide,
Filling the nether springs with deep revelation;
Which well in the valley will ever abide.
Darkness swiftly flying,

Light its room supplying.
His mind was refin'd above the rest of man;
What Moses' veil conceal'd
Was now to him reveal'd.
This was a glorious day,
When faith bore all the away,
And heaven's gate was set open for men.
  This was, &c.

3.

We are free from task masters rescued;
A yoke which our forefathers wore;
With Canaan's language we're greatly endued,
More than saints who liv'd heretofore:
Our souls, sore distressed, by the streams of Bable,
Sat weeping, while darkness did as surround;
To gain relief none on this earth was able,
Till the third record we found:
Here grace, true light, free offered,
And hearing likewise proffered;
Free *grace did* release us from the bond of woe;
What we deserved to feel
Was bruised in CHRIST's heel,
Even Jeshurun's mighty God,
Who left divine abode
To die for poor sinners, his seed below.
  Even, &c.

4.

Behold! O, ye faithful, how your God tremendous,
For you exerted his infinite power;
When dying freely, from ruin to rend us,
Did all power of death devour.
Then did he enter, O death, thy dark pavillion,
And by a power, superior far,
He conquered the keys of thy vast dominion,
This proved him, the mighty man of war.
This the freedom founded
In which our souls are grounded;
His life aton'd our strife to death's all conquering law;
In concert join your lays
On these three happy days,
And joyful let us be,
Since great Eternity
Did die for his seed when condemn'd by the law.
  And joyful, &c.

5.

Then hallelujah glory be to JESUS,
Hosanna sing to our crucified GOD;
The great deliverer from death did release us,
And from the serpent's devouring rod.
All he requires is only love each other,
Those that offend, rebuke in love;
Faith's life depends on love to its brother;
Love is the nature of God above.
His last *great* authorized,
Of his coming us apprised;
The signs of the times declare him at the door;
Then rest, my soul, in peace,
Waiting the grand release,
For you are sure to sing,
To CHRIST your glorious king.
In sweet hallelujahs when time's no more.
  For you, &c.

JOHAN PEAT.

SECOND SONG.

HAPPY Muggletonians who only
True faith have to receive;
Revelation ever new,
Gave to great *Muggleton* and *Reeve,*
Which makes us to CHRIST our king
Sweet hallelujahs ever sing.
  Which, &c.

2.

No more now we seek for rest,
Or wander up and down in strife;
Faith gives peace, and peacee possess'd,
Assures of eternal life,
Which makes us to CHRIST our king
Sweet hallelujahs ever sing.
  Which, &c.

3.

The bread of life, the very God,
By faith we now can plainly see;
Which does sweet content afford,
And fills us with satiety;
Which makes us to CHRIST our king

Sweet hallelujahs ever sing.
    Which, &c.

4.

The living water too we've, found,
Which does our thirsty souls suffice;
Faith, the balm, has cured our wounds,
The spring from whence all joys arise;
Which makes us to CHRIST our king
Sweet hallelujahs ever sing.
    Which, &c.

5.

His free grace we will adore,
Each sitting under his own vine,
Praises giving evermore,
Since we shall share in joys divine,
And to CHRIST our gracious king
Sweet hallelujahs ever sing.
    And to, &c.

6.

How shall we enough decline,
O GOD. thy vast unbounded love;
When thou didst in CHRIST appear,
And left mankind, thou GOD above:
We'll to thee most gracious king,
Sweet hallelujahs ever sing.
    We'll to, &c.

7.

This mystery the world cannot know,
Nor we it fully comprehend;
What GOD in man did undergo,
O CHRIST our Saviour, GOD and Friend,
We'll to thee most gracious king;
Sweet hallelujahs ever sing.
    We'll to, &c.

8.

No *other* GOD we'll ever own,
No other majesty adore;
Thou art the self-existing one,
GOD-Man, Man-GOD for everyone.
We'll to thee, most gracious king,
Sweet hallelujahs ever sing.
    We'll to &c.

Divine Songs

9.

O Father, Son and Holy Ghost,
Triune in titles, never thee;
Lord JESUS CHRIST; denied by most,
Is this hid sacred mystery.
God and everlasting king,
To whom we'll hallelujahs sing.
    God and, &c.

10.

This is the *Muggletonians'* faith,
This is the GOD which we believe,
None salvation knowledge hath,
But those of *Muggleton and Reeve.*
CHRIST is the *Muggletonians'* king,
With whom eternally they'll sing.
    Christ is, &c.

JAMES MILLER.

THIRD SONG.

O CHRIST our Saviour,
Tis our endeavour,
In time and ever,
Thee to adore.
What but faith can behold
Those glorious crowns of gold,
Which God will unfold
When time's no more.
    What but, &c.

2.

See the skies rending,
And faith's ascending,
Angels attending
In clouds above,
While reason here below
Opens their eyes in woe,
Torments to undergo,
And never move.
    While, &c.

3.

While faith with faith will rise

Above the falling skies,
Entering to endless joys,
Which ne'er will cease;
In *odes* of endless love,
As we to heaven *move,*
With GOD shall sing above,
In perfect peace.
   In odes, &c.

JAMES MILLER.

FOURTH SONG.

LOVE with unconfined wings,
 Hovers within my breast,
And by divine revelation brings
 My soul true peace and rest:
As I was musing by my faith
 On pure eternity,
I find no monarch on this earth
Enjoys such liberty.
   As I, &c.

2.

By faith I now have truly found
 The worship GOD requires;
Obedience is the perfect ground
 By which my heart's inspired;
Rejoice therefore, my mortal soul,
  That thou dost live to see,
  That no man living can controul
 This perfect liberty.
   Rejoice, &c.

3.

There's many men hath riches store,
 Yet are so worldly bent,
Tho' they have much, they crave for more,
 And never are content;
But I that am the poorest of all,
 From worldly cares am free,
Which makes me know they live in thrall,
 And I at liberty.
   But I, &c.

4.

'Tis neither pardon from the Pope,
 Nor prayers made to saints,

That I do value, no, nor hope,
    Nor ever make complaint;
'Tis CHRIST above, the Lord of love,
    That for true saints did die;
    'Tis only he has *pardoned* me,
    And gave me liberty.
        'Tis Christ, &c.

5.

By faith and patience, now my guide,
    My conscience is made clear;
And now the LORD is on my side
    I need no foes to fear:
I neither fear the stroke of death,
    Nor Devils' tyranny;
But freely can resign my breath,
For perfect liberty.
        I neither, &c.

6.

Patience, that virtue is so pure,
    It waiteth for the change,
It makes true faith for to endure,
    And never more to range;
It settles all the state of man
    In true content to be;
No other worship ever can
    Have perfect liberty.
        It settles &c.

7.

Should persecution flow amain,
    I do value it as dirt;
True faith it is I now retain,
    And never fear the hurt:
Before I would from this commission turn
    In fiery flames I would fry,
Tho' soul and body to ashes burn,
    I shall have liberty.
        Before I, &c.

8.

You firm believers every one,
    With hearts loving and true,
These lines of mine to muse upon,
    I dedicate to you:

Let faith and patience be your guide,
    And shortly you shall see,
CHRIST JESUS will for you provide
    A perfect Liberty.
Let faith, &c.

WILLIAM WOOD, *Joiner.*

FIFTH SONG.

COME all yo thirsty souls that's dry,
    To Jacob's well repair;
And drink your thirst to satisfy
    For Jacob's GOD is there;
This well will free your souls from hell,
    If in your souls it flow ;
For all that drank at Jacob's well,
    They Jacob's GOD do know.
        For all, &c.

2.

In Egypt's land I often fell,
    For I'd lost both my eyes;
But when I drank at Jacob's well,
    My soul was filled with joys;
I held GOD fast until he blest,
    And would not let him go;
Says he, 'go rest, now you are blest,
    I am Jacob's GOD you know.'
        Says he, &c.

3.

I see myself at liberty,
    Which made me GOD adore;
I see GOD'S soul had died for me,
    When blood from CHRIST did pour;
I drank, and drank, and had my fill,
    And wash'd me o'er and o'er;
For all that drank at Jacob's well,
    Can never thirst e'er more.
        For all, &c.

4.

From strength to strength my soul did rise
    To Zion's holy hill;
No reason can my joys surprise,
    Nor none my peace can kill;

For when I at that well do knock,
    With joys my soul did flow;
For all the sheep that are God's flock,
    Are wash'd as white as snow.
        For all, &c.

5.

This water, like the widow's oil,
    It never can me fail;
Nor neither will it ever spoil,
    It never can grow stale;
    Great Euphrates and Jordan
    When time does end will fly;
But I'll pass hell to Jacob's well,
    For that can ne'er be dry.
        But I'll, &c.

6.

That hell it is the grave of death,
    Wherein my soul must lie,
And when I have immortal breath,
    To Jacob's well I'll fly;
That well it is GOD's spirit pure,
    Which for me here did die;
And then I'll drink new wine secure,
    With GOD eternally.
        And then, &c.

7.

The flesh of Devils great and small,
    I with my GOD shall eat;
And all the cursed priests of Baal
    We'll trample under feet;
And when justice does them attend,
    We'll turn from them our eyes,
And with our glorious GOD ascend
    Into eternal joys.
        And with, &c.

8.

'Come, death and hell, give up your dead,'
    Our glorious GOD will cry;
'Go, cursed serpents, take your bed
    Of burning sand so dry!
And you, my saints, whom once I bless'd,
    When for you I did die,
Ascend with me and take your rest

In bless'd eternity.
    Ascend, &c.

9.

'Great Babylon, now tumble,'
    Our glorious God will cry;
'For now your saints I'll humble
    In blood eternally!'
And when our God has spoke the word,
    All peace from them will fly,
And drown the whore in her own blood
    To all eternity.
    And drown, &c.

10.

'Unjust, unjust!' the Devils cry,
    When I give them their doom,
'Tis you that ought, not I, to die,
    And misery assume;
Brit I need not for to fear them,
    They can't my peace destroy ;
For every Devil I condemn,
    It floweth forth now joy.
    For every, &c.

11.

For when my God calls me from death,
    To him I'll swiftly fly.
And leave curst Devils here to Weep
    In pain eternally.
For, like St. PAUL, I'm freed from Sin,
    And am well satisfied,
Though nothing else to glory in,
    But CHRIST once crucified.
    Though nothing, &c.

                                BOYER GLOVER.

SIXTH SONG.

Ask me not, whence all this joy;
Whence does songs my time employ,
Why I chant forth praise divine;
Freedom, freedom, freedom's mine.
    Why I chaunt forth praise divine;
    Freedom, freedom, freedom's mine.

Divine Songs

2.
Darkness long kept me fast bound,
Sin and death my soul did wound,
Reason's chains made me to groan;
Freedom, freedom then unknown.
  Reason's chains, &c.

3.
But when Reeve and Muggleton
Shew'd three titles in the SON;
Then assuredly I knew
Freedom, freedom, Freedom true.
  Then assuredly, &c.

4.
When I saw the Serpent's head,
In man bruised, my sorrows fled;
CHRIST's ascension from the grave,
Freedom, freedom, to me gave.
  Curtin's ascension &c.

5.
Freedom such as ne'er was known
Till that GOD resum'd his throne;
Long the myst'ry lay conceal'd,
Freedom, freedom now reveal'd.
  Long the mystery, &c.

6.
Tell me not wing reason saiths;
Reason hath not light of faith ;
Reason doom'd to endless woe
Freedom, freedom cannot know.
  Reason doom'd, &c.

7.
Though he long has claim'd the field.
The last fight shall make his yield;
Adam's sons shall then regain
Freedom, freedom, lost through Cain.
  Adam's sons, &c

8.
Till that time all we can know,
Revelation does bestow;
By the power of faith therein,

Freedom, freedom's plainly seen.
    By the power, &c.

9.

Brethren, now come join with me
In praise for your liberty,
Till we chaunt in heavenly bowers,
Freedom, freedom, freedom's ours.
    Till we chaunt, &c.

GEORGE HERMITAGE

SEVENTH SONG.

ONCE a captive in Egypt I was,
    A stranger in a foreign land;
There ruled by rigorous laws,
    While under proud Pharoah's command:
A task there was set me to do,
    Too great for me to perform,
Which made my poor soul for to rue,
    A long time day and night for to mourn.
    A task, &c.

2.

At length joyful news to me came
    From my father, who is King of kings;
His ambassadors brought me the same,
    Who were messengers of glad tidings;
They shew'd me I was noble born.
    And a captive no longer should be:
My rags then I throw off with scorn
    For *my* Father had ransomed me.
    They shew'd, &c.

3.

They shew'd me I was of royal seed,
    Then my lima descent I could trace;
And noble born I was indeed,
    Enrich'd with pure spiritual grace:
Although I was lost, I am found,
    And my Father me dearly doth love;
With joy my soul did abound.
    When I found of me he did approve.
    Although I, &c.

Divine Songs

4.
Now there is put upon me the best robe.
    And also a ring on my hand,
My feet with true peace now are shod,
    So I am able to walk and to stand
The fatted calf for me was killed,
    I have had a dainty rich feast;
A cup of rich blessings was filled,
    I have drank, and my joys are increased.
        The fatted, &c.

5.
This my Father for me did provide,
    I hunger and thirst now no more;
For my soul is well satisfied,
    And I have treasure in store.
Now on Jacob's pillow I rest.
    And there I can sweetly repose,
I know I am eternally bless'd.
    This the prophets to me did disclosed.
        Now on, &c.

6.
I am seal'd with the seal of God's love,
    And assured of a heavenly crown ;
Now reason can't of me approve.
    How fain would they trample me down;
But I'm arm'd with my sword and my shield,
    And joyfully I sit and sing.
Sweet truths royal dainties doth yield,
    And pleasure that's fit for a king.
        But I'm, &c.

7.
My raiment is curious indeed,
    'Tis of needle-work that's rich and rare;
From my GOD alone it doth proceed,
    He wrought it fit for me to wear;
The rich jewels of truth and of faith.
    And sweet revelation divine,
With such grace adorned me hath,
    As hath caused my faith for to shine.
        The rich, &c.

8.
My soul hath been washed from sin,
    And is clothed in bridal array;
The king's daughter's all glorious within,
    And will shine in an eternal day:
Then the church of GOD will be complete,
    Like a glorious bride she will shine,
The bridegroom with joy will her meet,
    And behold her bright beauty divine.
        Then the, &c.

9.
My heart it is cheered with wine,
    And oil makes my face for to shine;
My God hath prepared me in time,
    To meet him in glory divine:
With faith and with patience I wait,
    Till my soul takes a sleep in the clay.
To be raised then in a royal state,
    On my glorious coronation day.
        With faith, &c.

10.
Oh then, with the wings of a dove,
    Whose feathers are of yellow gold,
With joy I shall soar up above,
    My bridegroom and king to behold;
He will honor me with a bright crown,
    And give me a noble repast,
In his kingdom I then shall sit down,
    And drink the best wine at the last.
        Ile will, &c.

11.
Then my pleasures eternal will be,
    My joy will never have end;
I shall live with God eternally,
    My father, my bridegroom and friend:
My tongue will then harp divine lays,
    I sweet hallelujah shall sing,
My voice will sound forth the praise
    Of Zion's most glorious king.
        My tongue, &c.

REBECCA BATT.

EIGHTH SONG.

OH, CHRIST, eternal GOD alone,
Who was eternally,
Self pre-existing source of love,
From all eternity;
Before that men or angels were,
With glory thou alone,
Or any creature did appear,
Fill'd the imperial throne.

2.

When the rude chaos huddled lay,
With all things there confin'd;
Death, hell and darkness did obey
Thy powerful word divine;
Whatever should created be,
Thou fully didst descry,
Would unto all eternity
Thy glory magnify.

3.

Thy wisdom and almighty power,
   Before this world look date,
The angels saw and did adore,
   In their created state;
United all with now-born praise,
   Did hallelujahs sing,
To thee they tun'd their tuneful lays,
   Their great eternal king.

4.

But one superior far was made,
   Of the angelic host,
Whom reason's quitessence display'd,
   Should greater wisdom boast:
His person brighter than the rest,
   He did the rest excel,
'Twas he our parents dispossess'd,
   The tree by which they fell.

5.

This glorious orb which now you see,
   So beauteous fair and fine,
The Almighty made, by who's decree
   'Twill stand as long as time;

From senseless dust he call'd it forth,
    And Adam too also,
Eternal Ruler of the earth,
    And LORD of all below.

6.

When from his high eternal throne,
    The LORD his work surveyed,
And found his Image man alone,
    With no assisting aid;
A deep and silent sleep be sent,
    Which did his soul invade,
Until that power omnipotent,
    A lovely woman made.

7.

Awaking then he soon did rise,
    As from a swooning nod,
View'd the fair product with surprise,
    Of his Almighty GOD;
'Woman,' says he, 'shall be thy name,
    For nothing can I see
Throughout creation's beauteous frame,
    So like myself as thee.'

8.

Before she did a being come,
    She was by GOD design'd,
A net to catch the Devil in,
    And propagate mankind.
The way by which the Holy Ghost
    O'er shadowing would come down,
That all that were in Adam lost,
    In CHRIST should all be found.

9.

The anointed cherub now above,
    From whom the LORD withdrew,
No longer join'd the bands of love,
    Or paid obedience due;
But his Creator look'd on
    With Luciferial pride;
And whom he had his being from
    He secretly defied.

Divine Songs

10.
His damn'd ambition was so great,
    He rather chose to be
Deprived of that happy state,
    Than share supremacy:
For which from heaven was be hurl'd,
    And sealed here below
Left in the midst of this fair world.
    The harbinger of woe.

11.
With envy he beheld the pair
    The LORD had here placed,
Contriving bow he might ensnare
    And bring them to disgrace,
The great Jehovah did at length
    Withhold his helping hand.
Left both to their created strength,
    The Devil to withstand.

12.
The subtle serpent soon did come,
    The woman to accost;
An instrument prepared by whom,
    He'd be forever lost.
His comely person and address
    She did too much admire;
He courted her with such success,
    As to obtain desire.

13.
O'ertopping of her present light,
    For faith then dormant lay,
Appear'd to her so seeming bright,
    Her innocence betray'd;
To his unchaste embraces obey'd,
    Where he was soon entomb'd;
As swift as thought himself convey'd
    Into her silent womb.

14.
Dissolving there himself in seed,
    Her soul polluted through;
And with unlawful lust indeed,
    Beguil'd poor Adam too;
Naked, disrob'd of innocence,

Both did their Maker shun;
Conscious enough of their offence,
   Did from his presence run.

15.

The curse I need not now relate
   Each was to undergo;
Adam's posterity does share
   Enough while here below.
Come, true believers, envy not
   What wicked men attend;
For all their treasure soon will rot,
   Their heaven will have an end.

16.

Since you're enlighten'd from above,
   In praises join with me,
Adoring GOD's elective love,
   To all eternity;
Knowing. when CHRIST our GOD does come
   To put an end to time,
Reason will here with reason burn,
   While we in glory shine.

                              JAMES MILLER.

NINTH SONG.

HAIL! Hail! two prophets great,
Whose message does relate
To the state of Adam's seed,
Them to free from bondage;
      And to show,
      Joys that flow
      Here below,
In us from GOD that fountain;
Blessed are those eyes that see,
GOD here died to set him free,
Says Reeve and Muggleton.
      Blessed are, &c.

2.

Their mission does record,
That GOD our mighty Lord,
That two beings here gave breath,
Died to redeem all
      Adam's seed,
      Who did need,

Divine Songs

    To be freed
From everlasting bondage;
In his agony below,
Sweat from GOD like blood did flow,
Says Reeve and Muggleton.
    In his, &c.

3.

This Record it is clear,
A wounded heart will cheer,
If by faith he here can see
This great and secret treasure ;
    When death's sting,
    Down did bring
    Heaven's king
As low as mortal creature;
All the Godhead life did die,
God did languish, bleed and cry,
Says Reeve and Muggleton.
    All the, &c.

4.

Look up, lost souls, and see,
Your Maker on a tree;
Dying here by serpents' hands,
'Who was void of pity,
    For they cried
    When he died,
    Satisfied:
Now we have slain this traitor;
But their power was no more,
When they'd shed the purple gore,
Says Reeve and Muggleton.
    But their, &c.

5.

For in earth's silent womb,
The faithful did entomb;
Heaven's God and senseless king,
Till his appointed hour;
    Then he rose
    To oppose
    Death and those,
Who here had brought him under;
And when he quickened from the ground,
Death receiv'd that conquering wound,

Says Reeve and Muggleton.
    And when, &c.

6.

When he rose from the grave,
He power had to save
All the faithful in the dust,
To live with him for ever;
    Ever sure
    To endure,
    Quite secure,
In everlasting pleasure;
Then we all in love shall join
For to praise the God divine
Of Reeve and Muggleton.
    Then we &c.

7.

These prophets now asleep,
Death long them cannot keep;
For God's promise it is sure,
There's nothing can impede it;
    Death will fly,
    And will die,
    At the cry,
Surrender all to judgment!
And now I'll reverence with my pen
The memory of two pious men,
John Reeve and Muggleton.
    And now, &c.

8.

I them no worship pay
Now they're in silent clay;
For all praise it does belong
To our dear Redeemer;
    He is king,
    And I'll sing
    To that spring,
Which floweth love for ever;
Though I them reverence with my pen.
With God they are but mortal men.
Nam'd, Reeve and Muggleton.
    Though I, &c.

Divine Songs

9.

Who did glad tidings bring
From heaven's glorious King,
That the strews of life will run
Through our souls for ever;
    When we fly
    Up on high,
    And do cry,
All praise to Christ for ever:
Then through death our course is run.
To surround that glorious Son,
With 'Reeve and Muggleton.
    Then through, &c.

10.

When we rise from the grave.
And glorious bodics have.
Oh! how swift we shall ascend
Up to that glorious fountain;
    For to drink
    At that brink,
    When we think
What he suffered for us;
Death and hell will fly away
At the dawning of the day,
Says Reeve and Muggleton.
    Death and, &c.

                                      BOYER GLOVER.

TENTH SONG.

Now will I rejoice and sing
To Christ Jesus my God and king;
Who joyful news to me did bring,
   And to all true believers!
Thou formed the earth and heavens high,
And in a virgin's womb did lie;
And also thou did chuse to die,
   From death to relieve us.
      Thou formed, &c.

2.

All glory and honour be to thee,
Who shewed such mercy unto me,
Thy precious blood by faith I see,
   Which makes my election sure;

Who can but love such a God as this!
I believe in him, I cannot miss
Enjoying of eternal bliss,
   Forever to endure.
      Who can, &c.

3.

In ignorance: I have been led,
And could not find the living bread;
But now with it I'm daily fed,
   Through God's continual blessing:
He sent John Reeve and Muggleton;
Brought me from Sinai to Zion;
Which caused me to sing this song,
   With joy beyond expression.
      He sent, &c.

4.

The devils of us do complain:
We know they are the sons of Cain,
And all their prayers are in vain,
   For their God cannot hear them;
He has no ears; how should he hear?
His formless ghost cannot appear;
For this strange God they must pay dear,
   Therefore let us not fear them.
      He has, &c.

5.

Their nothing God I care not for,
Their false worship I do abhor;
I know it often causes war,
   And daily breeds confusion.
There is seven churches full of spite,
Each church doth plead that they are right,
When they are all more dark than night---
   Nothing but mere delusion,
      There it. &c.

6.

Therefore, my friends, come join with me
In praises to his Majesty;
Who from false gods has set us free,
   By this his lost commission;
Christ's holy name let us adore,
He is our God, we have no more,
He has for us great joys in store,

And without intermission.
    Christ's holy. &c.

    JOHN GATES, *once Clerk of Egham, Berkshire.*

    ELEVENTH SONG.

WHEN I view my God's creation,
  Oh! what wonders great I see!
When I think of his redemption,
  What a sight it is to me!
    To see that none could die,
    Justice to Satisfy,
    But the alone eternal *God.*
      To see, &c.

          2.

When he left his boundless kingdom,
  Of immortal glories bright,
And for us became a creature---
  How I wonder at the sight!
    To see that none could die,
    Justice to satisfy,
    But the Alone eternal God.
      To see, &c.

          3.

Tho' I see him here a creature,
  When in mortal flesh below,
When he grew mature by nature,
  All perfection he did shew.
    And when he here did die
    Justice to satisfy,
    Then died the whole eternal God.
      And when, &c.

          4.

On a cross I see a dying
  God's great spirit, which was pure,
Curs'd devils him envying,
  O what pain did he endure,
    When he was crucified,
    The blood flowed from the side
    Of the alone eternal *God.*
      When he, &c.

5.

Here the Devil's power ended,
  They no more him could do;
By the power of his spirit,
  He the chains of death broke through:
    And tho' he here did die.
    Justice to satisfy,
    Now lives the alone eternal God.
    And tho', &c.

BOYER GLOVER.

TWELFTH SONG.

WHEN first the truth I heard,
  My soul was dead with sin,
To die I was afraid,
  Such horror I was in;
I knew not where to fly
  Or where to find relief,
Afraid I was to die.
  This fill'd my soul with grief.
    I knew, &c.

2.

The scriptures I compared,
  As many more had done;
And found that I was noble born,
  Of God I was a son;
The more my soul did gaze,
  The more my faith did see.
That I my God should praise
  To all eternity.
    The more, &c.

3.

This is a treasure sure,
  Which none can take away;
It ever will endure,
  My night is turn'd to day;
My prayers are turned to praise,
  My glorious God and king,
Who me from death will raise,
  Redeeming love to sing.
    My prayers, &c.

4.

No envy can destroy,
   The peace which I. possess;
The gift of God is joy
   And endless blessedness;
Obedience to God
   Surpasses sacrifice,
Obey the prophet's word,
   And you to bliss will rise.
      Obedience to, &c.

5.

Then you'll wise virgins be,
   Your lamps all fill'd with oil;
The bridegroom's face you'll see,
   None can the marriage spoil,
And when your God you see,
   In his burning throne above,
Faith will that oil then be,
   Returning praise for love.
      And when, &c.

                                      BOYER GLOVER.

THIRTEENTH SONG.

Made to welcome the Prophet Muggleton into Braintree, Essex.

Now no more may monsters boast,
Nor reason's god the elect deceive;
Poor despis'd ones thrown down mountains,
Whilst in truth we do believe;
Grace and truth hath long abounded,
And all monsters are confounded.
      Grace and, &c.

2.

Then let each soul that's here be glad,
Rejoicing now with faithful zeal,
See the conduit of salvation,
Where we all have set our seal;
Whilst the mountains catch at small things,
Still our conduit floweth forth all things.
      Whilst the, &c.

3.

You, great Sir, we greet in love,
The object vipers would destroy,
Since your company in Braintree,
Now once more the saints enjoy;
By a power that divine is,
Makes our water sweet as wide is.
      By a, &c.

4.

Then let all saints in raptures join,
With joyful souls to make a choir;
To praise the God of our salvation.
Which did first your souls inspire;
And protected you so long too,
And with armour made you strong too.
      And protected. &c.

5.

Perils great have you endured,
Because you charge the world with sin;
You are the mark of all their malice,
Shot against by every fiend;
But you armour is your defence, Sir,
Until death release you hence, Sir.
      But your, &c.

6.

Then In dust a silent sleep
You take, and bid the saints adieu;
Till all time be gone and ended,
Then our God makes all things new;
Mountains then will shake and shiver,
Then we saints are blest for ever.
      Mountains then, &c.

7.

See the saints in clouds ascending,
With acclamations fill'd with joy;
Persecutors then beholding,
Which did oft the saints annoy;
We attending you ascending
Into glories never ending.
      We attending, &c.

8.

Sad and dismal will that be
To reason and his blind desire;
Seeing the weakest are made strongest,
Adds more fuel to their fire;
Fears and horrors whelm them under,
Whilst they perish all with wonder.
      Fears and &c.

                    WILLIAM WOOD, *Painter.*

FOURTEENTH SONG.

AN uncreated essence,
From all eternity;
Was the great Jehovah,
Which by faith I see;
His eyes like flames of fire,
His feet like brass do shine;
How can you but admire,
A God that is so divine.
      His eyes, &c.

2.

His voice like many waters,
St. John he doth compare;
But sweeter is than roses,
By exceeding far;
In him is no desire,
His spirits to confine;
How can you but admire,
A God that is so divine.
      In him, &c.

3.

His body clear as chrystal.
More softer is than down;
In him is all perfection,
With an immortal crown;
The beams of his bright glory,
The sun it doth out shine;
How can you but admire,
A God that is so divine.
      The beams, &c.

4.

At his own will and pleasure,

More swifter is thou thought;
In a kingdom without measure,
Which by faith I am taught;
He is altogether lovely,
So glorious and so fine;
For ever let us admire,
A God that is so divine.
   He is, &c.

5.

Thousands of bright angels,
Do in his presence stand;
Beholding of his bright glory,
And waiting his command:
Delighting in his service.
They readily do obey
The commands of their creator,
Which he on them shall lay.
   Delighting in, &c.

6.

Then let us return our praises
And thanks unto that king,
Which at his own time appointed,
His saints will likewise bring
Into his blessed mansions,
Full union for to have,
In his everlasting kingdom,
Who raised us from the grave.
   Into his, &c.

         ROBERT PICKARD.

FIFTEENTH SONG.

COME, raptur'd souls, rejoice and sing
 Your dear Redeemer's praises;
For he is our only God and King,
 The divine Rock of Ages;
Who from his glorious throne above,
 Into this earth descended;
Let us adore his matchless love,
 Ne'er to be comprehended.
   Let us, &c.

2.

A Virgin's womb did God contain,
 The very Lord of glory;

Yet unconsumed, amazing strange!
  Seek not but still adore thee:
JESUS an Infant pure was born;
  In Bethlehem, oh! ponder,
How mean his birth, and how forlorn,
  Which made proud reason wonder.
      How mean, &c.

3.

Herod, that mighty prince of hell,
  Sent forth his bloody edict,
And many thousand babes there fell,
  But Christ was safe in Egypt;
His great Vicegerents did him protect,
  And kept him from all danger,
Till freely he resign'd his breath,
  When in the hands of strangers.
      Till freely, &c.

4.

Here he obeyed his own decree,
  Submitting to death's power;
Immortal God, by faith I see,
  Sin, death and hell devour;
Death was too weak for to detain
  A precious life so pure;
The conquering hero rose again,
  By which death's death is sure.
      The conquering, &c.

5.

Eternal life he has regain'd
In a triumphant manner,
Or we for ever should have lain
Under pale death's dark banner;
Now God's ascended far on high,
Into those realms of pleasure,
Centre of bliss, eternity,
Believers' only treasure.
      Centre of, &c.

                      JAMES MILLER.

SIXTEENTH SONG.

Curst serpents often bruised,
The seed of Adam's heel;

When they false Gods refused
Their reason did them kill
But When that God came from above,
The wine-press for to tread,
His power did unite with love,
To break the serpent's head.
        But when, &c.

2.

Great locusts God surrounded,
Men mighty in dispute;
But God them all confounded,
Their reason could not root;
For there lay boundless purity
In his pure flesh below,
No reason could inherent be,
Where purity did flow.
        For there, &c.

3.

Two creatures God created
Out of the dust below,
His nature there he placed,
Which in their souls did flow,
Their souls were always pure divine
When faith in them did flow,
Hut reason came with a curst design,
His nature for to sow.
        Their souls, &c.

4.

The serpent he infused
His reason into Eve,
His counsel she refused
Till that she did receive;
Thus like a God did reason rove,
So powerful was he,
That reason in her soul did move
For to eat that cursed tree.
        Thus like, &c.

5.

When that this cursed serpent
In Eve had taken root,
She overcame her husband
To eat that cursed fruit;
But in their souls they did repent,

To lose such harmony,
Relenting light made them repent.
And they to God did cry.
      But how, &c.

6.

Then did the great Creator
A glorious promise make,
To take on human nature,
For his last image sake;
Says God, I will fulfil my word
To break the serpent's head;
I will tread out your sins in blood
Until my soul is dead.
      Says God, &c.

7.

'My glorious person you once see
In silent death shall lie;
I will a captive to death be,
That you may live on high;
My body on a cross shall bleed,
My justice to repay,
That you and all your righteous seed
May have eternal day.
      My body, &c.

8.

'You, reason has subjected
Now to a mortal death,
Because I you respected,
I'll vail immortal breath;
And then grim death I'll overcome
In pure mortality,
Then call you to my glorious home
In the boundless heaven's high.
      And then, &c.

9.

'I will pursue the enemy
Into a virgin's womb,
And there my Godhead life shall die
Pure flesh for to assume;
And in that body I will smite
Death, Devil, hell and grave;
My soul is mercy shall delight
You and your seed to save.

And in, &c.

10.

I will go up from Bosrah
With garments dyed red,
And suffer cursed serpents
For you my blood to shed;
And those that drink that blood in love
Shall live with me on high,
But all that drink that blood in wrath,
Are damned eternally.
    And those, &c.

11.

Your righteous seed they must relent
When justice they offend,
When in their blood they do repent
I will my prophets send;
Who shall declare to them my word
When unto me they cry,
I'll give them strength to drink my blood
That they may never die.
    Who shall, &c.

12.

I'll give to them a certain sign
That they may know the seed,
That unto mercy does resign,
And who in justice bleed;
He that can but stretch out his hand,
Shall touch me when on high;
But he that has the withered hand,
Is damn'd eternally.'
    He that, &c.

BOYER GLOVER.

SEVENTEENTH SONG.

O COME, my friends, and join with me
In praises to Christ's majesty,
Who freely did resign'd his breath,
And pour'd out his soul even unto death.
  Oh! my glorious God and redeeming king.
    Who freely, &c.

2.

And when he quickened from the dead,

O, there he broke the serpent's head,
The sons of Adam to set free,
That we may praise him eternally.
    Oh! my glorious God and redeeming king.
        The sons, &c.

3.

O what a glorious sight to see
The power of death conquer'd by thee;
Royal prerogative did thee compel
To conquer the enemies, sin, death and hell.
    Oh ! my glorious God and redeeming king.
        Royal prerogative, &c.

4.

And now he'as opened the book of life,
That in my soul has banished all strife;
A new name in the book has wrought,
The work of redemption by faith I'm taught.
    Oh! my glorious God sad redeeming king.
        A new, &c.

5.

O Lord, thou art the living bread,
And is alive tho' you were dead;
That when thy glorious face I see,
I shall live with thee eternally.
    Oh! my glorious God and redeeming king.
        That when, &c.

6.

And leave behind the seed of Cain,
Upon this earth for to remain;
The face of God ne'er to behold,
For reason's curst, tho' he is so bold.
    Oh! my glorious God and redeeming king.
        The face &c.

7.

God sent two prophets great I see.
Those glorious truths to shew to me,
And to all those that do truly believe
The declaration of great John Reeve.
    Oh! my glorious God and redeeming king.
        And to, &c.

8.
And great Muggleton by faith I see.
Was chose by God's glorious decree;
And those that great Muggleton disown,
Upon this earth will be left to groan.
   Oh! my glorious God and redeeming king.
       And those, &c.

JOHN WILLIAMS.

EIGHTEENTH SONG

WHY should I make freedom a slave,
Although the world be unkind, Sir?
Since my servant reason I have
Each critical monster to mind, Sir;
My reason shall draw. make brick and find straw,
It shall have no lime to be idle;
It early shall rise, each knave to surprise,
And put on the bit and the bridle.
       It early, &c.

2.
The children of this world are in arms
To kill and destroy for a season;
Not one bewailing another men's harms,
Thus it is to be ridden by reason;
Go on with work, fight Devil fight Turk,
Your reason and you are accurst too;
Since reason's your lord, and you rule by the sword
And suck up men's blood till you burst too.
       Since reason's, &c.

3.
Dust it's for which you do strive,
No treasure like that they can savour;
Each moment'tis for those that survive,
To take from the dead as a favour;
For still I perceive, if they could but live
Until this world's end, were it longer;
They'd still it enjoy, and kill and destroy;
The weaker must fall by the stronger.
       They'd still, &c.

4.
Let reason fight and plunder and kill,
And he'll continue fomenting;

Until with blood they all have their fill,
Without the least dram of repenting,
Let them fill their cup up, and drink every sup.
For reason on blood will be feeding;
My life shall stand in the promised land,
While mountains of reason lie bleeding.
      My life, &c.

5.

Then let my soul rejoice and be glad,
With raptures of sweet elevation;
What tho' this world be drunken and mad,
It shall not stop my revelation;
My sword in my mouth shall still defend truth,
And make reason's children to wonder.
It early shall fly and soar to the sky,
And sound in their ears like thunder.
      It early, &c.

6.

Then since the sword so ripe in mankind,
And ushers the soul to the grave too;
I'll keep house at home in my mind,
And enjoy those riches I have too;
I'll neither borrow nor lend---I cannot it spend,
It will be my portion to-morrow;
Whilst Devils that fight, must bid all good night,
And enter a deluge of sorrow.
      Whilst Devils, &c.

7.

And thus poor Cam will finish his days.
And solace his soul with delighting
In sounding forth his God's divine praise,
Whilst monsters and Devils are fighting;
My faith unto me a castle shall be,
Of impregnable strength and defence, Sir;
Each handler of steel my sentence shall feel,
Before that poor Cam goes hence, Sir.
      Each handler, &c.

                       WILLIAM WOOD, *Painter.*

NINETEENTH SONG.

WHO comes here
From Edom with dyed garments?

Our God so dear;
With blood he was made red.
When the wine-press he did tread
For his lost elect,
Whom he lov'd so dear.
      With blood. &c.

2.

For sin we
Justly all deserve to die,
The law makes it appear;
But God came down to die,
Justice to satisfy,
For his lost elect
Whom he lov'd so dear.
      But God. &c.

3.

Look and see
The boundless love of God,
When he suffered here;
He laid his glory down,
And of them he wore a crown,
For his lost elect
Whom he lov'd so dear.
      He laid, &c.

4.

His power and glory
With him he brought down,
When he centred here;
And naught he did divide,
For the God-head wholly died,
For his lost elect
Whom he lov'd to dear.
      And naught, &c.

5.

With power on high
He left his regency,
While he suffered here;
This power bore such away,
That they could not disobey
The commands of their God,
And Creator dear.
      This power, &c.

6.

Great Reeve and
Muggleton they do declare
That God suffered here ;
And when Christ was crucified,
The eternal Father died,
For his lost elect,
Whom he lov'd so dear.
       And when, &c.

7.

His body nail'd
Upon a cursed tree,
To the world it is clear;
But none are satisfied
What it was in him that died,
But his lost elect,
Whom he lov'd so dear.
       But none, &c.

8.

In love now let
Us all together join,
While we are mortals here;
in praises for to sing
To our dear redeeming king,
For his boundless love,
When he suffered here.
       In praises, &c.

                                      BOYER GLOVER.

TWENTIETH SONG.

O God of all Gods, and prince of all peace.
To sing forth thy praises let the saints never cease;
Who in thy divine love makes mortals thy guest,
By kind invitations to peace and to rest:
What love can be greater, can any one tell,
Than our God by his death to redeem us from hell?
Then let all that are elected his praises forth shew,
That had bowels of love to poor mortals below.

2.

For in the beginning when man was quite lost,
Out of life into death by the enemy toss'd,
Oh, sweet was thy promise thy own to redeem.

By promising life out of pale death again;
By faith thy babes saw it, tho' not in their days,
And lay down in peace, to thine eternal praise.
  Then let all, &c.

3.

A tower of water God built to men's wonder.
To keep the elect and the rebels asunder,
It stood on twelve pillars so bright and so clear,
The sun was seen thro' them all the whole year;
The pillars were faithful, beautiful and strong
To hold up the tower though ever so long.
  Then let all, &c.

4.

The next was a temple which God himself rais'd,
From the womb of a virgin, (his divine name be prais'd)
For himself to dwell in, which had twelve pillars strong,
And the powers of hell could do them no wrong,
This temple by serpents was trampled down plain
And in three days and nights it was reared up again,
Oh, mystery or mysteries! and blessed is he.
That hath faith to look into this great mystery.

5.

When the Holy of holies ascended on high,
And over grim death he had got victory,
The pillars stood fast, and like stars they did shine;
Their mouths breathed forth revelation divine;
And now in the dust death doth them retain,
Till Jehovah with power will raise them again.
  Then let all, &c.

6.

In process of time thick darkness did grow,
That it compass'd about this whole region below,
That men went a groping to find out the way,
But all to no purpose is these darksome days;
Till at length a bright light from heaven did shine
Which all that are elected' can witness divine
  Then let all, &c.

7.

In God's decreed time, in fifty and one,
In the month February, from his heavenly throne,
He made himself known unto all elect men,
The third and last time he shall ever come again;

He sent forth two champions his truth to maintain,
And to shut up all mouths that prattled in vain.
      then let all, &c.

8.

And out of their mouths proceeds spiritual fire,
To burn up all those that against them conspire;
With the sword of the Spirit, divine truth to defend,
And to cut them all down that with truth do contend;
They have also the keys of heaven and hell,
No champions like those in this region doth dwell.
      Then let all, &c.

9.

These champions have with them rare Gilead balm,
Which in a great earthquake will make a great calm;
It cures all wounds that are made by death's sting,
It makes the dumb speak, and sing praise to their
    king;
It makes the blind see these glorious days,
It makes the lame walk, and give God the praise.
      Then let all, &c.

10.

It makes the deaf hear their divine revelation,
Which expels all the fears of eternal damnation;
The knowledge of God in them is inspired,
Which all the elect have so long time desired;
The nature and form of angels they know,
What heaven. is above, and what hell is below.
      Then let all, &c.

11.

And of the right Devil, and rise of his seed,
They have satisfied all true men indeed;
The soul it is mortal they truly do say,
Tho' Devils and monsters of men do say, nay;
With many more secrets they are fully replenish'd,
Their work it is done, and God's mystery is finished.
      Then let all, &c.
                        WILLIAM WOOD, *Painter.*

TWENTY-FIRST SONG.

ETERNAL life it is to me,
  Now I by faith do know

That God has died upon a tree,
  To save my soul from woe;
For justice was wroth with sin,
  For which God did atone,
Or else in darkness I had been,
  And God should ne'er have known.
    For justice, &c.

2.

The holy city was brought down,
  Which Jerusalem did typify;
This was when God he vail'd his crown,
  And for to redeem us did die;
In the sanctum sanctorum of love,
  Did the Holy of holies dwell;
When God he came down from above,
  For to conquer death and hell,
    In the, &c.

3.

At Cana, A town of Gallilee,
  A miracle great was wrought;
Christ made the water wine, I see,
  When the water to him was brought:
This miracle it did show,
  Those souls which are divine,
When revelation it did flow,
  That their waters then were wine.
    This miracle, &c.

4.

Christ unto his apostles said,
  'In glory you shall shine;
And when I am dead, be not afraid,
  In my kingdom shove there is wine,'
And when by faith they did know,
  They should in glory shine,
Oh! how their spirits then did glow,
  When they drank that spiritual wine.
    And when, &c.

5.

When Moses he the rock did smite,
  He made the waters flow;
This did the soul of man delight,
  Who thirst did undergo;
The water gush'd forth like a flood,

To allay the thirst of man;
That water typified Christ's blood,
　　When he was God and man.
　　　　The water, &c.

　　　　　　6.

All that believe the third record,
　　They do drink of this spiritual wine,
And have the promise of the Lord,
　　That they ever in glory shall shine;
For by faith in the prophet's word,
　　Their souls are made divine;
They live by drinking of God's blood,
　　And their waters are turn'd to wine.
　　　　For by, &c.

　　　　　　　　　　　　BOYER GLOVER.

TWENTY-SECOND SONG.

Versus sung upon the Prophet Muggleton's coming down to Braintree, in Essex, in 1687, after being persecuted.

ALL saints that are present, come forth and rejoice.
Shew forth your elevations with heart and with voice,
For the storms they are past, and the winter is gone,
And the spring begins to flourish by virtue of the
　　　　Sun.
　　　　For the, &c.

　　　　　　2.

The lambs have their freedom, their joys have
　　　　abounded,
Since the wolves that would tear them, in their chase
　　　　are confounded;
They gnash with their teeth, and are sorely offended,
That the lambs have their freedom, and their power is
　　　　ended.
　　　　They gnash, &c.

　　　　　　3.

The shepherd is come for to see us once more,
To view those young lambs that, he ne'er saw before;
Where is such shepherd that dwells in the plain,
Can give his sheep water that they ne'er thirst again?
　　　　Where is, &c.

4.

And now, divine Sir, you are welcome to me,
And to the rest of our friends by their joy you do see;
We greet you in love as our shepherd and pastor,
And prostrate our souls to the grace of your master.
    We greet, &c.

5.

The Almighty God, which is the man Jesus,
Came down from his throne, of our burden to ease us;
Then let's sing to the praise or our heavenly king,
Till we with our voice do make the room ring.
    Then let's, &c.

6.

All praise, hallelujah and honour be given
To our God, Redeemer and Creator of heaven,
Who in his divine power doth nourish and cherish
All his elect lambs, that none of them perish.
    Who in, &c.

WILLIAM WOOD.

TWENTY-THIRD SONG.

On the Fourteenth, Fifteenth and Sixteenth of February.
(Tune, 'Fanny blooming fair')

ARISE, my soul, arise!
  Salute this glorious morn,
And tell the flowing joys
  Which should this day adorn;
When Muggleton and Reeve,
  From God's imperial throne,
Their mission did receive,
  To give to faith alone.
    When Muggleton, &c.

2.

On these three happy days,
  God did his mind declare,
That we might ever praise,
  His wonders every year;
These annual offerings bring,
  And unto Christ above,
In hymns of praise we'll sing,

Divine Songs

Thy love, O God, above.
    These annual, &c.

3.

Then saints united meet,
   In union let us join,
Our joys will then be greater,
   Our pleasures more divine:
'Tis such communion grace,
   Thus loving saints will be
Resemblers here of that blest place
   Of immortality.
      'Tis such, &c.

4.

There joys, will know no end,
   There's pleasures without pain;
When we shall there ascend,
   We shall no more complain;
But in sweet songs of love,
   We evermore shall sing,
Uninterrupted then above,
   The wonders of our king.
      But in, &c.

5.

Thy death, O God, will be
   Our ever grateful theme;
Thy sufferings in mortality
   Elect men to redeem:
Our subject then will be,
   In everlasting lays;
Tho' endless in eternity,
   It won't tell all thy praise.
      Our, &c.

JAMES MILLER.

TWENTY-FOURTH SONG.

A GLORIOUS throne in the heavens, me thinks I see,
A noble court bedeck'd with majesty;
A canopy of State, what tongue can tell,
The untold glories, where our God doth dwell?

2.

But to unfold what we don't understand,

God's holy prophet, we have in our land,
Who hath a soul adorned with matchless faith,
Winch is God's nature, as the scripture saith.

3.

But to his court, where God proclaims a call
To the elect angels for to see his fall;
The Almighty seats him on a matchless throne,
The elect admire the serpent all alone.

4.

A prisoner stands at the celestial bar,
Where guilt transports him from that kingdom far,
The judge unto the prisoner speaketh now,
Where direful anger seized the Almighty's brow.

5.

Which to behold the angels trembling lay,
The heavens seamed vail'd, then did the Almighty say,
'Pernicious actor of a deed so base,
The affects reap nothing to thee but disgrace.

6.

'Dost think that I who gave a life to thee,
Will suffer this rebellion against me;
No, thou shalt know my power shall extend,
To force thee hence, and downward thee to send.'

7.

The Almighty God, who then with power calls,
Which made heaven crack, and down the angel falls
Into a new found world, he did not know
That ere God's power had extended so.

8.

Nor has God done his crimes for to pursue
But woe to the earth, the Devil comes to you,
With whom he doth a new invention try,
In hopes to unthrone the eternal majesty.

9.

Which to prevent, great God the anger dear,
Decrees new ways, nor will he leave him here;
Then he into our parent Eve did come,
God nooz'd him there, and then decreed his doom.

10.
Thus was he cast by our great God's command,
Which to behold the angels trembling stand,
But straight new glories from their God appears
Into their hearts, and frees them of their fears;
   For which all praise and glory be ascrib'd
   Unto heaven's King for ever to abide.

JOHN LADD.

TWENTY-FIFTH SONG

FAITH, hope and charity recommended are
   To us by those who only know,
How far extends those heavenly paths so fair,
   And unto us the certain way doth show,
How to perform, and how to rightly do
   Such things as heaven's reward must be unto.

2.
First faith takes place, and then behold it draws
The heart from what delights it had before,
And then from things unjust it also awes,
The heart and mind from wand'ring out of door;
Oh! happy is he that can this faith retain,
And not fall back into the hands of Cain.

3.
And if he once though faith doth firmly gain
The way whereby temptations for to shun,
Then may he very well lay claim,
Unto the crown of life, which he hath won
Unto himself by having faith in them,
Whose language is more like to God's than men.

4.
For if we have faith, we hope also must have,
That we the rewards of faith shall once attain,
And if we do not believe that he will save,
Wo have not charity added to the same;
For charity believes the apostles, say,
That truth which is revealed in our days.

5.
Then Paul expresseth charity to be the chief;
The reason is, because we cannot have it
Before we are settled in a sure belief;

And then to gain it will be most requisite,
For when the foundation's sure, and is built well,
It will not fall with all the storms of hell.

        M. HATTER.

TWENTY-SIXTH SONG.
(Tune, 'Life of poor Jack')

OH! God, how shall I all my joys relate
 Unto whom shall I open them to?
It is not to the world of those things do I prate,
 Muggletonians, I speak unto you;
For the joys that do run thro' my breast could I write,
 It's too great for my pen to declare,
And my heart, was it possible I could indite,
 Then reason would go in despair;
For I see things past, present, and things for to come,
 By my faith, which is quicken'd in love.
Those glorious truths which is known but by some,
 The knowledge which came from above.

2.

When I view my God's plan to redeem his elect,
 His wisdoms is clearly made known;
How my heart thrill'd with joy when I feel the effect,
 That my God himself became a son,
He suffer'd himself to be servant to all,
 To redeem us, consented to die;
Then, rejoice Muggletonians, I am saved from the fall,
 He died, for such sinners as I;
So I'll praise and give glory to God in my theme,
 For his infinite unbounded love;
My pardon is sealed, and the means I esteem
 The knowledge which came from above.

3.

Before this commission was to me made known,
I knew not how my God to address;
When l pray'd to the father, I knew not the son,
My mind was always in distress;
His merciful Spirit to me did direct,
In a mysterious and wonderful way,
The hand that induced it, I am bound to respect,
My darkness is turn'd into day;
So I'll praise and give glory to God in my theme,
For his infinite unbounded love;
My pardon is sealed, and the means I esteem,

The knowledge which came from above.
                              JAMES DALE.

TWENTY-SEVENTH SONG.

ONE great Eternal God there is we own,
Who reign'd from all eternity alone;
Essential one, the only spring above
Of joy, of pleasure, and eternal love.

2.

Two sacred prophets, Reeve and Muggleton,
Inspir'd came from God's imperial throne,
Unravelling the sacred mystery
Of Christ, one God triune, but never three.

3.

Three glorious, dispensations now we find,
Extant on earth, to which is reason blind;
To Adam's seed they're given, for whose sake
The mystery's done this, threefold cord can't break.

4.

Four attributes thereof God will be,
Rever'd above to all eternity:
Wisdom and power will apparent shine,
Justice adore, and mercy praise divine,

5.

Five books did Moses write, in which the law
He well expounded, which reason keeps in awe;
This is a flaming sword has caus'd such strife,
To guard that seed still from the tree of life.

6.

Six points of worship there is, which to believe,
As they're laid down by the great prophet Reeve,
Eternal life will be the sure reward,
There is no salvation but in this record.

7.

With seven churches Asia did abound,
In which the true and living God was found;
Obscure the second, did one God declare,
Which now the third has manifested clear.

8.
Eight persons did the great eternal God
Preserve from the impending flood;
Triumphant rode, for new increase were sav'd,
While the whole world lay in one watery grave.

9.
Nine months the great Jehovah lay entomb'd,
Obscure lay buried in the virgin's womb;
No God there was in heaven or earth, till he
Appeared essential in mortality.

10.
The law ten sacred people did contain,
Which reason crav'd, but in observance vain,
Thinking to save themselves by it will be,
For not fulfilling, damn'd eternally.

11.
The eleven met, according to record,
And earnestly in prayer, invok'd the Lord;
Two lots were cast for one instead of him,
Whose cup now full, asunder burst with sin.

12.
The twelve complete, there mission did receive,
Impower'd on high. the Holy Ghost did give;
Twelve sorts of fruit these twelve apostles bore,
Yet Christ, the Son of God, did all adore.

CONCLUSION.

Mark well this sun dial with a single eye,
Observe, my friends, what truths therein do lie,
I dedicate to you all, while I live,
That you, with me, to God may glory give.
                    JAMES MILLER, 1738.

TWENTY-EIGHTH SONG.
(TUNE, 'Scots wha hae wi' Wallace bled.)

REEVE and Muggleton who led
The sons of God, and have them fed,
And shew'd who was the Lamb that bled,
   To gain the victory.

From the day God gave them power,
Reason's seed would them devour.
But they bound them down that hour,
   In chains and slavery.

2.

When the Devils they did rave,
Great Reeve the sentence to them gave,
Eternal torments they will have,
   And God shall never see;
But when I their writings saw,
Freedom's sword struck me with awe.
Free I'll stand, or free I'll fae, *(fall)*
   Or die for liberty.

3.

If oppress'd by reason's hand,
Faithful to my faith I'll stand;
Faith and peace go hand in hand
   To the land of liberty;
When proud reason ne'er shall go,
Thin earth will be their place of woe,
Burning torments undergo,
   And never shall be free.

4.

Then all those who do believe
In great Muggleton and Reeve.
A crown of glory will receive,
   And Christ their God shall see;
This will be the all-saints day.
When my God will to us say.
Come ye blessed, come away,
   And live eternally.

                                     WILLIAM CATES

TWENTY-NINTH SONG.
COMMISSION SONG.

HARK! hark! I hear the Almighty's voice,.
Saying, 'John Reeve, I have made choice
Of thee, my messenger to be,
To publish secrets hid from thee.
      Of thee, &c.

2.

And to assure what I have said,
The chiefest judge I have thee made,
My mind in scripture for to know,
To publish it to saints below.
    My mind, &c.

3.

'O Lord,' said I, 'I thee desire
some other person thou'lt inspire;
For my great inability,
Too mean thy messenger to be.'
    For my, &c.

4.

'If thou refuseth to obey
My great commands, to thee I say,
Both in thy body thou shalt see,
Curst hell and blest eternity.'
    Both in, &c.

5.

'Then, Lord,' said I, I'll thee obey,
With thy great Spirit, I thee pray,
Thou'lt me inspire, that I may be
A faithful witness unto thee.'
    Thoul't me, &c.

6.

Then said the Lord, 'it shall be done,
Go take thy cousin Muggleton,
Him I declare thy mouth to be,
And a high priest to wait on thee.
    Him I, &c.

7.

If he refuseth to obey
My sacred message, to him say,
That he for ever be accurst,
That God's commands refuseth doth.
    That he, &c.

8.

Then said the Lord, and spoke it soon,
'Go take thy choice companion,
And to John Tanee strait repair,
And seal him when thou comest there.

Divine Songs

And to, &c.

9.
Now I command thee, swift as tide
Take Muggleton, thy faithful guide,
Go to new Bridewell, where thou will see,
The Antichrist that opposeth me.
    Go to, &c.

10.
And when thou do his face behold,
Tell him from me, I've heard him bold
Against me broach his blaspheme,
For which curse him eternally.'
    Against me, &c.

11.
Next motion said, 'go summons all
Those cursed lying priests of Baal,
And know by what authority
False incense offered up to me.
    And know, &c.

12.
Bid them desist, or else do thou
Show them my fierce and angry brow
But my true prophets whom I send,
My favor's with them to the end.
    But my, &c.

13.
Say, who sent you to proclaim,
Under such falsehoods, my great name?
Therefore desist---me strait obey,
Or with my sword I will thee slay.
    Therefore desist, &c.

14.
Next motion said, declare to all,
Whose ignorance misguided call
Me their true God---to them declare,
Salvation doth to them appear.
    Me their, &c.

15.
Then first declare to them my form

And nature, which is yet unknown;
My form a spiritual man all o'er.
My nature's faith, which is all power.
    My form, &c.

16.
In me their God where ere I give,
It teacheth duty to believe;
Make them to know my dreadful stroke,
Unless they come and take my yoke.
    Make them, &c.

17.
Next go describe the Devil plain,
Whose first appearance here was Cain,
He once was Lucifer on high,
But fell, and became mortality.
    He once, &c.

18.
Then shew the nature of my throne,
It's spiritual I have thee shewn;
Likewise the angels' nature tell,
It's rational thou knowest full well.
    Likewise the, &c.

19.
Their bodies spiritual declare,
My sacred message swift to bear,
For I that am thy God can do
Wonders as yet unknown to you.
    For I, &c.

20.
Then tell my flock their souls must die,
That compounds all mortality;
They silent sleep until the day
I raise them to immortal ray.
    They silent, &c.

21.
Last, tell the place where hell shall be,
Its nature, torments, fuelly
This earth, where they their sins commit,
Is the place they suffer must for it.
    This earth, &c.

22.

Then shall their 'bodies be their hell,
Their cursed spirits the Devil,
Which burneth with such horrid flame,
They'll curse for to provoke their pain.
    Which burneth, &c.

23.

But you, my flock,' say to the blest,
'The Lord, by me, proclaim your rest,
With him for ever to possess
A glorious seat of happiness.'
    With him, &c.

24.

Then, praise the Lord, all you that own
His prophets Reeve and Muggleton,
For his most vicious free decree,
Peculiar you his saints to be.
    For his, &c.

                                JOHN LADD.

THIRTIETH SONG.
(TUNE, 'The Lillies of France')

All praise to my God, and his prophets I'll sing,
Since they unto me such glad tidings did bring;
They brought me from death unto a new life,
They have fill'd me with joy, and have banish'd all
      strife.
    They brought, &c.

2.

I in reason's line liv'd many a day,
And unto reason's God, I oftimes did pray;
But by this commission, I plainly do see,
One personal God is sufficient for me.
    But by, &c.

3.

For in reason's line I had a wounded soul,
But by faith in the truth, I now an made whole,
So let reason pray unto the persons three,
Since from that bondage I now am set free.
    So let, &c.

4.

My joy it is great, and my peace it is sound,
Since that the one personal God I have found;
So now I'll rejoice all the rest of my days,
Since that my prayers are all turn'd to praise.
      So now, &c.

5.

'Tis of that great God, who the wine-press has trod,
And purchas'd my soul, at the price of his blood,
Which by faith I see, is salvation to me,
And this is my earnest to eternity.
      Which by, &c.

                                   MATHEW HAGUE.

THIRTY-FIRST SONG.

ALL dominion and glory
Be to our great God,
Who hath made us partakers
Of his third record;
The knowledge of which
Doth make us rejoice:
That he of his clemency,
Thus 'should wake choice,
We his heirs to be
And in heaven to dwell
Beholding his glory,
Which do all things excel.
      We his, &c.

2.

Oh! the heavenly raptures,
We there shall possess,
The tongue nor the pen
Of no man can express;
Since the love of our God,
To us is made known,
Let us sing hallelujah,
To his heavenly throne:
And whilst we are here,
Let us all live in love,
To resemble the union
We shall have above.
      And whilst, &c.

3.

And as for the troubles
We here must endure,
Let this be our comfort,
Our reward is sure:
For what we here suffer
On account of our faith,
Will augment to our glory,
Then let us rejoice
That he, by his prophets,
To us hath made known,
Both his form and his nature,
With his heavenly throne.
      That he, &c.

4.

Likewise the right Devil,
They also unfold;
With the place of his torment,
Which none never could,
In this our dark age,
Discover his form,
That murdering Cain
Was the first Devil born,
They also affirm,
That the soul it must die,
And be raised again
To immortality.
      They also, &c.

5.

The nature of angels,
Is reason all pure;
This we certainly know,
And likewise are sure,
That all the whole world
Doth in wickedness lie,
O'erspread with blind guides
And vain falacy;
Who are striving by reason,
The scriptures to know,
And like wandering stars,
They run to and fro.
      Who are, &c.

6.

Then let us not waver.
But still stand our ground,
Our God will come quickly,
Our foes to confound;
With his heavenly host,
True judgment to give,
On the seed of the serpent,
Whilst we that believe
Shall stand in the clouds,
And see them receive
The sentence eternal,
Which none can reprieve.
    Shall stand, &c.

JOHN NICHOLLS, SEN.

THIRTY-SECOND SONG.

As I was musing all alone
  On great eternity,
Redeeming love so bright then shone.
  Salvation I could see,
The form of God by faith I see,
  His nature I do know;
This is eternal life to me,
This is eternal life to me,
  As prophets great do show.

2.

A formless God, without a head,
  Blind reason will adore;
This is a God will serve the dead,
  But faith wants something more;
Tho' in distress they oft have cried,
  No help they ever found;
Their God as yet has never died.
Their God as yet has never died,
  To heal the serpent's wound.

3.

O wretched man who dies in sin,
  What horror you will see;
'Twere well for you, you ne'er had been,
  To know such misery :
Should you weep rivers full of blood.
  No comfort could you find;
For want of faith in my God's word,

Divine Songs

For want of faith in my God's word.
  To ease their troubled mind.

4.

How dreadful is the stroke of death
  To reason here below,
When he does loose his mortal breath,
  And into silence go;
But with the faithful 'tis not so,
  The face of God they'll see,
When in his glory here below,
When in his glory here below,
  He sets all prisoners free.

5.

To courage, all you saints in love,
  And for your sins don't weep;
Eternal life, the God above
  In silent death did steep;
He left his great divine abode,
  The lofty heaven's high;
Immortal man there sat God,
Immortal man there sat as God,
  While God as man did die.

6.

God's justice it was wroth with sin,
  Which none e'er could atone,
All must in silent death have been,
  If God had not come down,
And kept the law, which none could do,
  Justice to satisfy,
For Adam's seed, 'tis very true,
For Adam's seed, 'tis very true,
  Whom sin had caused to die.

BOYER GLOVER.

THIRTY-THIRD SONG.

BEFORE I viewed this glorious mission,
  Which the Lord of life did send,
I was in a lost condition,
  Knew not how my life to spend.
      I was, &c.

2.

I implor'd the Lord of heaven,
  To relieve me in distress;
Still to me no comfort given,
  No regard, nor no redress.
    Still to, &c.

3.

When perusing on the letter,
  Which I oft times did survey,
Still my soul was ne'er the better,
  For, alas! I lost my way.
    Still my, &c.

4.

Then in scenes of sad dejection,
  Fearing that my soul might dwell,
Thus in shades of dark reflections,
  I was teaz'd with fears of hell.
    Thus in, &c.

5.

Thus was reason ever creeping,
  All my senses to invade,
For my faith lay then asleeping.
  And no reply to reason made.
    For my, &c.

6.

Now whilst reason was existing,
  Conscience was his whole abode,
Said the outward form subsisting,
  Was the way to worship God.
    Said the, &c.

7.

Then to homage with the devil,
  Dress'd up artful in disguise,
I, alas! did bow to evil,
  Thinking there to gain the prize.
    I, alas, &c.

8.

I to duty was so zealous,
  Lest my God I should offend
Reason's righteousness was jealous,
  Lest I should with him contend.

Reason, &c.

9.
I oft wished my life defeated,
  That my soul to heaven might fly,
But, alas! how I was cheated,
  When I found my soul must die.
      But, alas! &c.

10.
Faith and reason soon commanded,
  Both their forces to appear,
Reason's army soon disbanded,
  Faith alone did him cashier.
      Reason's army, &c.

11.
Reason's flocks I then viewed feeding,
  Under heavy burdens led;
When the letter they are reading,
  'Tis but husks on which they're fed.
      When, &c.

12.
View the world in all its splendour,
  Hypocrites that hold in scorn
Faith was never their commander,
  They are cursed reason born.
      Faith was, &c.

13.
Reason are those swine a feeding,
  They their bellies make their God,
Wars and bloodshed they are breeding,
  Hell eternal's their abode.
      Wars and, &c.

14.
Blessed be that glorious morning,
  Blessed be the hour when I
Saw the day star me adorning,
  Blessed to all eternity.
      Saw the, &c.

15.
It's the rock of my salvation,

It's my castle and my shield,
It's divine pure adoration,
　It's the bread of life reveal'd.
　　　It's, &c.

16.

Its those joys that so resplended,
　In those mansions so profound,
Pleasures that are never ending,
　When with glory we are crown'd.
　　　Pleasures, &c.

17.

In sweet elevated mountain,
　His eternal love we'll sing,
He's our light, our life, our fountain,
　He's our dear redeeming king.
　　　He's our, &c.

THOMAS SCUPHOLME.

THIRTY-FOURTH SONG.

COME all you that are dry,
　And in love now draw nigh,
For to drink of the infinite fountain;
　Do but step in the pool,
And the law will be cool,
　When you're wash'd in that infinite fountain.
　　　Do but, &c.

2.

God's prophets do shew,
　That the blood which did flow
From God's side, is that infinite fountain;
　And your souls it will clean,
If by faith you have seen
　That glorious and immortal fountain.
　　　And your, &c.

3.

If your souls they are red,
And with sin almost dead,
　You will live, if you drink of that fountain;
'Tis a water that's pure,
And your souls are secure,
　When you're wash'd in God's blood, that red
　　　fountain.

Tis a, &c.

4.

Let us set snide strife
While we are in this life,
   And think of the love of that fountain;
For the God of all love,
Came down from above,
   That his blood might become a pure fountain.
      For the, &c.

5.

Now the water is free,
To all those that can see,
   That God's blood is an infinite fountain;
Tho' the devils at strife,
Conquer'd eternal life,
   Yet they never can dry up that fountain.
      Tho' the, &c.

6.

My experience can tell,
That it extirpates hell
   In a soul when it drinks of that fountain;
When by faith I did fly,
Into eternity,
   Then my soul it was wash'd in that fountain.
      When by, &c.

7.

When Christ he here died,
The blood flow'd from his side,
   And did witness the death of that fountain;
And when Christ he was dead,
The Almighty God bled;
   What a scene was the death of that fountain!
      And when, &c.

8.

How the devils did shake,
When they felt the earthquake,
   In their souls, at the death of that fountain;
When the sun did appear,
Like sackcloth of hair,
   At the death of that infinite fountain.
      When the, &c.

9.

The Apostles, 'tis clear,
Did very much fear,
  And they mourn'd for the loss of that fountain;
But when God did arise,
It did them much surprise;
  Thomas cried, here's that infinite fountain.
    But when, &c.

10.

And when they did him know,
How their spirits did glow
  At the sight of that infinite fountain
And when Christ soar'd above,
He sent down in his love,
  The Holy Ghost' from that infinite fountain.
    And when, &c.

11.

And when they did receive,
They as freely did give
  Of the wine that they drew from that fountain;
And declar'd by the word
Of an Almighty God,
  All should live that did drink of that fountain.
    And declared, &c.

12.

Those that did believe,
They did power receive,
  For to lay down their lives for that fountain;
When their lives they laid down,
They were sure of a crown,
  By the blood of that infinite fountain.
    When their, &c.

13.

And by the third record,
We do know that the Lord
  Jesus Christ is that infinite fountain;
And in love now let us join,
To sing praises divine
  To our God that great infinite fountain.
And in love, &c.

                        BOYER GLOVER.

THIRTY-FIFTH SONG.

HAIL! blessed dawn, all hail! we sing,
  Distinguish'd glorious day;
When heaven's great immortal king,
  This record did display.
    This record, &c.

2.

In fifty-one, that happy year,
  This truth began to shine;
His last two prophets then appear'd,
  With tidings all divine.
    With tidings, &c.

3.

Come, raptur'd saints, rejoice with me,
  Admire redeeming love;
For it is by love alone I see,
  Our God came from above.
    Our God, &c.

4.

Oh! heart, amazing, matchless worth!
  To which there's no compare;
Jehovah great was born on earth,
An helpless infant there.
    An helpless, &c.

5.

Infinitedness! oh! wond'rous strange!
  Did finite like become;
Let us adore his glorious change,
  'Twas God became a son.
    'Twas God, &c.

6.

O, could my soul know how to trace,
  With sympathetic woe,
His toils amongst that cursed race,
  Whilst journeying here below.
    Whilst journeying. &c.

7.

Who can his mighty sorrows know,
  Or who the grief can tell,

Which Christ, our God, did undergo,
  To save his seed from hell,
    To save, &c.

8.

Submissive he resign'd his breath
  Unto the victor's power,
By which he was the death of death,
That very self-same hour.
That very, &c.

9.

Now death to us has lost its sting,
  No more the grave can boast;
We shall ascend with heaven's king,
  The mighty Lord of hosts.
    The mighty, &c.

10.

To Father, Son and Spirit too,
  That great and glorious One,
By faith in Jesus Christ we view
  Who did this work alone.
    Who did, &c.

THIRTY-SIXTH SONG.

IN a virgin, God entombed
In his burning glory bright;
Yet the virgin unconsumed,
Vail'd this great eternal light;
Clothed with flesh, blood and bone,
God here was born a son,
And vail'd eternity in night.
    Clothed with, &c.

2.

Now, behold a matchless wonder,
God an infant pure was born,
Spotless flesh did keep him under,
Former glory veil'd and gone;
No reason's gold had he,
No ruling majesty,
But like a subject all forlorn.
    No reasons, &c.

Divine Songs

3.
His vicegerents did protect him,
And did keep him from all harm;
Reason often did reject him,
Tho' he often did them charm,
When they his wonders see,
Then they amazed would be,
But knew not what did them alarm.
   When they, &c.

4.
When he had all things fulfilled,
Which he did come here to do,
Then by devils he was killed;
How in wrath their malice flew,
Filled, with envy and strife,
They slew the Lord of life,
And filled their father's cup anew.
   Filled with, &c.

5.
How their malice it extended,
When they took him from the tree,
That devil whom God never offended,
Him did pierce unjust we see;
But when he has made known,
God died in that son,
Oh! what a horror it will be.
But when, &c.

6.
Bright will be that glorious morning,
When God does to judgment come;
Bright will be that glorious dawning.
Of that great eternal Son;
That head with thorns once crown'd,
Bright glories will surround,
And streams of joy will through us run.
   That head, &c.

7.
Look, lost souls, for your redemption,
See your Maker on a tree;
Bleeding there without relention,
From grim death to set you free;

Think of his boundless love,
How he came from above,
And left his blest eternity.
    Think of, &c.

8.
God himself was a great winner,
When by devils he was slain;
And mortal man, a wretched sinner,
By God's death did life obtain,
Eternal life so sure,
By his God's blood so pure;
That crimson dye has washed sin's stain.
    Eternal life, &c.

9.
O, how blest is our condition,
Who by faith now lives to see,
How God gave John Reeve commission,
From sins wound to set us free
Freed from mount Sinai's strife,
To feed on mount Sion's life,
The soul of God eternally.
    Freed from, &c.

                              BOYER GLOVER.

THIRTY-SEVENTH SONG.
(Tune, 'The Queen of the May')

How blest is that soul who from death is set free,
Whose sins with its Saviour were nailed to a tree,
When mighty Jehovah resigned his breath,
And freed him power of eternal death.
    And freed, &c.

2.
This, none but a God of all glory could do,
By conquering him that did all things subdue;
He burst thro' death's bands his own seed to set free.
That they might reign with him to all eternity.
    That they, &c.

3.
What tho' the condition of my God was changed,
His eternal spirit remained the same;

This freely did offer which did death destroy,
'Twas infinite power; what could it annoy?
      'Twas, &c.

4.

Behold, elect jewels, your Saviour who died,
And for your transgressions death's pangs did abide;
And now your salvation to you hath made known,
Sing praise to Christ Jesus who Is God alone.
      Sing praise, &c.
                                 THOMAS PERRY.

THIRTY-EIGHTH SONG.

O DEATH, Where is thy dreadful sting?
   Grave, where thy victory?
Since God salvation down did bring,
   And for lost souls did die;
For when Christ was by devils slain,
   The victim then did die;
But when he rose to life again,
   He gain'd all victory.

2.

Here death, your mighty power fell,
   Though you so boldly trod,
And trampled down in silent hell,
   The very soul of God;
Though you a moment here did reign,
   When God for us did die,
When he arose to life again,
   You lost the victory.

3.

The sharpness of your sting is sin,
   The strength of sin the law;
But God no reason had in him,
   So no corruption saw;
But like a mighty lion bold,
   His power for to try,
He brake your chain, too weak to hold,
   And gain'd the victory.

4.

For when that God rose from the grave,
  'All power now says he,
'My lost elect mankind to save,
  Is given unto me;
My very soul in blood has trod,
  My wrath to satisfy;
And now I am a conquering God,
  In power and victory.

5.

'Three nights and days my soul did lay
  Within thy jaws, O death;
But longer you could not me stay;
  I re-assumed now breath,
For to fulfil my word so great,
  Which I spoke when on high,
I quickened from that latent state,
  And gained all victory.

6.

'For when that my first image fell,
  Your power fast him bound,
You brought him down to silent hell
  And sorely him did wound;
But I a gracious promise made,
  To him that I would die,
And when my soul in death had laid,
  I'd rise in victory.

7.

'And now, grim death, you are subject
  Unto my mighty power,
And I will call forth my elect,
  At my appointed hour;
At my command you'll disappear,
  You at my word shall fly,
And when my glorious voice they hear,
  They'll rise in victory.'

8.

Since God had such & promise made,
What need we for to fear,
For when our souls in death are laid,
There endeth all our care;
The word of God it doth suffice,

Divine Songs

Since he resides on high,
He'll call us forth to endless joys,
And give us victory.

BOYER GLOVER.

THIRTY-NINTH SONG.

CEASE, my soul, no more perplex,
Thy faith is on Jesus fix'd;
He is thy salvation true,
Fear not what vain man can do;
Tho' a mighty prince he be,
What signifies that to thee;
If persecution it should come,
Faith says 'Lord thy will be done.'

2.

If earthly crowns before thee lie,
Wouldst thou for them thy God deny?
Wilt thou not death much rather chuse,
Than thy salvation for to lose?
Or if a fire was prepared,
Faith could never be afraid,
But with raptures singing say,
'My dear God, I came to thee.'

3.

But all their father's subtil wit,
Cannot act, without permit;
Tho' they without number be,
God from all can set me free;
Then can God's elect be afraid?
They have alone the Saviour's aid;
Put the Lord's armour on,
Enemies thou shalt overcome.

THOMAS PERRY.

FORTIETH SONG.
(TUNE, 'My fond Shepherd of late are so blest.')

How blest and how happy am I,
  Who from eternal death am set free;
My hours, my bouts, serenely pass by,
  For I am one of God's elect I see.

2.

Hail! blessed and glorious three days,
  In which a commission was given;
My soul can rejoice and sing praise, and sing praise,
  For transcendent news sent from heaven.

3.

How beautiful are those divine feet,
  Which glad tidings of joy here do bring,
The news of salvation so sweet, so sweet,
  From Christ, our most glorious king.

4.

Now I know who it was for me did die,
  'Twas no less than the eternal God;
A spear there was thrust in his side, in his side,
  When alone here the wine-press be trod.

5.

Then forthwith blood and water did come,
  When the wound in his dear side was made;
Which proves that God died in the Son, in the Son,
  When his vesture with blood was made red.

6.

Then he bowed his glorious head and did die,
  Our debts then he fully did pay,
He, his justice did then satisfy, satisfy,
  And gained us an eternal day.

7.

By faith, my dear God, I have seen
  On the costs in bitter agony;
My soul in his blood is wash'd clean, is wash'd clean.
  And I shall live eternally.

8.

Christ Jesus, thou joy of my soul,
  What sorrow and pain thou went through,
And all to make thine elect whole, elect whole,
  All glory and praise is thy due.

9.

My dear God he will come once again,
And raise me to glory on high;
Then eternal praise I shall sing, I shall sing,
  To his transcendant bright majesty.

REBECCA BATT.

FORTY-FIRST SONG.

O GLORIOUS day which once more does salute us, We
will thy hours in praises spend;
Wherein God's mystery did end,
Which in sixteen hundred, fifty and one was given
To two prophets of renown,
John Reeve, the great; and Muggleton.

2.

The third, and last record on earth, is extant;
No more there'll be to man below;
And this the seed of faith doth know;
For spiritual principalities and powers,
So high exalted were brought down
By Reeve, the great; and Muggleton.

3.

Witness John Robins, that mighty prince of devils;
Who with lying signs appeared,
Which poor deluded souls received,
To their ruin here, and hereafter;
But his power did bow down,
To Reeve, the great; and Muggleton.

4.

And Tane too, exalted up to heaven,
Was, by them, brought down to hell;
This the saints do know full well,
Because they're left behind, by them recorded;
And now those powers few do own,
Since damn'd by Reeve and Muggleton.

5.

What havock has been made, what woeful sad
 destruction,
Among their followers here below;
Ranters and Quakers this do know,
For which their curs'd reason's so enraged;
That had they power, they'd kill all who own,
John Reeve, the great; and Muggleton.

6.

But by this last and spiritual commission,

All their power does decline;
And the law too does combine
Against them to protect what is against their natures;
Saints, I mean, who now do own,
John Reeve, the great; and Muggleton.

7.

Then Muggletonians, all sing praises to Christ Jesus,
For he is God, and only he---
This alone, by faith we see:
For reason cannot know the deep and hidden secrets,
Which all of this faith do own,
By Reeve, the great; and Muggleton.

8.

And now since they're dead and in the dust are lying,
And we, alone, can judgment give;
Let us, like true believers live;
And when we find that reason is blaspheming,
Let us pronounce their final doom,
The rule of Reeve and Muggleten.

9.

Why should we not, while in this world remaining,
Strive our talents to Improve;
Those that believe, embrace in love;
Those that despise, to death that's ever dying,
By the sentence, cast them down;
The rule of Reeve and Muggleton.

10.

Can we do too much for his eternal glory,
Who has been pleased to let us know
Our own salvation here below;
If so then, be not slack his will in executing;
But on devils pass their doom,
The rule of Reeve and Muggleton.

11.

Now to the Lord of Lords, Christ Jesus, our redeemer,
Let us in sacred anthems join,
And in songs of praise divine,
His holy name extol throughout all ages,
Since by him, we are made to own,
John Reeve, the great; and Muggleton.

JAMES MILLER.

FORTY-SECOND SONG.
(TUNE, 'Cassius and Pompey was both of them hated.')

My heart is as light as a bird in the spring,
And God's divine praise I will cheerfully sing;
I am assur'd for me he did die,
For which I shall praise him to eternity;
And tho' this truth many devils are scorning,
We shall see God in a glorious rooming.
      And tho', &c.

2.

Our God he will certainly call us from death,
And cause us to breathe there an immortal breath;
His bright burning glory will cause the first dawning,
When in his love he calls us in that morning;
And tho' this truth many devils are scorning,
They'll none see God in that glorious morning.
      And tho', &c.

3.

We have God's royal word, which there's nought can
      impede;
He died on a cross, for our sins he did bleed;
He sent forth two prophets, this secret to tell,
That he by his death has redeem'd us from hell
And tho' this truth many devils are scorning
We shall see God in that glorious morning.
      And tho', &c.

4.

When we are oppressed we soar up on high,
There drink of a fountain which ne'er can be dry;
Its virtues I now by experience can tell;
It extirpates death, and the fear of dark hell;
And tho' this truth many devils one scorning.
We shall see God on that glorious morning.
      And tho' &c.

5.

Blind reason does think, that our God he shall see,
When that he does raise him in eternity;
But guilt in their souls, it will quite veil that dawning,
When that they are rais'd in that dreadful morning;

And tho' this truth many devils are scorning,
It will be to me a bright glorious morning.
    And tho' &c.

6.

If God in his love had not died for my sin,
A captive in death, I for ever had been;
But to my comfort, I see I'm set free,
And surely with God, I for ever shall be;
And tho' this truth many devils are scorning,
We shall see God in that glorious morning.
    And tho', &c.

7.

How great was God's love to come down here and die,
For to attain power to raise us on high;
While devils in darkness beneath here will cry,
Because in their father they fell from on high;
And tho' this truth many devils are scorning,
We shall see God in that glorious morning.
    And tho', &c.

8.

A dry burning sand they will have for their bed,
Tho' always dying, yet ne'er will be dead;
Their cursed blasphemy the law will be forewarning,
When that they are rais'd on that dreadful morning;
And tho' this truth many devils are scorning,
It will be to me a bright glorious morning.
    And tho', &c.

9.

1 am joyfully feeding on that daily bread,
The flesh of my God, which for me once was dead;
And of his coming I have such a warning,
1 am always longing for that glorious morning;
And tho' this truth many devils are scorning,
We shall see God in that glorious morning.
    And tho', &c,

10.

The malice of devils to us it is great,
The faithful their fathers in time past did hate;
Nay, when that our God he came from on high,
Curst devils they caused his soul for to die;
And tho' this truth many devils are scorning,
We shall see God in that glorious morning.

And tho', &c.

11.

But their weak power him could not detain,
For on the third day he did rise up again;
And now he reigneth in glory on high,
Where we shall live with him to eternity
And tho' this truth many devils are scorning,
We shall see God in that glorious morning.
    And tho', &c.

BOYER GLOVER.

FORTY-THIRD SONG.

WHILE the herdsmen swine are feeding,
With their worship factions breeding;
Causing envy, noise and strife;
All strangers to the way of life.
    Causing envy, &c.

2.

But the Muggletonian's grounded,
In the worship God has founded,
Seeks no more, but sits secure;
He knows his God, and be is sure.
    Seeks no more, &c.

3.

While blind guides about do wander,
Pinch'd and starv'd with spiritual hunger,
Seeks the cleanest paths for rest;
Tho' there, they still are more perplex'd,
    Seeks the, &c.

4.

But the Muggletonian knoweth
What true peace the soul affordeth,
Rest contented all his days,
Because his prayers are turn'd to praise.
    Rests contented, &c.

5.

While these letter-mongers bawling,
Three and one, when none's their calling
For their God has ne'er a head,
But that's a God will serve the dead.

But their, &c.

6.
But the Muggletonian, making
Christ his God, his faith unshaking.
Knows he's safe, while Christ's his friend;
No other God will serve his end.
  Knows he's, &c.

7.
While these vagabonds are teaching,
And an unknown God are preaching,
Instead of giving hearers food,
They under-handed suck their blood.
  Instead of, &c.

8.
But the Muggletonians proffer,
All true bread, which none can offer,
Freely give that heavenly food,
To save their souls, and know their God,
  Freely give, &c.

9.
While these bastard pulpit roarers,
Devils incarnate, spirituals whorers,
With damnation scares the meek,
And squeezes money from the weak.
  With damnation, &c.

10.
But the Muggletonian's notion,
Knows damnation is their portion,
Bound in everlasting chains,
Till hell has being where they remain,
  Bound in, &c.

11.
These the wolves are, in sheep's clothing,
Which devour all before them,
Loves public greetings, and at feasts
The parson is the head of guests.
  Loves public, &c.

12.
These, the thieves are, and the robbers,
Which the scriptures plain discovers;

And For money they will paint
The very devil like a saint.
      And for, &c.

         13.
Truth they hate, 'cause it discovers
What they are; of what they're lovers,
Those saint-like, yet 'tis plain,
The scripture makes a trade for gain.
      Those saint like, &c.

         14.
But when Christ, in flames descending,
Hosts of angels bright attending,
Will this firmament divide,
And on the clouds in glory ride.
      Will this, &c.

         15.
Where will then pretended teachers,
Or the sin-absolving preachers
Then appear, for they can't face
Our glorious God that has a face.
      Then appear, &c.

         16.
Where will then their saints retire,
But with them into hell-fire?
For on earth our God they scorn'd,
Because he had a glorious form.
      For on earth, &c.

         17.
Then in fear, for mountains calling,
But none then, will mind their bawling,
Hull's begun, they feel the rod,
And fain would hide themselves from God.
      He'll begun, &c.

         18.
But all's over; no more scarlet,
Will bedeck a scripture varlet;
But to hell; oh, dire disgrace!
And there to have the hottest place.
      But to, &c.

19.
While poor Adam's seed ascending,
With their shouts the heavens rending,
Swift as thought to Christ repair,
And meet their Saviour in the air.
  Swift as, &c.

20.
Then the lights of this creation,
Which were made for time's duration,
Will no longer give their light,
Bus vanish in eternal night.
  Will no, &c.

21.
Endless horror, perturbation,
And eternal dissolution,
Then will hypocrites attend,
In racking torments, without end.
  Then will, &c.

22.
While the saints their God surrounding,
Feel eternal joys abounding,
With their king ascend above,
To realms of everlasting love.
  With their, &c.

         JAMES MILLER.

FORTY-FOURTH SONG
(TUNE, 'Stilla, darling of the Muses.')

Praises to my Maker's glory,
 Great immortal, only king,
Deeds which fill the secret story,
Let my muse attempt to sing;
While my soul with wonder traces,
 All thy attributes divine,
All thy goodness, all thy mercies,
 which in thee, I find combine.

2.
Love and joy, and admiration,
 In my breast alternate rise;
Who can view thy great creation,

Unastonish'd with surprise!
Man adorn'd with all perfection,
  Plac'd in heavenly paradise,
Thence he fell by thy permission,
  That he might more glorious rise.

3.

Death o'er all had reign'd triumphant,
  Adam sinn'd, and all must die;
But from mercy most abundant,
  Thou descendest from on high;
Man in all, but sin excepted,
  Thou for our sake didst become,
Leaving heaven, to be directed
  By thy guardians, in thy room.

4.

Wondrous strange, amazing wonder!
  The eternal Godhead died;
Thereby sin and death got under;
  He resplendant does arise;
Saints and cherubs now uniting,
  Sing a new song in his praise;
In a theme that's so delighting,
  Let us mortals join our lays.

GEORGE HERMITAGE.

FORTY-FIFTH SONG.

OH! praise the Lord my raptur'd soul,
  His mercy is great to thee,
Who from Egyptian darkness brought
  Me heavenly light to see;
Long in false worship I was lost,
  Guided by my blind zeal;
An idol worshipp'd for a God,
  That my soul could not heal.
      That my soul, &c.

2.

No other God I there could find;
  But praise to thee alone,
Who sent great Reeve and Muggleton,
  Thine elect to call home;
By them the shepherd's voice I heard,
  And I, a poor lost sheep,

Was brought unto the bar of God,
  Before his judgment seat.
    Before his, &c.

3.

Justly condemn'd, God justified,
  Oh! there I trembling stood;
There's naught could heal my wounded soul,
  But his most precious blood;
Which to attain I knew not how,
  Because of my great guilt,
Till prostrated I cried, 'Lord
  Do with me as thou wilt.'
    Do with me, &c.

4.

The Lord accepts my contrite heart,
  No more an angry judge;
He then appears to me in love,
  And heals me with his blood;
Without which from eternal death,
  There's none can be set free;
'Twas thou created and redeem'd,
  All glory lord to thee.
    All glory, &c.

5.

Oh! that my tongue could but express,
  Lord, how I thee adore;
So much as one poor single sand,
  That lies on the sea shore;
Although they without number be,
  Could I show that small part;
But all that thou require, Lord,
  Is a broken contrite heart.
    Is a broken, &c.

6.

But this thy third and last record,
Truth there is none besides;
Thy elect see that path of life,
Thy prophets are their guide,
Into those realms of light and life,
Where we shall ever sing,
All praise and glory to our God,
Our dear redeeming king.
    Our dear, &c.

Divine Songs

THOMAS PERRY.

FORTY-SIXTH SONG.

(A song made by a Believer when the Commission came first forth, and sung by the Prophet Lodowick Muggleton, at Braintree, in Essex)

WHEN men of learning leave discerning,
  Perfect truth then flourish shall,
The laity then wilt be esteem'd;
  Now mask what than there will befall;
No false speaking, no false seeking,
  Will be heard any more at all;
But uptight dealing without stealing,
  Evermore then flourish shall.

2.

The lion with the lamb may live then,
Peace will reign perpetually;
All strife and anger will be banish'd,
Things will go more equally;
No more error to breed terror,
Will be heard any more again;
For true believers are perceivers,
Neither will their faith prove vain.

3.

Not many wise, nor many noble,
  Ere embrac'd christianity;
They gave the world the shadow of it,
  Bat ever practic'd cruelty;
The conscientious, not contentious,
  Evermore were punished;
No compassion, but proud passion,
  Ever great men fancied.

THOMAS TURNER.

FORTY-SEVENTH SONG.

ARISE, my soul, sweet songs to sing,
In praise of Christ, my God and king;
Ye new-born saints come join with me,
Let us all join in sweet harmony,
To praise our God, who by words and voice,
Of Reeve nod Muggleton did make choice.

To praise, &c.

2.

His two last messengers to be,
His own elect for to set free
From reason's yoke and slavery;
Now we enjoy true liberty,
Which makes us chaunt sweet songs of praise,
To Christ, the ancientest of days.
    Which makes, &c.

3.

Tho' reason sometimes us annoys,
Yet often we have spiritual joys,
Which doth arise from our seed spring;
This makes the new-born saints to sing,
Sweet songs of praise, and divine lays,
To Christ, the ancientest of days.
    Sweet songs, &c.

4.

When our God hath put an end to time,
We shall be raised to joys divine;
Eternally with God shall be,
Most glorious sights we then shall see;
And that will raise new songs of praise,
To Christ, the ancientest of days.
    And that, &c.

5.

Reason will here be left in woe,
But saints will newer and newer grow,
Younger and younger we shall be,
New joys will spring eternally;
And that will raise new songs of praise,
To Christ, the ancientest of days.
    And that, &c.

6.

With glorious bodies we shall shine,
Have heavenly food that's all divine,
Which out of our own spirits will rise;
No want there be, but full supplies;
And that will raise new songs of praise,
To Christ, the ancientest of days.
    And that, &c.

7.

That glorious kingdom hath no bounds,
There divine music sweetly sounds;
As swift as thought we there shall move,
And be full of glorious Godlike love;
And that will raise new songs of praise,
To Christ, the ancientest of days.
      And that, &c.

8.

A spiritual glorious lore fire 'twill be,
Of new ravishing joys eternally,
So pure, so gentle, soft end sweet,
As will fill our souls with joys complete;
And that will raise new songs of praise
To Christ, the ancientest of days.
      And that, &c.

9.

There's a chrystal sea of burning glass,
And saints therein and out may pass;
And warbling birds on many a tree,
Turning their notes melodiously,
According to their wisdom praise
Our God. the ancientest of days.
      According to, &c.

10.

There is all such creatures as is here,
But spiritual, like chrystal clear;
All males, not made to generate,
But live in divine happy state;
They according to their wisdom praise
Our God, the ancientest of days.
      They according, &c.

11.

There is nothing there that can offend,
But all to peace and union tend;
The lion with the lamb doth play,
And down in peace together lay;
And saints will chaunt sweet songs of praise
To Christ, the ancientest of days.
      And saints, &c.

12.
Thousands of angels we shall see
Attending on God's majesty;
Armies of saints we shall behold,
And prophets crown'd with crowns of gold,
All ascribing glory, honour and praise
To Christ, the ancientest of days.
  All ascribing, &c.

13.
The spiritual motions that in us now rise,
Ws: shall feed on with new Godlike joys;
We that commun'd together below,
Shall perfectly each other know;
And that will raise new songs of praise
To Christ, the ancientest of days.
  And that, &c.

14.
But this the greatest joy will give,
Eternally with God to live,
See his glorious person face to face,
And remember his mercy and free grace;
All which will raise new songs of praise
To Christ, the ancientest of days.
  All which, &c.

15.
And now, my friends, with one accord,
Let's fight the battles of the Lord;
If persecutions us surround,
It will add the more glory to our crowns;
And that will raise new songs of praise
To Christ, the ancientest of days.
  And that, &c.

16.
Think of that blest eternity
We new-born saints are sure to see,
Angels nor men can't comprehend
The glorious joys, world without end;
All which will raise new songs of praise
To Christ, the ancientest of days.
  All which, &c.

REBECCA BATT.

FORTY-EIGHTH SONG.
(TUNE, 'Twas when the Seas were roaring.')

You men quite void of fear,
  Who justice does defy,
When you to death draw near,
  God's justice will be nigh;
Come let us reason truly,
  And take Reeve for our guide,
And see if justice wholly
  Was ever set aside.

2.

For justice in our nature,
  God's watchman is, I see;
To tell the great Creator,
  When we here sinners be;
For where there's no impression
  For sin in a soul made,
That soul needs no physician,
  As Christ, our God, has said.

3.

But we through true repenting,
  Find joy and peace abound;
But where there's no relenting,
  No mercy can be found;
For when that justice cried,
  'Lost Adam, where art thou?'
It cannot be denied,
  But justice made him bow.

4.

But being of God's nature,
  Relenting light was found;
He pray'd the great Creator
  To heal his deadly wound;
For justice him subjected
  With pain and misery;
He saw himself rejected,
  But God he could not see.

5.

Thus Adam for transgression,
  Both death and hell here found;
God's law it took possession,

And fast his soul here bound;
But God, that mighty shepherd,
  Restored this lost sheep;
Tho' spotted like a leopard,
  God made him cease to weep.

6.

And we of Adam's nature,
  For sin doth bleed and cry,
To God, the great creator,
  His justice to pass by;
And when we have relented,
  When justice has us bound,
And truly have repented,
  We mercy's God have found.

7.

Then, the first resurrection
  From death to life, we see;
Our souls made pure perfection,
  As white as snow they be;
But for a fresh transgression,
  Fresh punishment is found,
And justice gets possession,
  And mercy can't be found.

8.

This was the case of David,
  As Muggleton does tell;
Tho' he knew he was saved,
  He for transgression fell;
And filled with fear and horror,
  When justice had him bound,
He mourned his days in sorrow,
  Till he fresh merry found.

9.

Thus justice, when offended,
  Will make a sinner cry;
And mercy not extended,
  That soul will surely die;
Thus dread is our condition,
  With some it is much worse;
He ever will be damned,
  That does God's justice curse.

                              BOYER GLOVER.

FORTY-NINTH SONG.
(TUNE, 'The Billows')

OH! how my soul does ponder
On great eternity;
To think there's no beginning,
Nor ever end will be;
Oh! how my soul is ravish'd,
Now I by faith can see;
God left his boundless kingdom,
And here did die for me.
      God left, &c.

2.

Oh! how I am astonish'd
To see that God came down,
And here in Human nature,
He veil'd his glorious crown;
It was for sinful mortals
He left divine abode,
And died a spotless creature,
But arose a perfect God.
      And died, &c.

3.

These joys they are an earnest,
While we are here below;
And when that we are raised,
Eternal joys will flow;
Then Comes our greatest comfort,
The face of God to see,
Assured in his presence
To live eternally.
      Assured in, &c.

4.

When devils they are rais'd,
And from the grave set free,
They'll always be a dying,
Yet never dead will be;
Then comes their greatest horror,
Within their souls they'll see;
They'll always live in sorrow,
To all eternity.
      They'll always, &c.

5.

When God he was a dying,
No pity they did show,
And from his spotless body,
They caus'd the blood to flow,
And when that they are rais'd,
God will relentless be,
And leave them here in horror
To all eternity.
     And leave, &c.

6.

When God he was a dying,
What joy their souls did see;
Not dreading in that hour
The great eternity:
But when that they are rais'd,
God's law so quick will be,
They'll cry with pain and horror,
'Endless eternity!'
     They'll cry, &c.

7.

And now with grateful praises,
Sing to our God and king,
Who for our soul's redemption,
Salvation here did bring;
For there's no God like Jacob's,
Lord Jesus Christ on high,
Who lives one God in glory,
Above the starry skies.
     Who lives, &c.

                                BOYER GLOVER.

FIFTIETH SONG.

BEHOLD our great God
  When he bled on the cross,
Sin, death, hell and grave,
  He soon conquered for us;
Who are his elect seed,
  Like gold we've been tried,
Now we feed on his blood,
  That was spilt when he died.

Divine Songs

2.

Now, all who do hunger and thirst,
  They may feast;
There's a banquet prepared,
  For spiritual guest;
Tho' the prophets do serve it
  In homely attire,
There's plenty to satisfy
  All our desire.

3.

This banquet provided for
  None but the poor;
Wine, oil, milk and honey,
  Received without store;
To purchase with money,
  Or works would be theft,
As none may enjoy it,
  But as a free gift.

4.

We are all on a level,
  At this royal feast,
As no one is greater
  Than him that is least,
The donor excepted;
  But this may seem odd,
We are joint heirs with Christ,
  And Christ is our God.

5.

We don't invite reason;
  It never could scan
God's glorious person,
  When he became man;
So they're not invited
  With us for to dine,
For they truly can't relish,
  Such dainties divine.

6.

For pastime and pleasure,
  We joyfully sing,
Of the glorious feats done,
  By Zion's great king;
The song of redemption,

Both ravish each heart,
When saints, sweet enraptur'd
　　Their joys do impart.

7.

Christ pour'd out his soul;
　　See death down it goes;
None ever shall rise, who
　　Thro' seed are his foes;
To snatch his lost sheep
　　From an eternal grave,
Is worthy of Jesus,
　　Who conquered to save.

　　　　　　　　　　　　JAMES DALE.

FIFTY-FIRST SONG.
(TUNE, 'Christ my precious bleeding God.')

THOUGH reason prates of mighty things,
They know not of that king of kings;
'Twas he alone the wine-press trod,.
When he became my bleeding God.
　　'Twas he alone the wine-press trod,
　　When he became my bleeding God,
　　When he became my bleeding God.

2.

The great Jehovah did the work;
The man Christ Jesus is the same,
Who died upon a cursed tree,
From eternal death to set me free.
　　　　Who died upon, &c.
　　　　From eternal, &c.

3.

Oh! then what pain his soul went through,
No one was there that could him help;
'It's finished,' my God he cried,
His head he bow'd, his soul then died.
　　　　'It's finished,' my, &c.
　　　　His head, &c.

4.

I saw my God next in the grave,
It was my mortal soul to save;
But death could not him long detain,
By his own decree he rose again.
  But death could, &c.
  By his, &c.

5.

No other God but this I'll have,
He conquer'd death, hell and the grave,
His own elect for to set free,
To praise him in eternity.
  His own elect, &c.
  To praise, &c.

6.

When all is over, and time's no more,
O, then our joys they will increase;
Then reason will lose their mighty things,
Whilst we shall praise the king of kings.
  Then reason will, &c.
  Whilst we, &c.

BOYER GLOVER.

FIFTY-SECOND SONG.

IN the first of St. John, it is very clear,
That God blame flesh, as the prophets declar'd;
In the womb of a virgin he died, I see,
And again he did live, his elect to set free.

2.

That Word that was God, became flesh and did live,
And dwelt amongst men, their sins to forgive;
He came unto his own; they received him not;
These devils they knew not that he was God.

3.

The prophet Isaiah, in old times did tell,
God would become flesh, and with as will dwell;
That wonderful Counsellor, the mighty God, I see,
Was the everlasting Father that died on a tree.

4.

He that descended down in his love,
Ascended again to his kingdom above;
There he will reign for ever, I see,
Praise him, ye saints, to all eternity.

5.

And when he ascended, gave gifts unto men,
The gift of true prophecies, I do mean;
They that can believe they were sent of God,
Will surely have a prophet's reward.

6.

All you that have faith in this third record,
And truly believe, that Christ is the only Lord; Patiently wait till your change it doth come,
Then Jesus, your Lord, will call you home.

7.

At the voice 'Come my bless'd,' we shall arise,
And meet our almighty God in the skies;
With great Reeve and Muggleton, there we shall see,
Our God, face to face, to all eternity.

WILLIAM CATES.

FIFTY-THIRD SONG.

HARK! hark! I hear the trumpet speak,
Saying 'awake from your dead sleep,
The time is come that you must fly
To your God in all eternity.

2.

'Make haste, I say, all you that own
The prophet Reeve and Muggleton;
Make haste, that you with them fly
To your God in all eternity.'

3.

'Then Lord,' said I, 'our lamps are trimm'd,
We are are ready on you to attend;
We are ready at your feet to fly,
And live with God eternally.'

4.

The second sound will then be heard,
Wakening the devils full of fears;

Then they'll lament, and howl and cry,
That they are damn'd eternally.

5.

No glimpse they'll have of God on high,
To add unto their misery;
No more they will the light then see,
But remain in hell eternally.

6.

While we are with our God above,
With golden harps and songs of love,
Praising his name that set us free,
And shall live with God eternally.

CATHERINE PEERS.

FIFTY-FOURTH SONG

LAUGH, and reason's God despise,
All ye saints that are made wise;
Reason's god is in all life,
Human, brutal, vegetive,
Which, at first, from nothing came,
And must to nothing return again.

2.

Reason has its delights here,
Worldly riches are his care;
While faith with plenty here are bless'd,
Of a jewel they are possess'd
Of the brightest magnitude,
Which does blind the Cainish brood.

3.

Its brightness from a substance shine,
Which proud. reason can't define;
Reason's eye look to and fro
For the God they do not know;
So being of their father's trade,
A nothing god themselves have made.

4.

Of nothing God made worlds, they say,
A nothing, well their God may be;
Nothing working on nothing,

Of nothing can come nothing;
So their whole system, where they rest,
Is but nothing at the best.

5.

To the faithful is proclaim'd,
How this notion nothing came;
Cain, when in angelic state,
God's forming beings of matter, did hate,
And would from God his power take,
And of nothing all things make.

6.

This author of nothing, is cost down,
From God's presence he is thrown;
Because, he god of god's would be,
And do all things more wise than he;
God to this earth has him confin'd,
And never more to know his mind.

RICHARD WYNNE.

FIFTY- FIFTH SONG.
(TUNE, 'When first by fond Damon.')

No more of your canting and preaching, no more,
With external forms which have charm'd me before,
Your vain supplications and crocodile tears,
Nor your cries to the Lord you have made without ears;
Your fetters I drop, from your thraldom I'm free,
Hypocritical priests, now your falsehood I see.
  Your fetters, &c.

2.

You who by long prayers do prey on the poor,
The bread and the substance of widows devour;
Of external righteousness make a fair show,
While nothing but praise and gain's in your view;
Ye vipers, ye serpents, ye seed of the devil,
How can you escape the last great day of evil.
  Ye vipers, &c.

3.

I bid you adieu, while I trust on my God,
My glorious redeemer, and sov'reign Lord;
Behold the great work which he wrought on the tree,
'It is finish'd,' he cried, 'it is finish'd for thee;'
Content with his merits, my weakness I'll own,

And rely on his power, and mercies alone.
    Content with, &c.

4.

For on earth all have sinn'd, and no one is good,
Salvation's alone in the blood of our God;
For the sin of his seed, he was smitten and bruis'd,
By the children of reason, was mock'd and abus'd;
The chastisement for our peace upon him was laid,
By his stripes we are heal'd, and our debt he has paid.
    The chastisement, &c.

5.

Then, O may the seed of the dear bleeding lamb,
In spiritual wonder, adore his great name;
Beholding the kingdom of heaven their own,
Without works of righteousness which they have done;
While hypocrites cry up their prayers and their tears,
'Tis finish'd, 'tis finish'd, will calm all our fears.
    While hypocrites, &c.

                          HENRY BONEL, 1763.

FIFTY-SIXTH SONG.

ALL hail to our redeeming king,
  For all his boundless love;
With raptur'd joy of praise we'll sing,
  'Twill be our theme above;
Where discords will for ever cease,
  Eternal love abide;
True saints shall all be crown'd with peace,
  And pleasures sweetly glide.

2.

Incessantly we there shall praise
  This great end glorious God;
Eternal hallelujahs raise,
  In that most bless'd abode.
What mortal can define the joy
  That is laid up in store,
Where nothing never shall annoy
  The faithful evermore.

                          MILLER, 1744.

FIFTY-SEVENTH SONG.
(TUNE, 'By a prattling stream, on a midsummer's eve.')

By faith I can see how my God did come down,
In flesh he vailed his glorious crown
The eternal Father transmuting I see,
And hiding his Godhead in humanity.
    And hiding, &c.

2.

His spiritual body was changed to seed,
With which Mary's mixed as he had decreed;
This became a fitclothing for his spirit so pure,
And vail'd from devils his infinite power.
    And vail'd, &c.

3.

Thus God became man; O! how glorious the sight,
To see as I can, fills my soul with delight;
To see God a dying upon a curst tree,
Assures me of living to eternity.
    Assures me, &c.

4.

A part of Jehovah could not set me free;
'Twas this whole I AM that did die on a tree;
These things seen in order has made my soul good,
And when reason would drown me, I drink Godhead
    blood
    And when, &c.

5.

His blood all-sufficient my wounded soul heal'd;
What made it sufficient, the infinite spring kill'd;
No half of a God could redeem one from hell;
No, it was Paul's God, where all fullness do dwell.
    No, it, &c.

6.

Oh! how I behold him in three glorious roads,
Which he has entitled, three heavenly records;
Each a form and a nature most glorious I behold;
The first quite external like the fathers of old.
    The first, &c.

Divine Songs

7.
But when he descended, his Godhead conceal'd,
And none knew where God was, but were 'twas
      reveal'd;
They preach'd the Son, tho' the Father was he;
They preach'd his wisdom in a mystery.
    They preach'd, &c.

8.
Lord, this is a mystery, most glorious to sec,
God manifest in flesh, great eternity;
His blood savour'd life, where the veil was look'd
      through,
And his blood savour'd death, in those who said he's,
      not true.
    And his, &c.

9.
When it was his decreed time that the third record
Should reveal the two seeds, and who's very Lord,
It witness'd the Father in the Son does remain;
The Holy Ghost proceeding from the mustard grain.
    The Holy Ghost, &c

10.
This pure chrystal fountain my thirst does suffice,
I see the Godhead dead, the true sacrifice;
This sight makes me sure all my sins are pass'd by,
This sight lights me safe Into eternity.
    This sight, &c.

JOHN PEAT.

FIFTY-EIGHTH SONG.

BEHOLD a wonder! two messengers are sent,
By voice of words, with a new testament;
O, strange expression! is there more than two?
(To wit) the old testament, and the new:
Yea; now in this last age there is come forth,
The third record of God upon this earth.

2.
For the two witnesses spoken of by John
In the book of the Revelation,

Are now extant on earth, their names are known,
Call'd John Reeve and Lodowick Muggleton;
These two are sent the true God to declare,
His form and nature both, and what they are.

3.

The right devil, his form and nature tell,
With the place of heaven, and the place of hell;
The angels and their persons, and withal,
The rise of the two seeds, and of the fall;
And how the soul is mortal, and must die:
These things are declar'd with great majesty.

4.

So that the scriptures now stand on their feet,
The Spirit of Life is pour'd into it;
For this is the commission of the Spirit,
Which doth the law and gospel both interpret;
No prophet, or apostle, heretofore,
Did know so mach; but these prophets knew more.

5.

Yea; and their knowledge doth excel all men,
That ever spoke, or ever writ with pen;
So doth their power; for in their mouths is put
A two-edg'd sword, and it doth surely cut;
For life and death in these same words do lie,
Two seeds seal'd up to all eternity.

6.

For God hath given them a greater power,
Than over mortal man had to this hour;
Let none despise this, lest they feel the stroke,
The sentence past, it is without revoke;
Renown'd prophets, let this your motto be,
You are the last to finish prophecy.

ELIZABETH GOODWIN.

FIFTY-NINTH SONG.

COME reason, now let's reason,
  And hear what I shall say;
For words when spoke in season,
  Will glorious truths display;
Yet, tho' by reason spoken,
  Mind what I here unfold,
My reason's but the token,

By faith these truths are told.
    Yet tho', &c.

2.

Yet useful 'tis, I own it,
   If faith its master be;
But ever shall disown it,
   To have the mastery;
For 'tis itself rebellious,
   And full of cursed pride,
And of its own is jealous,
   All other works deride.
    For 'tis, &c.

3.

But when by faith 'tis given,
   A power how to shew
The mysteries of heaven,
   How sweetly does it do;
The best of servants, surely,
   For mortals, but the worst,
Of masters, 'tis most truly,
   For't brings eternal curse.
    The best, &c.

4.

Then saints who know its power,
   Your praises ever sing,
And Christ's free love adore,
   Your everlasting king;
Who that you might be heirs,
   He clos'd the breach so wide;
Immortal God prepares
   A mortal womb, and died.
    Who that, &c.

5.

Thus heaven's great Creator,
   His spiritual body chang'd
Into a spotless creature;
   Oh! wonderfully strange,
That the eternal Spirit
   Should lay his glory by,
That we might life inherit
   With him eternally.
    That the, &c.

6.
This mystery admire,
  How God did flesh assume,
And yet without desire,
  Tho' both were in the womb;
But when our God descended,
  That cursed seed lay dead;
And only faith defended
  The very God's Godhead.
    But when, &c.

7.
Now, saints, behold your Maker,
  A spotless infant born;
In all with us partaker,
  Excepting sin alone;
Tho' angels from all danger,
  Protecting did him keep;
Yet no place but a manger
  Was found where God could sleep.
    Tho' angels, &c.

8.
Then think not much while here,
  Necessity to know
For Christ, as it appears,
  The same did undergo;
For, when to Bethlehem guided,
  The wise men brought relief;
Besides, he was despised,
  Acquainted much with grief.
    For when, &c.

9.
Are you unjustly treated?
  Consider he was worse;
For sin on sin repeated,
  Deserv'd eternal curse;
But he no sin committed,
  Yet charged wrongfully;
For they a thief acquitted,
  And doom'd our God to die.
    But he &c.

10.
Believers, read the story,
  And ever be content;
Think how the God of glory
  All sufferings underwent,
That we might be possessors
  Of an immortal crown;
He was number'd with transgressors.
  And died to save his own.
    That we, &c.

11.
Then, humble with submission,
  Think not your troubles strange,
Or pine at your condition,
  But patient wait your change;
For after grief comes pleasure,
  Where we shall ever sing
With Christ, our only treasure,
  Our suffering God and king.
    For after, &c.

JAMES MILLER.

SIXTIETH SONG.
(TUNE, 'In a Virgin God entombed.')

DEATH thou mighty king of terrors,
  To all mortals here below,
I shall feel thy stroke of sorrow,
  Ere I to my God can go;
Welcome, grim death, to me,
  Your power will end, I see,
When I ascend to God on high.

2.
Oh! how sharp's thy sting of horror
  To lost mortals here below;
Oh! how dreadful is the sorrow
  That they'll ever undergo;
But saints that God does know,
  With them it is not so;
They die to live with God on high.

3.
Though you got the great Creator,
  Once within your darksome cell;

He was of a quick'ning nature,
　　There your mighty power fell;
Had you ne'er been at strife
　　With the whole Godhead life,
Then death you'd reign eternally.

　　　　　　　　4.
Here the devils they were blinded,
　　Tho' they Christ as God denied,
Eternal death they need not have minded,
　　If by them God had not died;
Then all would silent be,
　　No joy, nor misery,
To the elect, nor lost mankind.

　　　　　　　　　　　BOYER GLOVER.

　　　　　SIXTY-FIRST SONG.
　　　(TUNE,' Eternal life it is to me.')

How happy is that soul that sees
　　His God for him has died,
And has his conscience set at ease,
　　By the blood that flows from Christ's side;
His spirit is sanctified,
　　By tasting boundless love;
When soul and body here have died,
　　He shall soar to God above.
　　　　His spirit, &c.

　　　　　　　　2.
God's blood is a fountain pure,
　　Which in our souls does flow,
It makes us here to sit secure,
　　For we know that to God we shall go;
This, this is the water of life,
　　Which thirst does satisfy;
The devils with us are at strife,
　　We shall live eternally.
　　　　This, this, &c.

　　　　　　　　3.
This is a glorious truth indeed,
　　And happy is he that can see
That God here on a cross did bleed,
　　From sin to set us free;
This, this is a wondrous light,

When God in death here lay,
External light was vail'd in night,
　For to spiritualize his clay.
　　This, this, &c.

4.

No other way could God here find,
　When he came from his kingdom above;
So unto death himself resign'd,
　As a manifestation of love;
Oh! I am amazed at the sight,
　In death the Godhead lay,
That eternal light might pass thro' night,
　For to see an eternal day.
　　Oh! I am, &c.

5.

My soul it does in splendour live,
　When I drink of the water of life;
I have none to sell, nor none to give,
　For I have just but enough to save life;
My spirit is sanctified,
　By feeding on God's love;
When soul and body here have died,
　I shall live with God above.
　　My spirit, &c.

6.

Tho' soul and body here must die,
　We long in the grave shall not be,
For God he will come from on high,
　To raise us to eternity;
Oh! how we rejoice at the sight,
　Death's power is done away;
For eternal light once past thro' night,
　To give us an eternal day.
　　Oh how, &c.

7.

The world they are astonish'd,
　To hear that God did die;
And, if that he was wholy dead,
　How he can live on high;
This, this is the water of life,
　And eternal life to see;
And eternal life, when kill'd by strife,

Did quicken by God's decree.
      This, this, &c.

8.
For God he said, 'three nights and days,
   My soul and my body shall lie
In silent death, and then I'll raise,
   And soar to my kingdom on high;
And then I will quicken from death,
   That my elect may see,
I have resum'd immortal breath;
   By virtue of my decree.'
      And then, &c.

9.
As God and man, Christ here did die,
   And a creature appear'd to be;
But in his body there did lie
   The soul of all infinity;
For when he from death arose,
   Nought could impede, I see;
Not hell, nor devils could oppose
   The power of his decree.
      For when, &c.

10.
God he to Elias said,
   'I will go down and die;
And when in silent death I have laid,
   I will soar up on high;'
And when God did relate,
   He died alive to be,
The power of his word so great,
   Became a firm decree.
      And when, &c.

BOYER GLOVER.

SIXTY-SECOND SONG.
(TUNE, 'Happy Muggletonians, who only.')

COME, all true saints, who do believe,
   And own this third and last record,
Which to great Muggleton and Reeve
   Was gave from heaven by the Lord;
Come join with me, to Christ we'll sing,
   Who only is our God and king.
      Come join, &c.

Divine Songs

2.

Who for his image man came down,
   And in the virgin's womb did lie;
Left for awhile his glorious throne,
   And here assumed humanity;
A man of sorrows did become,
   And suffer'd death to save his own.
      A man, &c.

3.

Eternal seed and nature came,
   The very God himself above;
And in the virgin's womb did change;
   Oh sacred mystery of love;
Immortal seed itself did die,
   And quicken'd in mortality.
      Immortal seed, &c.

4.

Redemption is a theme too high,
   The glorious garment of our God,
Which now he wears eternally,
   Seated on his divine abode;
Angels nor men can't comprehend,
   So great a God, so good a friend.
      Angels nor, &c.

5.

The joys which do continually flow,
   In the eternal God on high,
From all his sufferings here below,
   While he was in mortality;
Eternity can ne'er relate,
   They're so superlatively great.
      Eternity can, &c.

6.

Come, true believers, every one.
   Lay all dissensions by, and strife,
Since the same God we all do own,
   The only Lord of light and life;
With heart and voice together join,
   To praise this God that's so divine.
      With heart, &c.

7.
While reason here do vainly boast
  Of their imaginary God,
We will adore the Lord of hosts.
  And sing to him with one accord;
For death itself could not confine
  A God so great and so divine.
    For death, &c.

8.
True, the proud victor did invade,
  And o'er the Godhead life did reign,
He to his own decree obey'd,
  Death of itself had prov'd but vain;
But this he did that we might be
  With him to all eternity.
    But this, &c.

9.
Death was too weak long to detain,
  In the cold grave, a life so pure;
For at the time he pre-ordain'd,
  He conquered death, broke through death's power;
The glorious hero did arise
  Triumphant, crown'd with victories.
    The glorious. &c.

10.
Sin, death and hell at once o'ercame,
  By his eternal spirit's death;
No other way could God regain
  Eternal life, but pass thro' death;
No way could the Almighty find
  But this to save elect mankind.
    No way, &c.

11.
With joy and wonder magnify
  Our saviour Jesus, God alone,
Who's now ascended far on high,
  Seated on his immortal throne;
To him, with me, for ever sing.
  And praise this great immortal king.
    To him. &c.

12.
Proud reason here may do their worst;

Their hell-bound-reason still adore;
With which they'll be for ever curs'd;
  While we are in pleasures evermore,
They'll all be howling here below,
  In lasting pain and endless woe.
     They'll all, &c.

13.

Oh! glorious God, Almighty King,
  To thee we'll give our mortal praise;
And to our dear Redeemer sing,
  The residue of our short days;
And when from death we are call'd on high,
  Praise him to all eternity.
     And when, &c.

JAMES MILLER.

SIXTY-THIRD SONG.
Lines on Exodus, chapter xxv. Beginning verse 22.

JEHOVAH three different modes hath explain'd,
  Where his prophets he'd meet to commune,
Of all things he to Israel would give in command,
  In the most holy place there it's shewn;
From above the mercy-seat, which is on the ark,
  And the two cherubims (ek'd) between;
By faith only (while reason is chain'd in the dark)
  Is the light of God's Countenance seen.

2.

Our forefathers who liv'd in Moses' days,
  And those during the time of the law,
Tho' by shadows and types they did give God the praise,
  They the substance thereof clearly saw;
When at the altar they offered an innocent ram,
  They see God would become flesh, and die;
And when its mingled body ascended in flames,
  They saw Jesus ascending on high.

3.

They, with gold overlaid, had an ark made of wood,
  Which the manna and law did contain;
And to shew reason lusted for Aaron's priesthood,
  Aaron's rod in the ark must remain:
This figure did the angelic nature present,

Which glories in an external show;
Unto whom the first record on this earth was sent,
  Reason's nature to hold up in view.

4.

Up above on the ark, see the pure mercy's seat,
  Which was made of the finest of gold;
Neither covered, nor lin'd, but a substance complete,
  With one nature throughout, here behold;
Thus did created faith man's first nature display,
  (To it the second record was sent,)
Which was Abraham's seed God took un him that day,
  He in Mary that change underwent.

5.

In the two golden cherubims seated below,
  There the Spirit of God doth appear;
See his wrath in Elias; in Moses his love,
  Both his justice and mercy declare;
So in the third record both Muggleton and Reeve,
  By the same Holy Ghost were inspired,
Did the two edged sword of God's spirit receive,
  With his justice and mercy were fir'd.

6.

Thus, the three dispensations, by figures were shewn,
  With the saints that in each offered prayer;
Those pure hearts, (like the censor, with incense
           thereon,)
  The sweet righteousness of faith do bear;
That doth send forth sweet odours of gracious perfume,
  Which the sanctum sanctorum receives,
There into the presence of the Lord it doth come
  From those that in each record believe.

7.

While the first record lasted, two vails did exist,
  By which two future records were shewn;
For the first stood the people, the second the priests,
  And within went the high-priest alone;
When the second record rent in twain the first vail,
  Then the sanctuary did appear;
The second, the holy of all, did conceal,
  But by this third record 'tis made clear.

8.

On a table exalted within the first vail,

Stood the vessels of gold which contained
The twelve loaves of shew bread, twelve apostles
      reveal'd,
  Jesus Christ him the true bread explain'd
Before the shew bread stood a candlestick of gold,
  Which did bear seven lamps full of light;
Of one faith seven churches of Asia behold,
  Shines before twelve apostles, as bright.

9.

Now both veils were within as a kingdom of priests,
  We the Holy of Holies are shewn;
Where the way is prepared for the kings of the east,
  And the ladder of Jacob made known;
Which in three from earth unto heaven did reach;
  Witness---ark, mercy seat, cherubims;
In three missions the Lord sent his prophets to preach
  The true worship of the king of kings.

10.

We have cause to rejoice, who are christians indeed,
  For on us the third record doth shine;
We do know what we worship, for this is our creed:
  Jesus Christ with three titles divine;
As Creator, a Father, Redeemer, a Son,
  As Holy Ghost, when he sanctifies;
All to whom the true God in Christ Jesus is known,
  Unto eternal life will rise.

CONCLUSION.

How should we have known, that Moses and Elias were the spiritual protectors of heaven and earth, and of God himself, from his incarnation to his ascension, even as a spiritual God, if this Commission had not come forth? therefore it is the commission of the Spirit, because it opens all the counsel of God.

WILLIAM MATHEWS.

SIXTY-FOURTH SONG.

COME, loving saints, with me behold
  These glorious happy days,
Returning now to fill our souls
  With wonder, love and praise;
Assist my muse, exalted king,
  Dear saviour God above,
And teach my soul with joy to sing
  Thy mercy and thy love.

2.

Before creation's morning light,
  Thy radiant glory shone,
Or mighty hosts of angels bright,
  Existed all alone;
Matter, a chaos, dark and dead,
  Did in his presence lie,
Quite void of motion, sense and life,
  From all eternity.

3.

His piercing eye survey'd the mass,
  Where all seeds hidden lay,
Almighty power spoke the word--
  Darkness and death obey'd
The spring of light, of life and joy,
  From whom all beings sprang,
In heaven above, or earth beneath,
  And lastly Godlike man.

4.

Erect majestic here did shine,
  More like his God than all;
His body pure, his soul divine,
  Lord of this earthly ball;
By violating God's command,
  The serpent sow'd his tares;
Then sin and death came hand in hand,
  The source of all our cares.

5.

Transgressing thus their Maker's law,
  With sorrow did deplore,
The loss of innocence they saw;
  Immortal now no more;
Nature in all did feel the curse,

By our first parents' sin;
The heavenly orbs now took their course,
   For time did then begin.

6.

Redeeming love, amazing strange,
   I now would strive too speak,
The great Creator's wondrous change;
   But, oh! my soul's to weak;
Immortal fire will tune my lyre,
   Bright angels to outshine;
Whose highest lays are borrowed praise,
   But ours is faith divine.

7.

Jehovah great did man become,
   To save poor Adam's seed;
Thus David's Lord was David's son,
   The very God indeed,
Disrob'd of glory did descend,
   Invisibly entomb;
'Twas faith alone could God defend,
   While in the virgin's womb.

8.

Shrouded within a manger here,
   Thus Israel's God was born;
An infant helpless he appear'd,
   So mean and so forlorn;
How pure and innocent his life,
   In him no guile was found;
Which put proud reason oft at strife,
   Their hellish fury drown'd.

9.

Let's trace him to Mount Calvary,
   Where he resign'd his breath,
Triumphant gain'd the victory,
   O'er sin, o'er hell, and death;
He then ascended far on high,
   His stewards did adore,
Resigning power and majesty
   To him for evermore.

WILLIAM MILLER.

SIXTY-FIFTH SONG.

COME all true saints who have believed
   In this great glorious mission,
Which Reeve and Muggleton receiv'd,
   Both join'd in this commission;
To Christ we'll sing, with heart and voice,
   Our God and our Redeemer,
And while time lasts, we will rejoice,
   When time's no more for ever.

2.

Thro' all eternity we'll raise
   Our souls in elevation;
But, oh! eternity's too short
   To praise his transmutation;
God here did very man become,
   And left his habitation,
For to beget himself a son,
   The saints' true adoration.

3.

He manifested was in flesh,
   And destroyed death's power;
All Adam's seed this does refresh,
   And longing wait that hour,
When time shall end, for death's a friend
   Unto all true believers;
That glorious morn we shall ascend,
   And leave all damn'd deceivers.

4.

This mystery was never shown,
   Until this dispensation,
Wherein God's prophets have made known
   Assurance of salvation.
My friends, since we're assur'd of this,
   Let's sing, and still adore,
For mansions of eternal bliss
   Christ has for us is store.

5.

The prophets they are now no more
   Within this land so fam'd;
A jewel they've left us in store,
   Its value can't be nam'd;

Whereby we see eternal life
  Is in our souls abiding;
Then over banished be all strife,
  Since God's our only hiding.

6.

When he descends to put an end
  To time and this creation,
Where will proud reason find a friend,
  In that last conflagration?
With shouts the saints will all arise,
  To meet their dearest Saviour,
Ascending far above the skies
  To realms of light and pleasure.

7.

Then will our new created springs,
  Flow, ever to admire
The love of Christ, the King of Kings,
  While devils must retire
In lasting pain to yell and howl,
  From torments never raising;
Then shall each blessed faithful soul
  Christ God be ever praising.

                        WILLIAM MILLER.

SIXTY-SIXTH SONG.
(TUNE,---'Hark, hark, ye sons of faith.')

MUGGLETONIANS rejoice,
Of us God has mode choice,
To praise him in eternity,
For ever, and for ever;
Where we shall sing,
Praising him,
Immortal king,
He's Christ, our soul's redeemer:
His promise in our souls do shine,
We praising hint in heart divine,
Under Reece and Muggleton.
      His promise, &c.

2.

Our faith will ever shine,
Being of God's nature divine,
Eternal pleasure ever shine

In an immortal kingdom;
Where faith will rise,
Without surprise,
Immortaliz'd,
In a glorious condition;
Fashion'd like our God shall we,
When rais'd up in eternity,
Under Reeve and Muggleton.
      Fashion'd like, &c.

3.

Eternal life shall we
See in eternity,
Lord Jesus Christ died for we,
When in mortal condition;
Fulfilled he
His own decree;
Repriev'd we be
From everlasting torments;
For it we praise him here below,
While mortal breath in us do flow,
Under Reeve and Muggleton.
      For if, &c.

4.

Lord Jesus Christ is pure,
His blood I drink I am sure;
The third record I glory in,
It is those truths I feed on;
Them is reveal'd,
If it's believ'd,
Salvation seal'd,
To every true believer;
These are those joys I now possess,
Salvation lays within my breast,
Under Reeve and Muggleton.
      These are, &c.

5.

To truth I'll firmly stand
Against reason's hand;
Although the serpent bruise my heel,
My God his head has broken;
Now I'll not fear
Reason here,
Ever severe,
My faith it will support me;

For God he has made choice of me.
To praise him in eternity,
Under Reeve and Muggleton.
    For God, &c.
HENRY THOMAS PICKERSGILL.

SIXTY-SEVENTH SONG.

COULD the law give salvation, Christ never had died
Nor have suffer'd that passion with a spear in his side;
But to show forth his power, and redeem his own,
He descended to this earth, from his heavenly throne;
And when he had performed that great mystery.
Swift as thought he ascended to heaven so high.

2.

Let your faith then be strong, tho' this world as
    despise,
Tho' we sink in this orb, in the next we shall rise
To a glorious throne and a place that is sure,
To a heavenly kingdom that shall ever endure;
Where saints and blest angels hallelujahs shall sing
And for ever sing the praise of our heavenly king.
ANN WEEKS.

SIXTY-EIGHTH SONG.

IN Christ in whom we do believe,
  It is him our souls do love;
It's Christ alone became a son,
  To his own power above;
It's Christ himself that suffered death
  Upon a cursed tree,
And it is Christ that will raise the saints,
  To dwell eternally.

2.

Our blessed Saviour did not fly,
  From death, when offered him,
But willingly he did comply,
  To suffer for our sins;
Oh! here was love, was matchless love,
  Our God had before design'd,
To suffer a dreadful death,
  To redeem elect mankind.

3.
If God himself had not prepar'd
  For death, no man alone
Would ere have spilt his precious blood,
  No more than break his bones;
By this we see, devils were confin'd,
  And by true faith we know,
A chain they'll have, when rais'd from the grave,
  That will bind them here below.

4.
By this our faith, we likewise see,
  That Christ, by his own power,
Will raise the saints to dwell with him;
  Then comes the happy hour,
When we shall see ourselves set free,
  While the devils here below,
For all their cursed cruel deeds,
  Must suffer an endless woe.

5.
All true believers, join with me,
Rejoice both rich and poor,
Let's make no difference here below,
Our God made none, I'm sure;
He suffer'd death for all the elect,
Upon a cursed tree.
And those that do believe in him,
Tho' poor, may be net free.

                              MARY OUTRIDGE.

SIXTY-NINTH SONG.

CHRIST, thou dear redeeming king,
You salvation down did bring;
But when you to death did go,
Mercy, mercy, few did know.

2.
But when mercy rais'd its head,
Many souls rose from the dead,
And God's wonders great did show,
Which made mercy, mercy flow.

3.
Father, Son and Holy Ghost,
Was, through mercy, in death lost;
But your power did regain,
Mercy, moray lost it's plain.

4.
For when that you soar'd above,
And did send down in your love.
The cloven tongues of fire here,
Mercy, mercy did appear.

5.
For by justice all must die,
But to mercy we can fly;
Now Christ's blood has set as free,
Mercy, mercy we can see.

6.
Blest the soul by mercy crown'd,
Curst the soul by justice bound;
Now's the time from wrath to fly,
To mercy, mercy liberty.

7.
For the soul by mercy blest,
He has enter'd in God's rest;
For in mercy God rest found,
Mercy, mercy, love has crown'd.

8.
Mercy is that sovereign king,
Which true balsam here does bring
To a soul by justice bound;
Mercy, mercy heels that wound.

9.
Oh! thou great and mighty king,
Who thy mercies' praise can sing
Like the soul set free from hell!
Mercy, mercy he can tell.

10.

When for sin we lost are found,
Then does grace, grace abound;
And from hell our souls are free,
Mercy, mercy we can see.

11.

For when time is at an end,
We to mercy shall ascend,
And in harmony of love,
Mercy, mercy praise above.

BOYER GLOVER.

SEVENTIETH SONG.

LET us with lifted voices sing,
To Jesus, our great God and king,
Who doth such boundless mercy shew,
To us poor mortals here below;
Since he alone has set us free,
We'll join in love and liberty.

2.

Our God descended from above,
And left his great celestial throne,
To purchase life for Adam's seed;
He cloth'd himself with flesh and bone,
And nailed upon a cursed tree,
To bear down death's supremacy.

3.

He is the champion of our hope,
On whom alone we do depend;
His matchless love to us was shewn,
When with his life, he sav'd friend;
Let us adore his majesty,
Who gave us life and liberty.

4.

Let all who of his love partake,
Sit down beneath this shady vine,
And sing the praises of our God;
Let us in sweetest concert join,
Above the sky our notes will raise,
To sing the Lamb's new song of praise.

PHILIP LATHORP.

SEVENTY-FIRST SONG.

FAITH, like a sovereign balsam sure,
The wounds of sin does perfect cure,
Wipes all our sorrows quite away,
Assures us of eternal day;
Come saints, adore elective love,
For we shall reign in realms above.

2.
Substantial are those joys serene,
Which can by faith alone be seen,
Laid up for Adam's sons in store,
Where we shall shine where time's no more.
    Come saints, &c.

3.
The faithful in the first record
Believ'd Jehovah, their great Lord,
Would in his time pure flesh assume,
In the chaste virgin's blessed womb.
Come saints, &c.

4.
Believers in the next record,
Believed Christ, the Son of God,
Was nailed to a cursed tree,
And crown'd with thorns of infamy.
    Come saints, &c.

5.
The last record is now on earth,
Declar'd by prophets of great worth;
No more there'll be till Christ descends,
To put to time a final end.
    Come saints, &c.

6.
Now God's great mystery is done,
The Father was the only Son;
And he's the Holy Ghost we see,
One glorious God, with titles three.
    Come saints, &c.

7.
If life eternal 'tis to know,
The very God while here below,
To Christ alone then let us sing,
For he's our only God and king.
    Come saints, &c.

8.
Not knowing, must be endless pain,
When Christ our God does come again,
The tares and wheat will sever'd be,
According to his great decree.
    Come saints, &c.

9.
The seed of faith will then arise,
All glorious bodies with surprise,
Like unto him, their only Lord,
Singing new songs with one accord.
    Come saints, &c.

10.
Then faith will quite bear the sway,
For when we see that glorious day,
Sight will our ravish'd souls employ,
In pure divine seraphic joy.
    Come saints, &c.

11.
Fruition then will perfect be,
Each blessed saint his God will see;
Redeeming love we'll all adore,
In those blessed mansions evermore.
    Come saints, &c.

12.
Reason will here with reason lie,
Howling to all eternity;
A burning sand their bed will be,
And dying, live eternally.
    Come saints, &c.

13.
Jesus, our God, 'Come, come away,'
Our souls do long to hear thee say,
'Swiftly ascend, my seed, above,
Surrounding me your God of love.

Come saints, &c.

14.
Enter into your Lord's great joy,
Where nothing ever can annoy;
Eternal love alone will be
Our theme to all eternity.'
  Come saints, &c.

WILLIAM MILLER.

SEVENTY-SECOND SONG.
(TUNE, 'Upon a Summer's evening clear.')

My soul doth glorious scenes discern,
 Since I by faith do see
My God by his almighty arm,
 Salvation wrought for me;
I see he left his glorious throne,
 And died for me here;
The eternal God did man become,
 And paid the ransom dear.
  And paid, &c.

2.
He entered the virgin's womb,
 And there he did transmute
His spiritual body into seed,
 Christ Jesus was the fruit;
Of that blest seed which there dissolv'd,
 With which the virgin's united then;
Her seed the Godhead spirit clothed
 With a garment pure and clean.
  With, &c.

3.
Which was a body of flesh and bone,
That he perfect man might be;
And when he was of age mature,
He died upon a tree;
By reason's sons my God was slain,
Hit spirit then did die,
That his elect with him might reign
To all eternity.
  To all, &c.

4.

The great Creator, Jacob's God,
  Is my Redeemer dear;
It was he alone the wine-press trod,
  When the Godhead died here;
He has nail'd my sins unto his cross,
  And cancell'd all my guilt;
And now my soul is at no loss,
  Since I see God's blood was spilt.
      Since I, &c.

5.

Tho' my sins were as the scarlet dye,
  They are as white as wool become;
I have sought for them, but none could spy;
  They all away are done;
The blood of God hath wash'd my soul,
  And cleansed me from sin;
That sovereign balm hath made me whole,
  And taken out death's sting.
      And taken, &c.

6.

And now my prayers are turn'd to praise,
  My God he doth me love;
He'll come once more my soul to raise,
  Then I'll soar with him above;
Then I his glorious face shall see,
  A new song of praise shall sing;
But, eternity too short will be
  To praise my glorious king.
      To praise, &c.

                        REBECCA BATT.

SEVENTY-THIRD SONG.

OH! what a sight it is to see
Eternal God did die for me;
He suffered death upon a tree,
That I might live eternally.

2.

Infinite power he did bring down,
When here he vail'd his Godhead crown;
No other way but this, I can
See, how he was both God and man.

3.
The eternal Father died most sure
Within a virgin's womb so pure,
And quicken'd in humanity
The essence of eternity.

4.
When the devils put my God to death,
And he resign'd his sacred breath,
The eternal spirit then did die,
The fountain of infinity.

5.
The world of their three may boast,
But I'll adore the Lord of hosts;
Who for his seed did chuse to die,
That we might live eternally.

6.
I know my life is hid in him,
His death aton'd for all my sin;
From cursed envy I'm set free,
I'm longing for eternity.

7.
And now my soul flows o'er in praise
To Christ, the ancientest of days;
Redeemer dear, I'll praise thy name,
Eternally I'll sound thy fame.

JOHN PEAT.

SEVENTY-FOURTH SONG.

THE Lord is God, none else can be;
How say some then, that there are three?
If Christ be God, (which most do own.)
Besides him then there can be none.

2.
The father, Son and Holy Ghost,
We see doth blind the eyes of most;
But prais'd be God that I do see,
Christ Jesus is that glorious three.

3.
First as a Father to create,
And after left that glorious state,
For to redeem elect mankind,
And so become a Son I find.

4.
And by this third and last record,
We plainly see our blessed Lord,
His Holy Spirit forth did give
Unto great Muggleton and Reeve.

5.
Then come, my friends, and with me join
To praise the God that's so divine;
And when from death we're called on high,
We'll praise to all eternity

EDWARD FEVER.

SEVENTY-FIFTH SONG.
(TUNE, 'Could the law give salvation.')

THO' we live among devils, why should we repine?
'Twas the lot of our Master when he was in time,
Whom they treated with envy, with malice and scorn;
But with Judas 'twas better they'd never been born,
For hell is their portion, as our God has decreed,
Both for their grandsire and all his curst seed.

2.
Since this is their kingdom, then here let them reign,
Our glorious freedom they ne'er can obtain;
For their fathers, our God and his prophets did kill,
And the blood of the faithful their children would spill;
But our Lord shall descend from those mansions
      above,
And for ever will separate envy from love.

3.
Then we shell ascend with our God into bliss,
And leave these proud devils to howl and to hiss,
In blackness of darkness for ever to moan;
Their spirits did barr'd close in dark bodies will groan;
While saints in pure raptures their God shall adore,
And sing hallelujahs to him evermore.

MARTHA MILLER.

SEVENTY-SIXTH SONG

WHEN to false worship I did go,
  Darkness opprest my mind;
And when the law brought me to woe,
  No peace I there could find;
But when I saw the third record,
  God's prophets they did cry,
'Forsake false worship, serve the Lord,
  And you will never die.'

2.

Then faith and reason they did move,
And strive for mastery,
And fain my soul would have God's love,
Afraid I was to die;
But this was hard for to attain,
God's love I could not see,
The guilt of conscience did remain,
And guilt condemned me.

3.

I'd fain my conscience lull'd to sleep,
  God's law to pacify;
But justice made my soul to weep,
  As if God had stood by;
Guilt in my soul appear'd to me
  To be like scarlet dye,
Until God's blood, by faith I see,
  My soul to sanctify.

4.

Oh! how astonishing to think,
  That God he here should die,
And give lost souls his blood to drink,
  Their thirst to satisfy;
When Moses rais'd the serpent up,
  Those that the type could see,
They of God's blood did drink a sup,
  From hell to set them free.

5.

The serpent seed, when they were stung,
  They look'd and found relief,
Upon the serpent which there hung,

This eased their present grief;
Tho' they were heal'd externally,
   God's love they ne'er could know;
The sting of conscience oft did cry,
   Which fill'd their souls with woe.

6.

This dreadful state I once was in,
   When I was dark and blind;
But God has cleans'd my soul from sin,
   For mercy I'm designed;
His precious blood which here was shed,
   Did like a fountain flow,
And tho' my soul with sin was dead,
   By that is heal'd from woe.

7.

With joy my soul does now abound,
   Redeeming love to see;
But oh! what joys when we surround
   God in eternity,
And homage pay to my great king
   For his redeeming love,
And feed on that eternal spring,
   Dear Jesus Christ above.

8.

When that I in the grave do fall,
   To soar above the skies,
As swift as thought my God will call,
   As swift I shall arise;
And then my soul will sit secure,
   No reason there will be,
My glorious joys for to alloy
   To all eternity.

9.

I look'd and saw the tree of life
   In bitter agony,
I saw curs'd devils all at strife,
   When God died on a tree;
I saw the sun was darken'd,
   Which was God's flesh, I know;
When he fulfill'd his royal word,
   The blood from him did flow.

10.

The writings which against me stood,
  It was God's law, I see;
But God has shed his precious blood,
  And slew the law in me;
I see it nail'd upon a cross
  When Christ was crucified;
And now my soul is at no loss,
  For God for me has died.

                              BOYER GLOVER.

SEVENTY-SEVENTH SONG.
(TUNE, 'Love, what art thou that's so divinely bent.')

FAITH is a glorious crown for to behold,
A crown of blessings, not a crown of gold;
A crown of pearls that shine so clear and bright,
Bringing all saints to everlasting light.
    A crown, &c.

2.

Thro' faith alone all saints' rejoices are,
Of everlasting life, thro' God's great care,
In sending his two witnesses for to declare his name:
Look in the Revelations, and there you'll find the same.
    In sending, &c.

3.

Faith is a choice and precious thing,
Bringing all saints before their heavenly king;
A king of glory, as saints by faith do see,
A personal God, but not in persons three.
    A king, &c.

4.

Therefore doth faith alone out of them spring,
And God to them hath given a blessing;
Because thou art faithful on this wicked earth,
Thou shalt ascend to everlasting mirth.
    Because thou, &c.

5.

Unto that glorious throne which is on high,
Full of triumph and everlasting joy;
Not like reason that on this earth must be
Burning in hell to all eternity.

Not like, &c.

6.
Faith is a pearl which kings cannot retain;
Faith is attain'd, but not by learned men;
Faith is an eye which makes saints see so clear;
Faith's a saint's life, and death they need not fear.
    Faith is, &c.

7.
Faith is a pearl which in man's heart doth lie;
Faith's an assurance of eternal joy;
Faith is a purge, which to all saints is given;
Faith's a saint's life, because it comes from heaven.
    Faith is, &c.

WILLIAM TOMKINSON.

SEVENTY-EIGHTH SONG.

WHILST I by faith can soar above,
And view the object of my love;
I see that God who died for me,
Now reigns in power and majesty.

2.
I see that head now wear the crown,
Which once in glory he laid down,
This glorious mystery to complete,
And death lies conquer'd at his feet.

3.
Not long ere he will come once more,
Then will my love in joys flow o'er,
When I that glorious face shall see,
That has redemption wrought for me.

4.
What raptures do those saints possess,
That can this heavenly mystery see;
No mortal can the like express,
But those that share the same with me.

5.
To know my God, is bread divine,
With which my hungry soul is feed;
For since this glorious truth I've seen,
I am supplied with living bread.

Divine Songs

6.
By faith I see my God above,
Who once did suffer on a tree,
And did descend in tender love,
And took on him mortality.

7.
Clothed in flesh, with blood and bone,
That glorious garment he put on,
The wine-press of his wrath he tread,
And thus he broke the serpent's head.

8.
His soul they pierced with a spear,
Till blood and water gushed out;
With which my conscience is made clear,
My soul from guilt is purg'd throughout.

9.
Who can such heavenly scenes behold,
And not be ravish'd at the sight!
Serpents may please themselves with gold,
But this alone is my delight.

10.
No more proud reason dare presume
Unto this glorious mount to go;
To stand with faith there is not room;
No thou shalt hold an ass below.

11.
No clouds shall over-top my joy,
No guilt of sin my peace annoy,
When I from reason am set free,
Enjoying perfect liberty.

12.
Yet now I set me down and sing,
And rest my soul beneath the shade;
My faith is firmly built on him,
The rock that's in Mount Zion laid.

13.
Tho' I lay sleeping long in dust,
And many ages may survive;
Yet I in Christ shall safely rest,

Because in him I am sure to rise.
MARGARET THOMAS.

SEVENTY-NINTH SONG.

FAITH's the balsam like the olive green,
   Assures the soul of life;
Will cure the lethargy of sin,
   And ends all needless strife;
If with the heart you can believe,
   Then fancy, why oppress'd?
This last commission of John Reeve,
   Your mind will be at rest.

2.

Rouse then, my soul, with saints to sing
   To Christ our only God,
And praise this everlasting king,
   Who left divine abode;
Highly he honour'd Mary's womb,
   Dissolv'd himself in seed;
Where secretly he lay entomb'd,
   The immortal God indeed.

3.

Oh! matchless love, unbounded grace,
   That God should man become;
And man alone was in God's place,
   While he became a son;
In wonder lost, my soul above,
   Feasts by true faith upon
This great eternal God of love,
   Whose mystery is done.

4.

By Judas was the God of bliss,
   In Bethlehem's garden fair,
Betray'd with a dissembling kiss,
   As scripture doth declare;
A multitude, with warlike bands,
   Hurried our Lord away,
With vile, outrageous, impious hands,
   Before his judge that day.

5.

False witnesses were ready soon,
   The devil and his friends,

Sufficient none to seal his doom;
   Then how to gain their ends,
This question put, if Christ could be
   (No longer now at strife)
The Son of God? That's blasphemy!
   Resolve to take his life.

6.

What Satan would in heaven have done,
   Environ'd thus around,
On earth is finish'd by his Son;
   By reason guilty found,
Condemn'd to die without relief,
   Tho' innocent he stands;
They scourge and whip him like a thief,
   Now in their devilish hands.

7.

Pilate proceeds, his sentence read,
   That ignominious death;
Christ here a sacrifice was made,
   With thieves resign'd his breath;
Crowned with thorns of great disgrace,
   His royal head it bled;
The purple gore ran down his face,
   And soon he bow'd his head.

8.

Then with a spear they pierc'd his side,
   They thirsted still for more;
The streams flow'd from his wounds so wide,
   To fill their hellish score:
Thus Israel's mighty God was dead,
   No kind of life remain'd;
His valuable blood was shed;
   The earth was with if stain'd.

9.

The eternal Spirit did resign
   Unto the victor's power;
Tho' they could not our God confine,
   For in that very hour,
Swiftly than thought he rose again,
   As he before decreed ;
Eternal life he did regain,
   For his own faithful seed.

10.
The great Elijah did come down
　　To attend his gracious God;
Immediately roll'd back the stone,
　　The keepers trembling stood;
Seiz'd they were with guilt and fear,
　　To see what here was done;
So bright these angels did appear,
　　They to the senate run.

11.
Large gifts they gave, secret to keep,
　　And said, 'reveal to none;'
His disciples stole him when asleep,
　　What has this night been done:
Thus devils, tho' convinc'd will be,
　　But devils still the same,
Their portion's dark eternity,
　　In never ending pain.

12.
Our God's ascended now on high,
　　And triumph'd over death,
Leading captive captivity,
　　And was, O death, thy death.
Since we are heaven-born, let's sing
　　Praises, and still adore
This great eternal God and king,
　　Both now and evermore.

13.
The Father, Son and Holy Ghost,
　　Those glorious titles three;
One person answers still at most,
　　From all eternity;
Whose powerful word made man, who came
　　From dead and senseless dust,
A pure and undefiled frame,
　　From his great God at first.

14.
He was throughout by sin defil'd,
　　But God his promise gave,
Who came in flesh, and death has foil'd,
　　His lost elect to save;
Each faithful soul does here receive
　　Their pardon and remission,

By mighty Muggleton and Reeve's
   Most powerful commission.

15.

My dearest friends, beware to sever
   Those messengers of God;
Our Lord he join'd them both together,
   One glorious path they trod;
God's form and nature both inform,
   Divine content to be;
Bright burning glory did adorn
   His form eternally.

16.

The angels' nature they make known,
   Pure reason for to be,
With Godlike spiritual forms alone,
   In immortality;
Heaven's glorious kingdom is above,
   That starry orb we see;
Where Christ does reign in peace and love,
   To all eternity.

17.

Man is the devil here below,
   They likewise plainly prove;
This earth will be their hell we know,
   From whence they'll ne'er remove;
The soul that sins shall surely die;
   How vain does reason prate
While here of immortality,
   In this imperfect state.

18.

Then let discords for ever cease,
   And never more be known;
May all true saints live here in peace,
   Since the same God we own;
Come, true believes, live in love,
   Who have those truths embrac'd;
Rejoice, for we shall shine above,
   Behold him face to face.

19.

Who from the imperial throne above,
Of glory once again,

This glorious mission in great love,
Did give to mortal men;
The prophets they are now no more,
Their doctrine still do stand;
Believe, 'tis life for evermore;
Deny, you're surely damn'd.

WILLIAM MILLER.

EIGHTIETH SONG.
On the Fourteenth, Fifteenth and Sixteenth of February.
(TUNE, 'Dying Swain.')

BELIEVERS, now let us rejoice,
  And tune our joyful lays;
United all with heart and voice,
  On these three happy days;
On which great Reeve and Muggleton,
  Their mission did recieve
From heaven's high exalted throne,
  Of glory we believe.
      On which, &c.

2.

To sing the mystery so great,
  Of Christ our God above;
Angels nor man can ne'er relate
  His dear Redeemer's love;
Heaven descended into earth,
  Amazing 'tis to tell,
The wonders of his lowly birth,
  Who here with man did dwell.
      Heaven, &c.

3.

Immortal God thus man become,
  He laid his glory by;
And did beget himself a son,
  In pure mortality:
A man of sorrows Christ was here,
  Acquainted much with grief;
Let saints be fill'd with holy fear,
  'Twas God that brought relief.
      A man, &c.

4.

He conquer'd sin, death and the grave,
  And now's ascended high;
How mighty is our God to save
  His own eternally:
Bright burning glories round him shine,
  A triple crown does grace
Our God and king that's so divine,
  In that most blessed place.
      Bright, &c.

5.

Where myriads of angels sing,
  Melodiously they raise
Their voices to that mighty king,
  In pure seraphic praise:
Era long that last great trump shall sound,
  Whilst nature seems to nod;
'Twill shake and tremble all around,
  At our approaching God.
      Ere long, &c.

6.

The angels loudly will proclaim,
  That time is now no more;
Arise, you dead in Christ by name,
  To joys for evermore;
Then shall the faithful seed ascend,
  Behold him face to face;
Eternal pleasures without end;
  Oh! happy Adam's race.
      Then, &c.

7.

Reason adult will here remain,
  This earth will be their hell;
With everlasting grief and pain,
  In horror's darksome cell;
While saints in spiritual glory shall,
  Now hallelujahs raise;
And sing, O God thy wonders o'er,
  In never ending praise.
      While, &c.

WILLIAM MILLER.

EIGHTY-FIRST SONG.

CEASE, vain world, for to declare,
Your sinful souls immortal are;
And were so before Christ did die,
Who purchas'd immortality.

2.

If men's souls immortal were,
Before our saviour Christ came here;
In vain, in vain his blood was shed,
If that the better part was fled.

3.

Call, deluded world, no more
Our Saviour yours, if sated before;
For if to heaven your souls could fly,
No need had Christ For you to die.

4.

Sure Adam's soul was touch'd with sin,
Or fear had never enter'd in;
The soul that sins must die therefore,
And lay obscure till time's no more.

5.

When time's no more our glorious Lord,
The omnipotent, speaks the word;
Then soul and body both shall rise
To endless pain or lasting joys.

JAMES MILLER.

EIGHTY-SECOND SONG.

COME, all select souls,
That delight in full bowls
Of celestial wine from that fountain,
Which never is dry,
But their spirits supply,
While the sun scorcheth up the high mountain.
Which never, &c.

2.

The rabbies do think,
Because we thus drink,
That we are bereft of our reason;
But in time they shall see

    Who's in fault, they or we,
For we never can drink out of season.
        But in, &c.

3.

    For this we well know,
    When our cup does thus flow,
Our transports are sweet and exceeding
        All that reason can frame,
        Or on earth can be nam'd;
Thus you see our drinking's believing.
        All that, &c.

4.

    Likewise we do eat
    Of that spiritual meat,
That preserves our dear souls from all hunger,
        Whilst the devils are starv'd,
        And must have their reward,
When that we are parted asunder.
        Whilst, &c.

5.

    Then let's rejoice all and sing
    To our heavenly king,
That so of his bounty doth feed us;
        For we live here to die,
        To reign eternally
With that God who hath bought and redeem'd us.
        For we, &c.

JOHN NICHOLS

EIGHTY-THIRD SONG.

COME, true believers, join with me,
To praise God for this mystery;
For unto him we should bestow
The love that in our hearts do flow.

2.

For God he did his love forth show,
When he died for the elect below;
And it still further did proclaim,
When from the ground he rose again.

3.
And when ascended up on high,
In his own glorious majesty,
He did himself the power resume,
That he had left when in the Son.

4.
Since Christ he has such love made known,
When he on earth became a son;
We will admire and still rejoice,
While we're possess'd of heart and voice.

5.
So now, my friends, rejoice and sing,
Since we are sure our heavenly king
New glories for us has prepar'd,
That by his prophets he declar'd.

6.
And then our joys will be divine,
Ever in glory with him to shine;
For to be blest with God above,
Surely is a wondrous love.

ROBERT ROBINSON.

EIGHTY-FOURTH SONG.

COME saints, rejoice with heart and voice,
  To see our God has come down,
For to redeem his own elect,
  Himself became a son;
    Himself became a son;
And through this mortal life did pass,
  Temptations did not fear;
And on a cross his blood was spilt
  For them he lov'd so dear.
    For them, &c.

2.
Our Lord was dead, in sepulchre laid;
  What a glorious sight to see!
It was the power of his own word,
  He rose by his own decree;
    He rose by his own decree;
Of angels and Men no help he had,
  For none there could not be;

But, by the power of his own word,
  Our God rose perfectly.
    Our God, &c.

3.

Now he is risen from the grave,
  And was seen by men;
Dead bodies rose that were near,
  And in the city came;
    And in the city came;
Which made the people for to say,
  The son of God they'd slain;
But they not long did stay,
  Went back to their graves again.
    Went back, &c.

4.

This was not all that reason did,
  For the disciples they did kill;
And many saints did share the same fate,
  Their precious blood they spilt.
    Their precious blood they spilt.
When all is o'er and time's no more,
  Then, what will reason say,
To see us rise before their eyes,
  While they in darkness lay!
    While, &c.

5.

Our God is risen up on high,
  In glorious splendour shines;
And sent to us the third record,
  By two champions that are divine;
    By two champions that are divine;
John Reeve and Muggleton I mean,
  Two prophets that were pure;
And all that doth believe the same,
  Their souls are made secure.
    Their, &c.

6.

Blessed are they who can but see,
  Once more our God will come,
To his elect whom he respects,
  And for to call us home,
    And for to call us home;

Then patiently wait and you'll be great,
   With angels and saints divine;
Where they sing the new song, which will be long,
   While we in chorus join.
      While we, &c.

                THOMAS PICKERSGILL.

EIGHTY-FIFTH SONG.
(TUNE, 'As I was a walking for my creation.')

WHAT wonders great my soul doth see,
When the seed spring doth arise in me;
Water of life so sweet doth flow,
I have heavenly peace, and faith doth grow
      Water of life, &c.

2.

Then I my God can comprehend,
Who is my great eternal friend;
He left his glorious throne on high,
And for Adam's seed came down to die.
      He left his, &c.

3.

The eye and hand of faith doth find
Sweet food for to refresh my mind;
Now I my God in three paths can trace,
I admire his mercy and free grace.
      Now I, &c.

4.

My God eternally did shine,
In a glorious person all divine;
His nature is all faith I'm sure,
Above measure, and is all power.
      His nature, &c.

5.

He purer is than purest gold,
A bright glorious person to behold;
A garment down to his feet doth wear,
More transparent shines than crystal clear.
      A garment, &c.

6.

He softer is than softest down,
Crown'd with a most glorious immortal crown;
Sweeter than sweetest roses fine,
Purer than snow is my God divine.
      Sweeter than, &c.

7.

Swifter than thought he did entomb
Himself within the virgin's womb;
So that our God he enter'd there,
Before the virgin was aware.
      So that, &c.

8.

But by a wonderful change in her soul soon,
She felt him convert to flesh, blood and bone;
For there he dissolv'd into seed,
Which the virgin's mix'd, as he had decreed.
      For there, &c.

9.

Without desire her seed she shed,
Which cloth'd the very God's Godhead;
Thus of her he took Abraham's seed alone,
And cloth'd himself with flesh, blood and bone.
      Thus of, &c.

10.

This mystery of God's becoming flesh,
The tongues of Men nor angels can't fully express,
Neither can comprehend it fully;
So wonderful deep is this great mystery!
      Neither can, &c.

11.

His own glory, power, justice and love,
Did move my God to come down from above;
To be made capable to die;
That we might live with him on high.
      To be, &c.

12.

Oh! this was my God, the eternal God,
Who alone by himself the wine-press trod;
Justice was made wrath with sin indeed,

This made my God come down to bleed.
    Justice was, &c.

13.
His own righteous law he walked through,
Which none but a God of all power could do;
Upon a cross my God did die,
His justice for to satisfy.
    Upon a, &c.

14.
Great darkness did o'erspread the globe;
All nature trembled when my God
Upon a cross resign'd his breath,
When the eternal Spirit enter'd death.
    Upon a, &c.

15.
By his death, over death he gain'd victory,
So became death's death to set us free;
Death was too week my God to detain,
His own powerful word rais'd him again.
    Death was, &c.

16.
Thus my God hath broke the serpent's head,
Who'll be always dying, yet never dead;
The pit reason dug, he is fell in I see,
And he is justly damn'd eternally.
    The pit, &c.

17.
This victorious God almighty of love,
Is ascended to his bright throne above,
Where he reigns in power and bright majesty;
Praise him all saints eternally.
    Where he, &c.

REBECCA BATT.

EIGHTY-SIXTH SONG.
(TUNE, 'Young Nancy one morn.')

  Hail! hail! this new day,
    And your voices display;
Let them pierce through the natural sky,
  And feed upon him,

Who's the fountain and spring;
From whom floweth joys from on high.
    And feed, &c.

2.

Hail! prophets sublime,
  Who hath brought truth divine,
From heaven's imperial throne;
  Which the great prophet Reeve,
  In commission receiv'd,
And imparts to the faithful alone.
    Which the, &c.

3.

The first day behold,
  The Lord did unfold,
From a glimpse of his heavenly light;
  Revelation did show,
  The secrets which flow,
In scripture true prophets did write.
    Revelation did, &c.

4.

In the second appeal,
  The Lord did reveal,
And made him obedient to know;
  Experience should tell,
  Both heaven and hell:
Lord where thou would'st have me I'll go.
    Experience should, &c.

5.

In the third, let my verse
  As truly rehearse,
What the two former enjoin;
  And what hell conceal'd,
  Heaven once more reveal'd,
In two prophets both true and divine.
    And what, &c.

6.

True believers, then raise
  Your voices in praise,
To Christ, our redeemer and king;
  For he's God alone,
  Eternally one,

To him we'll eternally Sing.
    For he's, &c.

7.

On this side the grave
  Afflictions we have;
His merciful trials of love;
    The humbler we be,
    The higher will he
Raise us in his kingdom above.
    The humbler, &c.

8.

All glory and praise,
  The rest of our days,
To him we'll ascribe evermore.
    Who will rescue our breath
    From the power of death,
For ever to praise and adore.
    Who will, &c.

                              JAMES MILLER.

EIGHTY-SEVENTH SONG.

YOU saints and servants of the Lord,
  That do his ward obey;
Who by this third and last record,
  Are taught the righteous way.

2.

In spirit and in truth, as thus,
  To worship him alone,
As Father, Son and Holy Ghost,
  In one divine person.

3.

First sing his praise, as he is God,
  The father of us all;
Then as he by his precious blood,
  Has freed us out of thrall.

4.

Now as he is the Holy Ghost,
  Who sanctifies we find;
Sing praise to Christ the Lord of hosts,
  With heart and cheerful mind.

Divine Songs

5.

Three witnesses in heaven are
  Who bear a true record;
And he thereby is made appear
  To be both God and Lord.

6.

The Father by creation.
  Him for to be, doth show;
And by redemption the son,
  That he is God we know.

7.

Likewise by sanctification,
  It plainly is made known,
To him the glory doth belong,
  And to no other one.

8.

By works he thus appear'd as three,
  Which witnesseth right well,
Our Saviour Jesus Christ is he,
  In whom all Godhead dwell.

9.

Eternally those virtues three,
  His person doth contain;
Ere that the heavens created be,
  Or he the earth did frame.

10.

Eternal was the Father thus,
  Eternal was the Son,
Eternal was the Holy Ghost,
  In one divine person.

11.

Thus trinity in unity,
Appears to be but one,
One personal God, not persons three,
Our Saviour Christ alone.

12.

Then unto him eternally,
All glory be therefore;
Yea, and our God has titles three,

Now, and for evermore.
GASKCOYNE.

EIGHTY-EIGHTH SONG.
(TUNE, 'In ancient times.')

How shall we, bounded here, adore,
  Lord, thy unbounded love;
Or which why can we praise thee more,
  Until we get above?
Matter is gross, the world's confin'd,
  Our bodies cannot flee;
In contemplation, true, the mind
  May feast itself on thee.
    Matter is, &c.

2.

When the last trump shall raise the dead,
  And reason here confin'd;
The limbeck holds the dross and lead,
  By chymistry divine:
The world's the limbeck; matter, dross;
  The bodies which confine;
Proud reason's spirit is the lead;
  The chymist, God divine.
    The world, &c.

3.

But, the pure gold, with matter pure,
Purged by fire will rise,
And in its limbeck rise secure;
This is matter spiritualiz'd;
'Twill swift ascend, the heavens rend,
For nothing can impede;
True faith will tend to Christ his friend,
For 'tis like God indeed.
    'Twill swift, &c.

JAMES MILLER.

EIGHTY-NINTH SONG.

How blest are the saints when assur'd of salvation,
  Whilst all the world wallows in false alarms,
Heavenly raptures are our contemplations,
  New joys that far exceed all earthly charms.

Divine Songs

2.
Heaven's great majesty by our faith we do see,
  The glorious train that on God doth attend;
Hasten time, let us fly to that society.
  Where of our joys there shall be no end.

ANN WEEKS.

NINETIETH SONG.
(TUNE, 'Cupid, god of soft persuasions.')

Christ my precious bleeding God,
  This I by faith do comprehend;
'Twas he alone the wine-press trod,
  He is my glorious God and friend.
    'Twas he, &c.
    He is my, &c.

2.
The great Jehovah did the work,
  According to his owe decree,
He pour'd out his soul unto death,
  For to set his own seed free.
    Ho pour'd, &c.
    For to set, &c.

3.
Then who can praise this God enough,
  That for our ransom paid so dear;
His precious blood by faith I see,
  Has wash'd my sinful soul quite clear.
    His precious, &c.
    Has wash'd, &c.

4.
Within the silent grave I know
  My sinful soul must go to steep;
Until my God returns again,
  His glorious work for to complete.
    Until my, &c.
    His glorious, &c.

5.
Then shall I arise with the blest saints,
  For then I know the work is done;
A glorious army we shall be,
  To follow Reeve and Muggleton.

A glorious, &c.
To follow, &c.

AVIES SARAH TOONE.
(Afterwards Mrs. WALLIS.)

NINETY-FIRST SONG.

IT is by my faith I'm dictated to sing,
And that of a person no less than a king;
Whose kingdom's not here, tho' I see it's not afar,
Since his messengers come, my soul for to cheer.
    Whose kingdom's, &c.

2.

He two messengers chose, and he gave them to know,
That his kingdom was not on this earth below;
But by faith I can see, it was in mortality
He was slain for my sins, my soul to set free.
    But by &c.

3.

The King of all kings, O that is his name,
Tho' reason, proud reason, they do him defame;
They'll not be contented without persons three; But no
divided king e'er shall reign over.
    They'll not, &c.

4.

They despis'd his kingdom, and set it at naught,
And my king, like a lamb, to the slaughter was
    brought;
They hung him on a cross, and they pierc'd him I see,
Thinking from his power for to get free.
    They hung, &c.

5.

When that my king they had certainly slain,
And in a sepulchre three days he had lain,
He rose up again, it was by his own decree,
That they from his power no way should get too.
    He rose, &c.

6.

Now this is reason's kingdom, they in splendour it
    retain,
Until that my king he doth come once again,
With a mighty host, his true subjects to free,

And leave reason here to eternity.
>With a, &c.

7.
With weeping and wailing in horror to lie,
  Because that my king they do daily deny;
Whilst that his true subjects doth rejoice, aye and sing,
  All glory and praise be to their eternal king.
>Whilst that, &c.

MATHEW HAGUE.

NINETY-SECOND SONG.

CURST devils, once with malice fill'd,
The blood of our dear God they spill'd;
But those that caus'd our God to die,
Will all be damn'd eternally.
>Will all be, &c.
>Will all be, &c.
>But those, &c.

2.
Their children, the apostles kill'd,
And the blood of faithful me they spill'd;
And those that caus'd the saints to die,
Will all be damn'd eternally.
>Will all be, &c.
>Will all be, &c,
>And those, &c.

3.
What dreadful horror there will be,
When they are in eternity;
When they blaspheme, God's law will cry,
You are justly damn'd eternally.
>You are, &c.
>You are, &c.
>When they, &c.

4.
This thing within my soul I see,
When that God's law condemn'd me;
But now I see God died for me,
And I shall live eternally.
>And I shall, &c.

And I shall, &c.
But now, &c.

5.
Our God came down in love to die,
His justice for to satisfy;
That Adam's seed, which here did die,
Might live with him eternally.
      Might live, &c.
      Might live, &c.
      That Adam's, &c.

6.
A new commandment God did give,
To love each other while we live;
That by this love all men might see,
That we his true, disciples be.
      That we, &c.
      That we, &c.
      That by, &c.

7.
We ne'er are like our God above,
But when we are in perfect love;
For it is by love alone we see,
That we shall live eternally.
      That we, &c.
      That we, &c.
      For it, &c.

8.
My sins, my God has me forgave,
With none in envy now I live;
For I know all that in truth does die,
Will live with God eternally.
      Will live, &c.
      Will live, &c.
      For I know, &c.

9.
And all that doth the truth despise,
Above this earth will never rise;
They are doom'd in darkness here to be,
With cursed Cain eternally.
      With cursed, &c.
      With cursed, &c.
      They are, &c.

10.

When the elements do melt with heat,
The blood of God will be so sweet
To faithful souls which here did die,
For then they'll live eternally.
>   For then, &c.
>   For then, &c.
>   To faithful, &c.

11.

When my faith it soar'd up on high,
I saw God in eternity;
It was then my God he gave to me
An earnest of eternity.
An earnest, &c.
An earnest, &c.
It was, &c.

12.

And now I am not afraid to die,
Nor in the silent grave to lie;
For I have wash'd my soul in my God's blood,
And I am ready for eternity.
>   And I am, &c.
>   And I am, &c.
>   For I have.

13.

When the bridegroom, comes my lamp will burn,
I have oil enough to serve my turn;
When my lamp is lit, by God I see,
It will burn to all eternity.
>   It will, &c.
>   It will, &c.
>   When my, &c.

14.

When reason's from the grave set free,
They'll here in darkness ever be;
And for want of oil in their lamps I see,
They'll be damn'd to all eternity.
>   They'll be, &c.
>   They'll be, &c.
>   And for, &c.

15.

No envy can my peace destroy,
Which here on earth I now enjoy;
For I am compell'd the truth to see,
And am longing for eternity.
    And am, &c.
    And am, &c.
    For I am, &c.

16.

If I had immortality,
The face of God I soon would see,
I'd fly above the starry sky,
To my God in all eternity.
    To my God, &c.
    To my God, &c.
    I'd fly, &c.

BOYER GLOVER.

NINETY-THIRD SONG.

LET my soul soar up on high,
And survey eternity;
Where two prophets great do tell
That a glorious God does dwell;
Who came down and here did die,
And now lives eternally.

2.

There the faithful all will dwell,
When their God calls them from hell,
That silent sleep of death,
Here upon this mortal earth;
Then as swift as thought will fly
Far above the starry sky.

3.

There's a glorious king bright,
There's all day, and there's no night;
There a host of angels dwell,
Who God's wonders great can tell;
But the thing that comforts me,
Is, that I God's face shall see.

4.

In the presence of our king,
We his praise shall ever sing;
Because he here for us did die,
We shall live eternally,
His bright person to adore,
He's our God, well have no more.

5.

When our God calls us on high,
There to live eternally;
Joys celestial, joys divine,
We in glory all shall shine;
While the devils here below,
Live in pain and endless woe.

BOYER GLOVER.

NINETY-FOURTH SONG.
(TUNE, 'The King; God bless him.')

JOHN Reeve is God's prophet, I clearly do see,
  And Lodowick Muggleton too;
God chose them, that they might his mysteries declare
  To all those whom he doth love true;
They are God's last prophets, and God they've made known,
  And blessed is he that possest him;
For when to the truth he hath set to his seal,
  He then is assured God's blest him,
     God's blest him,
     God's blest him.
For when to the truth he hath set to his seal,
  He then is assured God's blest him.

2.

The faithful in Christ, they have tasted this cup,
  And now it is handed to me;
Come, come, my dear friends, let us take a deep sup
  Of Christ's most noble mystery;
Christ Jesus our God who for us here did die,
  And blessed is he that possest him;
For when to the truth he hath set to his seal,
  He then is assured God's blest him.
     God's blest him,
     God's blest him.
For when to the truth lie with set to his seal,

He then is assured God's blest him.

3.

When Gad he gate Moses those table of stone,
   Inscrib'd with the angelic law;
It was that the people the true God might own,
   If so, they nigh unto God draw;
The only one God which Moses testify,
   And blessed is he that's possest him;
For when to the truth he hath set to his seal,
   He then is assured God's blest him.
      God's blest him,
      God's blest him.
For when to the truth lie With set to his seal,
   He then is assured God's blest him.

4.

Three commissions God promised he'd send on this
        earth,
   And now they have all three appear'd;
The water, the blood, and the Spirit, I see,
   The souls of God's elect have cheer'd;
Christ Jesus, that God, who for us here did die,
   And blest is that soul that's possest him;
For when to the truth he hath set to his seal,
   He then is assured God's blest him.
      God's blest him,
      God's blest him.
For when to the truth he hath set to his seal,
   He then is assured God's blest him.

5.

The apostles and prophets are trees of our God,
   In the garden of God they do stand;
Christ Jesus the tree of life is in the midst,
   The faithful do stretch forth their hand,
And partake of the fruit of our only one God,
   And blest is that soul that's possest him;
For when he hath eaten of the tree of life,
   He then is assured God's blest him.
      God's blest him,
      God's blest him.
For when he hath eaten of the tree of life,
   He then is assured God's blest him.

                      ISAAC FROST, 1829.

Divine Songs

NINETY-FIFTH SONG.

LET'S lift up our souls and rejoice,
  This is the triumphing day;
When God's belov'd prophets were releas'd
  From monsters and beasts of prey;
Who for truth so long time were confin'd
  In a dungeon with vipers to dwell;
But the dragon, alas! was stark blind,
  To think to keep truth in a cell.

2.

For now he hath shak'd off the chains,
  And ministers truth to each brother;
Like the sun in the firmament shines,
  From one end of the earth to the other;
What power can extinguish such light,
  Which God's divine person inspires;
It is all the saint's delight,
  And all our forefathers' desires.

3.

Some serpents still fill'd with disdain.
  Think long to be shedding our blood;
Till this time they cannot refrain,
  To blaspheme against all that is good;
It is not the prophets alone,
  But each belov'd saint the same;
They trample under dirt the just one,
  And all that profess his name.

4.

In darkness they hover about,
  Expecting to find some rest;
With nothing but fear and doubt,
  Their reasonable souls are possess'd;
With their three-person God they can't help
  Disdaining our union and love;
In the midst of a plenty they want,
  When the sun it shines bright from above.

5.

Since serpents in darkness rejoice,
  Let us praise the true God for light,
And obey the true shepherd's voice.
  That guides all our souls aright;

For tho' we as pilgrims live here,
   As sojourners in a strange land;
We brisk and lively appear,
   When serpents they cannot stand.

                WILLIAM WOOD, *Painter*.

NINETY-SIXTH SONG.

ETERNAL Jesus, source of love,
   What praise in me will dwell,
When thou dost call me up above,
   From death and silent hell;
What raptures my soul then will see,
   When I praise thee for thy love;
Redeeming love the theme will be,
   In thy kingdom of glory above.
      What raptures, &c.

2.

Thy power it was infinite,
   When thou didst form on high;
But how thy love does us delight,
   When thou to redeem us didst die;
The work of creation above
   Was done by a power divine;
But how does thy redeeming love,
   Make Infinite power to shine.
      The work, &c.

3.

When you did form us here in love,
   No sorrow you then did know;
When you redeem'd us in thy love,
   What pain you then did know;
Thy infinite power, I see,
   Shines most when you was dead;
The virtue of the word from thee,
   Did raise thy glorious head.
      Thy infinite, &c.

4.

When that you did create above,
You infinite was no less;
But when you did redeem in love,
Then death did your Godhead possess;
But tho' in a finite-like state,
You died your elect to save,

The power of your word so great.
Did conquer death, hell and the grave.
    But tho', &c.

5.

Oh! how astonishing to think,
  That God once dead should be,
And give lost souls his blood to drink,
  From sin to set them free;
But that which astonishes more,
  Is, that when he was dead,
The word which he did speak before,
  Should raise his glorious head.
    But that, &c.

6.

Oh! God, what a great sight I see,
  Thy infinite spirit above
Came down and died upon a tree---
  What a manifestation of love!
And when you was center'd in death,
  Death could not your spirit devour;
You re-asssum'd immortal breath---
  What a manifestation of power!
    And when, &c.

7.

For tho' Elias sat on high,
  And fill'd your glorious throne,
He left your spirit here to die,
  And conquer death alone;
Tho' you as a creature here died,
  Nought could your word impede;
The word you spoke, I am satisfied,
  Was spoke from an infinite seed.
    Tho', &c.

8.

When great Jehovah form'd on high,
  He did infinite power possess;
When to redeem us he did die,
  His power could be no less;
He never was less than God,
  Sin could not him devour;
He raised Lazarus by his word,
  By virtue of infinite power.

He never, &c.

BOYER GLOVER.

NINETY-SEVENTH SONG.

My brethern in Christ,
The eternal Lord,
Attend and ascend to praise such a God,
  Who is our dear Saviour,
  The God we adore,
We'll love him while here, and then for evermore.

2.

Our voices we'll raise,
To sing forth praise,
In spite of the world, to the end of our day;
  To such a dear Saviour,
  Our praises are due,
We'll love him for ever; my friends, what say you?

3.

Are you so inclin'd
To praise such a God,
For his boundless love eternally good,
  To become our dear Saviour,
  And die on the cross,
To save us his children, that none should be lost?

4.

His blood did atone
For his elect alone,
Being flesh of his flesh, and bone of his hone;
  How great is his mercy
  And favor to us,
To free us from bondage and also the curse.

THOMAS LUTHER.

NINETY-EIGHTH SONG.

On the 17th of January 1676, being the day the prophet Muggleton was tried at the Old Bailey for Blasphemy; fixed five hundred Pounds, to be imprisoned till paid, and to stand three days on the Pillory, (two hours each day) at Temple Bar, at the Royal Exchange, and West Smithfield, in the city of London. His books were divided into three lots, and burnt before his face each day while he was on the Pillory.

ONE thousand, six hundred and seventy six,
Was a black dismal day which the devils prefix,
To bring a great prophet to their unjust bar,
Where reason was clouded and malice shown far;
An endictment of blasphemy, then was brought out,
And the question was ask'd, whether guilty or not?

2.

To reap up the venom, that senate did spit;
Too tedious it would be in verse to relate;
They belch'd out their poison, thinking to devour
The prophets of God, whose strong faith was a tower
Of impregnable strength against malice and hate,
In attempting to assault, which rebounds on their pate.

3.

When the jury, that for the same purpose was made,
Had brought in their verdict, the judge's thanks paid,
And Balaam Jefferys was left the court's sentence to
    pass,
Which he did with a voice that did bray like un ass;
And said, 'thou most stand in the pillory thrice,
And pay a small fine, of five hundred pound price.'

4.

Now, now the fight's done, for the prophet of God
Hath conquer'd his foes with the two edg'd sword;
Hell foam'd at his rest, while the nine days did
    last,
Which being expir'd the wonderment's past;
He rides the white horse and with joy he is crown'd
With the love of those saints that encompass him
    round.

5.

This, this was the day *(19th July)* fate sparkled disdain,
That a dungeon should longer God's prophet detain;
He hath now left your hell and that devilish place,
For a palace of joy, that is free from disgrace;
Then let us all rejoice, and for his bless'd sake,
And for his day of redemption, a jubilee make.

6.

Love, love be our bliss, and triumph our joy,

While malice and hatred damn'd envy destroy;
Let the devils below when we sing forth a choir
Of praises to God, for they can soar no higher;
Then this dismal black orb where our joys were
        suppress'd
By those who were stamp'd with the mark of the beast.
                ALEXANDER DELAMAIN.

NINETY-NINTH SONG.
(TUNE, 'Dear Chloe, come give me sweet kisses.')

FOR to look on the works of creation,
  It is wonderful great to behold;
So likewise the work of redemption,
  Which was by the prophets foretold,
That our God would in time become flesh,
  His own elect seed for to save;
Or else saint and devil would both have lain together,
  And never would have risen from the grave.
      Or else, &c.

2.
His prerogative royal did move him
  At first for to form or create,
Of a substance which was earth and water,
  His power is wonderful great;
The innumerable host that's in heaven,
  In a word let it fully suffice;
A grand specimen surely is plain to be seen,
  In the face of the natural skies.
      A grand, &c.

3.
In six days God's creation was finish'd,
  I see it stands so on record;
The man was the noblest of all creatures
  That ever was form'd by his word:
Now, behold, he who was the creator,
  In due time very man did become,
Transmuted himself into human nature,
  Of the substance of flesh, blood and bone.
      Transmuted. &c.

4.
There's three that bear witness in heaven,
  The Father, the Spirit and Word;
So likewise there's three that bear witness on earth,

The Spirit, the water and blood:
Now these, all do agree in sweet union,
  In communion I have them all found;
How God became flesh, and dwelt upon earth,
  His prophets to me doth expound.
      How God, &c.

            5.

God the Father, he was in creation,
  By the prophets in the law we are told;
God the Son, he was in redemption,
  As the gospel does clearly unfold:
On this God I depend, and no other
  Will I ever trust in or believe;
For my sanctification lies in the commission
  God gave to great Muggleton and Reeve.
      For my, &c.

            6.

While he walk'd his sore journey here.
  He had many bitter enemies 'tis true;
But their spite and their malice he never did fear,
  For the bonds of death he broke through;
So, woe be to those that despise him,
  'Twould been better they ne'er had been born
In the day of their doom, when their fear it does come,
  He surely will hold them in scorn.
      In the, &c.

            7.

He's a savour of life unto life,
  Unto those that do on him rely;
He's also a savour of death unto death,
  Unto all those that do him deny;
So, now let us all join together
  To praise him as our only Lord,
For he has promis'd life and salvation to all
  That believes in his last prophet's word.
      For he, &c.

                    WILLIAM SEDGWICK.

ONE-HUNDREDTH SONG.
(TUNE, 'Fanny blooming fair, and St. Osyth by the mill.')

OH! Christ my God and king,
  To thee we'll always raise
Our voices here, and sing
  Incessant, Lord, thy praise;
Thy mercy is so great,
  We can't too much adore,
Or all thy praise relate,
  Now, nor when time's no more.
    Thy mercy, &c.

2.

Oh! everlasting spring
  Of light, of life and joy;
When thus contemplating,
  No nature can employ;
But in transporting bliss,
  Faith does with faith combine,
And what. we have in this,
  Is exactly divine.
    But in, &c.

3.

Thy wonders, O my God,
  Too wondrous are to tell;
Who left divine abode,
  To conquer death and hell;
I may endeavour here,
  Thy boundless love to show;
But, bounded, cant declare
  Those joys I never knew.
    I may, &c.

4.

An earnest here we have
  Of joys which are sublime;
I've tasted and do know,
  That they are all divine;
But nature's clog prevents,
  Fruition can't be here;
These natural elements,
  Ere bliss must disappear.
    But nature, &c.

Divine Songs

5.
Faith cloth'd with earth will rise,
  Beyond this ending globe;
Meet God beyond the skies,
  Deck'd in divine robes;
Whilst wasting nature dies,
  And every orb of light,
Dissolving falls and lies
  In an eternal night.
     Whilst wasting, &c.

JAMES MILLER, 1740.

ONE HUNDRED AND FIRST SONG.

From Jericho to Jerusalem
I travell'd with faithful men;
But in my way, curs'd thieves I found,
  Who stole my peace, and did me wound.
  Who stole my peace, and did me wound.
  Who stole my peace, and did me wound.
  But in my way, curs'd thieves I found,
  Who stole my peace, and did me wound.

2.
False priests and levites pass'd me by,
And left me in my blood to die;
For they'd no oil nor wine I found,
To heal a poor lost sinner's wound.
  To heal, &c.
  To heal, &c.
  For they, &c.
  To heal, &c.

3.
Next came the good Samaritan,
Which was when Christ was God and man.
And in his blood by faith I found,
Both oil and wine to heal my wound.
  Both oil, &c.
  Both oil, &c.
  And in, &c.
  Both oil, &c.

4.
He sat me on his faith to ride,
Until that I was satisfied;
The third commission was the inn,

Which here did cleanse my soul from sin.
  Which here, &c.
  Which here, &c.
  The third, &c.
  Which here, &c.

5.

The two-pence he as earnest gave,
It was that he'd lie in the grave;
When he return'd from death, he said,
The debt it wholly should be paid.
  The debt, &c.
  The debt, &c.
  When he, &c.
  The debt, &c.

6.

The people that are call'd the host,
It is poor Adam's seed when lost;
The man to whom he gave the care,
It is true prophets that liv'd here.
  It is, &c.
  It is, &c.
  The man, &c.
  It is, &c.

7.

And when Christ died for Adam's sin,
The gospel was that very inn,
Which he returned, as he said,
And then the debt was wholly paid.
  And then, &c.
  And then, &c.
  Which he, &c.
  And then, &c.

8.

For justice it was wroth with sin,
And Christ the debt paid in the inn;
In the commission of the blood,
He died according to his word.
  He died, &c. He died, &c.
  In the, &c. He died, &c.

                                        BOYER GLOVER.

Divine Songs

ONE HUNDRED AND SECOND SONG.

OH! death, what is thy bitter sting!
  Thy thousand piercing darts!
Ten thousand pleasures, faith doth bring,
  To ease my dying heart.

2.

A glorious object I do view,
  Quite thro' thy gloomy way;
Which now my dying soul pursues,
  Through night instead of day.

3.

Since life with thee's no sympathy,
  Then finish soon the strife;
A friend I'm sure thou art to me,
  The way to endless life.

MARGARET THOMAS.

ONE HUNDRED AND THIRD SONG.

OH! what great and glorious treasure,
  Flow within my soul, I see;
Now I know by true repentance,
  What it was that died for me;
The Godhead spirit here did centre,
  In a human frame I see;
The whole Godhead here did enter
  Into silent death for me.
    The Godhead, &c.

2.

Altho' I am a wicked sinner,
  And justly do deserve to die;
Within my soul mercy is crying,
  You're blest, you live eternally;
Like faithful Noah, I great favor
  In the sight of God have found;
His precious blood, that glorious Saviour,
  Has heal'd the serpent's deadly wound.
    Like faithful, &c.

3.

Oh! how my soul is freed from sorrow,

Now I by faith my God can see;
While curs'd devils fill'd with horror,
   Dread the great eternity;
When my soul was almost dying,
   By reason's malice great to me;
In my soul a voice was crying,
   Oh! my God hath died for me.
      When my, &c.

4.

What tho' I live with cursed devils,
   And amongst them here shall die;
I shall have a glorious supper,
   When my God comes from on high;
On the flesh of mighty captains,
   With my God, I then shall feed;
On mighty men of that great nation,
   Which caus'd our glorious God to bleed.
      On the, &c.

5.

And on the flesh of smaller devils,
   I shall feed by faith, I see;
When my God comes in that morning,
   Of the great eternity,
Kings and priests will lose their power,
   None will bear supremacy;
All fill'd with horror in that hour,
   They'll be damn'd eternally.
      Kings and, &c.

6.

When upon them we are feeding,
   With our glorious God divine,
And do know they are a bleeding,
   Oh! how glorious we shall shine;
Fill'd with love and grateful praises,
   With acclamations loud will cry,
When our God from death us raises,
   Into blest eternity.
      Fill'd with, &c.

BOYER GLOVER.

ONE HUNDRED AND FOURTH SONG.

GLIDE swiftly, ye streams
  Of God's blood, through my soul;
How soft are the themes
  That does reason controul;
By the third commission
  God gave to John Reeve,
In a blest condition,
  We truth do receive.
    In a blest, &c.

2.

It's the blood of our God
  That sets lost mortals free,
And makes them assur'd
  They happy shall be;
For by eating God's flesh,
  True salvation is found,
And our drinking God's blood,
  Makes new joys to abound.
    And our, &c.

3.

Like the sheep that was lost,
  We have all gone astray;
Till we join'd the true flock,
  We were in the wrong way;
But the ninety-nine just ones
  Whom justice ne'er bound,
They never were lost,
  So they ne'er can be found.
    They never, &c.

4.

For no man on this earth
  Ever happy can be,
Unless a lost sinner
  Himself he can see;
And when justice has scourg'd us,
  That fiery rod!
Then mercy relieves us,
  And shows us our God.
    Then mercy, &c.

5.

No turnings nor windings
  In truth doth appear;
No alarms of false doctrine
  E'er fills us with fear;
For the way to salvation
  Is narrow and straight;
And sweet revelation
  Shows us heaven's gate.
    And sweet, &c.

BOYER GLOVER.

ONE HUNDRED AND FIFTH SONG.
(TUNE, 'God save the kind.')

GREAT Muggleton and Reeve,
True prophets I believe;
Great God's last choice,
His mind to make known
To the elect alone;
Therefore I'll him adore,
Israel's great God.
    His mind, &c.

2.

By faith, I plainly see
His blood was shed for me;
By reason's brood,
The Lord of life they've slain;
Eternal life we've gain'd;
Therefore let's him adore,
Israel's great God.
    The Lord, &c.

3.

'Tis by the prophet's word,
Declar'd in the third record,
And fully made known;
But reason cannot see
This noble mystery;
Therefore let's him adore,
Israel's great God.
    But reason, &c.

4.

Come, friends, and join with me
To see this mystery---

God wholly dead;
No assistance wanted he,
Rose by his own decree;
Therefore by faith I see
'Twas Israel's great God.
   No assistance, &c.

5.

No other God I'll have,
His love is all crave;
Therefore I'll sing,
His mercy is so sure,
For ever to endure;
Therefore let's him adore,
Israel's great God.
   His mercy, &c.

RICHARD SMITH, 1794.

ONE HUNDRED AND SIXTH SONG.
(TUNE, 'Jolly Sailor.')

OH! glorious Jesus, our eternal God,
How great was thy mercy and favor,
 To leave thy throne above,
 And come down here in love.
 Our bounds to remove;
 My glorious Saviour.

2.

Such love as thine surpasses all, as giver,
For none can compare with it ever;
 Heaven's great majesty,
 For us sinners did die,
 To raise us on high,
 To our God and Saviour.

3.

How happy's he who's the honour to know God,
And are sure to live with him for ever
 'Tis by faith we receive
 Great Muggleton and Reeve,
 And so to believe
 In our God and Saviour.

4.
These prophets have finish'd the mystery of God.
For he chose them in his love and favor,
   His truth to make known
   To his elect alone,
   For we are his own,
   He's our God and Saviour.

5.
The heavenly mysteries they have reveal'd,
Will rejoice and make us glad for ever;
   For by faith I do see,
   God died on a tree,
   And has redeem'd me;
   He's my God and Saviour.

6.
Three days and three nights in the grave God did lay,
Death was too weak for to keep him under;
   For with him, I see,
   Death had no sympathy;
   According to decree,
   Arose my God and Saviour.

7.
Said God, 'I have power to lay down my life,
And have power to take it again;'
   Now the prophet tells me.
   God's word was a decree;
   It was that God, I see,
   That did raise my Saviour.

8.
The infinite power of God's word speaking,
Must affect the thing spoken of sure;
   At the time he decreed,
   Life quicken'd in the seed,
   Then rose indeed
   My God and Saviour.

9.
God rais'd Moses and Elias to glory on high,
And invested them with great power;
   To represent God on high,
   Whilst God came down to die,
   Far to raise us on high,
   Like a glorious Saviour.

10.
His infinite properties he did bring down;
His glory he will not give to another;
  By inherent power did rise,
  And soar'd above the skies;
  Crowned with victories,
  Our God and Saviour.

11.
All glory and honour to our God alone is due,
There was none ever like him in power;
  'Tis his word will us raise,
  At the end of those days;
  To Christ alone give all praise,
  He's our God and Saviour.

                REBECCA BATT.

ONE HUNDRED AND SEVENTH SONG.

God's prophets now at rest,
Your writings have me blest,
And your praise I now will sing,
For this sacred treasure;
    For I see
    Yon are free
    From misery;
Which gives much pleasure;
You made my soul with joy abound,
You made my head with mercy crown'd,
Great Reeve and Muggleton.
      You made, &c.

2.
Your record's clear to me,
Both life and death I see;
Death the king of horror here,
You have captivated,
    And I know
    It is so,
    As you show,
Just as you have related;
For you blunt the sting of death,
Tho' you have no mortal breath,
Great Reeve and Muggleton.
      For you, &c.

3.

Through death new life we see,
By mercy's liberty;
Which makes us great conquerors bold,
Over the seed of reason;
    For we know,
    They will go,
    Very low,
And be damn'd for their treason;
You gave me a mighty sword,
For to cut down reason's lord,
Great Reeve and Muggleton.
    You gave, &c.

4.

For at God's very feet,
Under the justice seat,
We our souls do here delight,
By slaying cursed reason;
    When they cry
    Blasphemy,
    God can't die,
We kill him for their treason;
For your sword is not in vain,
Many devils it has slain,
Great Reeve and Muggleton.
    For your, &c.

5.

The olive leaf you brought,
Which justice set at nought;
For where mercy does abound,
Justice has no power;
    When we see
    Liberty,
    And are free,
And peace does wrath devour;
Then you do by Jordan stand,
And lead us to Canaan's land,
Great Reeve and Muggleton.
    Then you, &c.

6.

Gigantic men we see,
The sons of Anack be,
Mighty men of great renown,

Ready to devour;
    When they cry,
    Let them die,
    We let fly,
And cut down all their power;
With your sword I ready stand,
To obey your dread command,
Great Reeve and Muggleton.
    With your, &c.

7.

That great and mighty shield,
Which guards us in the field,
Sure it is the power of faith;
And justice is your sword, sir;
    Which does kill,
    Reason still
    That rebel
Against your mighty word, sir;
With that sword we them pursue,
To the gates of hell with you,
Great Reeve And Muggleton.
    With that, &c.

8.

Your doctrine it is clear,
Does lead to mercy here;
We have touch'd the tree of life,
And we shall live for ever;
    From that root,
    We bear fruit,
    Which will suit,
When we from death do sever;
Then we loudly shall abound,
Mercy, mercy, thou hast crown'd
Great Reeve and Muggleton.
    Then we, &c.

9.

And on that glorious day,
Like lambs we'll skip and play,
Round about great Zion's hill,
The fountain of fall pleasure;
    Then will be
    Liberty,
    For to see

An endless hidden treasure;
Then with joy we shall abound,
And through Christ, by God be crown'd,
With Reeve and Muggleton.
  Then with, &c.

10.

Though worms does us destroy,
And vaileth all our joy:
With our eyes we God shall see,
In his burning splendour;
 For that son
 Bright will burn,
 And return
To make death surrender;
For Christ is our mighty head,
Which will call us from the dead,
With Reeve and Muggleton.
  For Christ, &c.

11.

When you the truth did tell,
Great Babylon then fell;
And in the saints there did arise
A great and mighty city;
 Where they praise
 Mercy's rays,
 All their days,
Which shines on them in pity;
New Jerusalem come down,
And with joy the saints did crown,
By Reeve and Muggleton.
  New Jerusalem, &c.

12.

In peace we here do stand,
All wailing God's command,
Till he comes down from on high,
From death our souls to sever;
 Then we'll fly
 Far on high,
 Praise to cry
To Christ our God for ever;
For who God's loving praise can sound,
Like the soul by mercy crown'd,
Through Reeve and Muggleton.
  For who, &c.

13.

How sweetly does appear
God's prophets' words while here,
In our souls they peace do sound,
Which gives us much pleasure;
    When they cry,
    'Liberty!
    Quickly fly,
And dig for hidden treasure.'
Round your necks you pearls did wear,
And surpass'd the diamonds far,
Great Reeve and Muggleton,
    Round your, &c.

14.

Although your souls are dead,
Your power is not fled;
For that power it will stand
Until time's last duration,
    For to kill
    Reason still,
    That rebel
Against your inspiration;
Fur when that your God's wonders told,
Your souls surpassed burnish'd gold,
Great Reeve and Muggleton.
    For when, &c.

BOYER GLOVER.

HUNDRED AND EIGHTH SONG.

FARE ye well, ye dark Egyptians,
    To Agar and his sons, adieu;
Your Gods are only tales of fiction,
    And your doctrine's all untrue;
In your dark land I was a stranger,
    In chains and fetters was confin'd,
And a slave to cruel Pharoah,
    Justice my death-warrant sign'd.

2.

Death and famine me surrounded,
    Heavy burdens forc'd to bear;
Then aloud I cried for mercy;
    But formless Gods, how could they hear?
But at length my royal father

Sent his dear servants unto me,
They show'd me, he had paid my ransom,
　　And shed his blood upon a tree.

3.

From Pharoah's land I've now departed,
　　In vain he strove to keep me bound;
Awaken'd faith increases stronger,
　　And reason falls, till he's quite drowned;
Now in peace, I am possessive
　　Pleasures that can ne'er decay,
By faith my soul it's prepar'd
　　For the great rejoicing day.

4.

For my royal father's servants,
　　By his command, has me adorn'd;
With wedding garments I am clothed,
　　Waiting for that glorious morn;
Then will the royal bridegroom come
　　And claim his bride he loves so dear,
The virgins wise, will than arise,
　　And meet the bridegroom in the air.

5.

No saint can e'er describe the meeting,
　　When faith meets his lovely king,
And they have that glorious greeting,
　　Love ever flowing from the spring;
The Lamb, the three armies will follow,
　　Into heaven, their glorious home,
In the third it is commanded,
　　By great Reeve and Muggleton.

EDWIN KITCHEN.

Divine Songs

HUNDRED AND NINTH SONG.

ALL glory unto God alone,
Who for me here did die,
And led captive, captivity;
He was a glorious fountain bright,
      From all eternity.

2.

When God be sent the prophet Reeve,
And Muggleton also;
His works of creation and redemption,
In my soul did flow.

3.

God he descended from above,
To die here below for me,
To work the mystery of redemption,
Which work I plainly see.

4.

The blood of God it purifies,
My soul it is made clean;
And now I shall ascend and see
My dear redeeming king.

5.

Where I shall reign in realms above,
To praise the God of all love;
Come Zion's sons, rejoice and sing,
To praise Christ the redeeming king.

6.

For now redemption is made clear,
It doth my heart and soul so cheer;
Come Zion's sons, rejoice and sing,
To praise Christ the redeeming king.

7.

When the fiery serpent begins to sting,
It is the law I'm sure;
But when I look on the Son of man,
My soul is quite pure.

8.

The serpent it was lifted up,

To typify the Son;
And now the thing it is made clear,
By Reeve and Muggleton.

9.

And when my God doth come again,
To call me up on high;
Oh! then I shall ascend and see
His glorious majesty.

10.

Christ is the God whom I adore,
And shall now and for evermore;
Therefore I will rejoice and sing,
To praise Christ the redeeming king.

ROBERT DAWSON.

HUNDRED AND TENTH SONG.

HARK, hark, the trumpet sounds!
   Arise ye saints to joy,
Proud reason stands confound,
   No morn can you annoy.

2.

Hark, hark, the glorious cry,
   The royal bridegroom near,
Awake ye virgins wise,
   Your lamps with oil prepar'd.

3.

And with your God ascend,
   Into bright realms above,
To sup on all curst serpents,
   With Christ the God of love.

4.

Rejoicing o'er the race of Cain,
   Gods great supper will be;
Because all persecutors vain
   Are damn'd eternally.

5.

Then to God who died for us
   Eternal praises sing;
Hosannas be unto the Son

Divine Songs

Of Israel's shepherd and king.

EDWIN KITCHEN.

HUNDRED AND ELEVENTH SONG.
(TUNE, 'The Storm.')

ISRAEL's great God, he descended,
  By his infinite power divine,
Mystery never comprehended,
  By proud reason's lofty mind;
When the virgin's womb contain'd him,
  His decree became all power,
The great Gad and king of heaven,
  Here on earth did death devour.
      The great, &c.

2.

Infinite power all did die
  When Jesus Christ was crucified;
They could not longer boast of power,
  When they pierc'd his righteous side;
The holy temple was destroy'd,
  According to God's firm decree;
In three days rais'd for evermore;
  This I by faith can plainly see.
      In three, &c.

3.

Here God became the son of David,
  When he in this world abode;
He was the everlasting Father,
  Clothed in a mortal robe;
Eternity the glorious Father,
  When a son he became time;
Being infinite in power,
  Rose eternity divine.
      Being infinite, &c.

4.

'Twas Adam's nature God took on him,
  When transmuted into flesh;
The same originating from him,
  At end of time with him will rest;
The splendid rays of truth now shining.
  Dread not prosecution's threats;
Awake from slumber sons of Zion,

Know your birth's eternal great.
    Awake from, &c.

5.

Rejoice, you happy mortals here,
  Your happy fate you'll ne'er repine;
Believe the third record, ne'er fear,
  But you will drink spiritual wine;
That heavenly cup that God has offer'd,
  Here for Adam's seed below;
Rejoice, all you, that by this profit,
  None can wine like this bestow.
    Rejoice all, &c.

                RICHARD PICKERSGILL, 1807.

HUNDRED AND TWELFTH SONG.
(TUNE, 'The Lillies of France, and the fair English Rose.')

In one thousand six hundred, fifty and one,
God chose two prophets his will to make known
To all elect men, that he did leave heaven;
All praise hallelujahs, and glory be given.
    To all, &c.

2.

To our great God, the eternal Father veil'd,
Wrapt up in flesh against death he prevail'd;
By power inherent in his prison I see,
He deliver'd himself from death's captivity.
    By power, &c.

3.

When God became man he'd no reason in him,
This must be allow'd, then how could he sin?
There's nothing could sin but reason I'm sure,
Christ's life was God's life infinitely pure.
    There's nothing, &c.

4.

The eternal Father the life of Christ became,
The purity ne'er alter'd, tho' its condition changed;
The Godhead in eternity, the Godhead here in time,
It ne'er sin'd in eternity, how could it sin in time?
    The God, &c.

5.

Then as he ne'er sinn'd, no power death could have,
No longer than decreed to keep him in the grave;
Sin and death in union together they do lie,
Christ's sinless life with death could have no
      sympathy.
    Sin and, &c.

6.

By Christ haring power himself to release,
O'er death he gain'd power to raise such to his feast
Of eternal pleasures that are of his faith,
When we soar up on high, and breathe immortal
      breath.
    Of eternal, &c.

                              RICHARD WYNNE.

HUNDRED AND THIRTEENTH SONG.

LIFE's but a journey to the grave,
Alike to monarch as to slave;
Where all mankind will levell'd be,
Under pale death's captivity;
Which makes me long to see the time,
When saints will all immortal shine.

2.

These gloomy mansions will retain
The breathless saint when freed from pain;
Submitting to all conquering power,
The victor will all life devour.
    Which makes, &c.

3.

Then reason, why this needless strife
Surely there's nought can die but life;
Both soul and body here must lie,
For all that's born must surely die.
    Which makes, &c.

4.

The time will come when time must be
Swallow'd up into eternity;
When Christ our God will summons all
Within this fair terrestrial ball;
Then shall we all immortal shine,

Praising our God that's so divine.

5.

The dead in Christ will first arise,
And ope' their new and wondering eyes;
Ascend as swift as thought above,
Surrounding Christ their God of love.
      Then shall, &c.

6.

'Come, my dear saints, come, come away,
Enjoy with eternal day,
Where endless pleasures are in store,
For you, my chosen, evermore.'
      Then shall, &c.

7.

With glorious bodies like to him,
Our great immortal God and king;
There we shall hallelujahs raise,
Singing the Lamb's new songs of praise,
      Then shall, &c.

8.

The serpent's seed will here be left
Of all their former joys bereft;
Centred in darkness, grief and woe,
Eternally to undergo.
      While we, &c.

9.

Then shall the righteous shine and sing
Unto their dear redeeming king,
Who did such matchless mercy show
Unto poor Adam's seed below.
      Then shall, &c.

10.

O come, my dear Redeemer, come,
And take us to our long'd-for home;
Where we shall sing with one accord,
Adoring of our suffering Lord;
Then shall we all immortal shine,
Centred in bliss that's so divine.

WILLIAM MILLER.

HUNDRED AND FOURTEENTH SONG.
(TUNE, 'Tweed side.')

IN darkness I wander'd about,
  When lost, and a servant to sin;
But now by God's blood I am free,
  As if lost I never had been;
The light of redemption doth shine
  More bright than the sun at noon-day;
And the eating the flesh of my God,
  Has taken all my fears away.

2.

My soul has the wings of a dove,
  And often to God it does fly;
But with him it cannot abide,
  Until that it first here does die;
This, this was the state of our God,
  When he assum'd humanity;
His kingdom he ne'er could could assume,
  Until that his soul it did die.

3.

Curst devils did put him to death,
  Tho' loudly they heard him to cry;
But nothing their wrath could appease,
  Until that our God he did die;
'Away with him!' loud they did cry,
  And doom'd our God for to die;
Believing, when he were dead,
  He'd lie there to eternity.

4.

But they are all mistaken, I see,
  Our God. he's ascended on high;
He'll call them forth under his law,
  To suffer to eternity;
They scourg'd him and crown'd him with thorns,
  Nail'd him to a cross for to die;
Their malice to make quite complete,
  A soldier pierced his thigh.

5.

The blood that then issued forth.
Its virtue there's few can it tell;

It takes off the fear of death,
Assures us we sha'nt live in hell;
And now I will patiently wait
Till our God calls me up on high;
His word will raise me from the grave,
To live with him eternally.

BOYER GLOVER.

HUNDRED AND FIFTEENTH SONG.

OH! Lucifer, of you I'm going to tell,
Your nature was reason, so you did rebel;
When you was in heaven, I do mean,
That your rebellion first was seen.

2.

For which God did cast you down,
From his high imperial throne,
Upon this earth for to remain,
And you will never return again.

3.

And you was that angel bright, I see,
That very serpent, tho' called a tree;
Your person most lovely did appear,
Unto Eve's sight, it is most clear.

4.

And your oily tongue did her deceive;
Oh! when your counsel she did receive,
Then her innocence you did beguile,
She brought you forth in a man child.

5.

That child, he yaw the devil, 'tis plain,
Who then did appear in cursed Cain;
All knowledge of God you wholly lost,
With all of your angelic host.

6.

For your children, my God did kill,
'Twas they his precious blood did spill,
For which they will be dam'd, I am sure,
Eternal torments they'll endure.

Divine Songs

7.
It was my glorious God they kill'd,
That promise might be fulfill'd;
That he for Adam's seed might die,
That they might live eternally.

8.
Oh! what great love our God did shew,
Such a cruel death did undergo,
That we might for ever be free,
And praise him eternally.

9.
I know all saints upon his earth,
Have reason in them from their birth,
That doth most sadly them perplex,
Whenever he doth play his tricks.

10.
Which he sometimes do try to see,
If he can but get the mastery;
All we can do while here, I own,
Is by our faith, to keep him down.

11.
For reason, you shall my servant be,
Tilt death doth come to set me free,
So patiently my soul shall wait,
Till death has finish'd this mortal state.

12.
For a glorious crown's prepar'd for me,
Then our dear prophets I shall see;
In a lovely kingdom we shall shine,
With our dear God that's so divine.

13.
When I reflect on my happy state,
My tongue cannot my joys relate,
For by my faith I clearly see,
For ever in glory I shall be.

14.
My glorious God I shall behold,
With joys too great for to unfold;
In raptures then we all shall sing,

To our dear redeeming king.

15.

While devils will be left behind,
And they no comfort then will find;
Time then ended, all will be o'er,
Their heaven's past and all their power.

16.

Oh! them their hell it will begin,
Where they committed all their sin,
Upon this earth they are doom'd to be
Unto all eternity.

SARAH FEVER, 1816.

HUNDRED AND SIXTEENTH SONG.

OH! how happy is that man,
Unto a truth that witness can;
That the eternal God did die,
To give him life eternally;
This is my Glorious God and king,
And I his praises e'er will sing.

2.

This God the Father did create
Man in a pure innocent state,
In his own form, which is a man;
A truth which none but devils deny can;
This is my glorious God and king,
And I his praises e'er will sing.

3.

This God to Adam a promise made,
That he would break the serpent's head,
For to redeem his elect seed---
This is the glorious God indeed;
This is my glorious God and king,
And I his praises e'er will sing.

4.

O, what a power God did show,
When he descended here below,
Transmuted in a virgin's womb,
Did very God and man become;
This is my glorious God and king,
And I his praises e'er will sing.

5.

Of a pure virgin never defil'd,
My God became a pure man-child;
This is the Father and the Son,
And Holy Ghost, in person one;
This is my glorious God and king,
And I his praises e'er will sing.

6.

This mystery did lay conceal'd,
Till God he from his throne reveal'd
How those wondrous works were done,
Declar'd by Reeve and Muggleton;
This is my glorious God and king,
And I his praises e'er will sing.

THOMAS WALTON.

HUNDRED AND SEVENTEENTH SONG

REJOICE, ye saints of God above,
And sing his dear redeeming love,
For very God did flesh become,
Vail'd all his glories in a Son;
Both Father, Son and Spirit too,
Has now declar'd himself to you;
Three glorious titles, but one God,
In time and in divine abode.

2.

Oh! wondrous strange it is to tell,
God should himself with mortals dwell;
That Adam's seed should be employ'd,
When Adam's daughter overjoy'd,
As mother to her God became,
The infant God did test the same;
When from her womb the spotless babe
His Godhead show'd, in flesh array'd.

3.

Well might the angels joy proclaim,
And greet in such pathetic strain;
When they descended to declare,
She'd more than man, for God was there;
While the shining angels too,
Appear to wandering shepherds' view,

To tell the joy was to man assign'd,
God man was born to save mankind.

4.

Oh! sacred news, redeeming king,
Thy love while here we'll ever sing;
And to time's end we'll strive to show
Thy love, O Lord, to us below;
Praise is the offering which faith brings,
True faith thou lovest, O king of kings;
Our all in this imperfect state,
Is this return for love so great.

5.

United, knit in love let's raise
Our voices then in mortal praise;
And on these days to Christ our king,
The glorious tidings yearly bring;
But when translated up to thee,
In realms of blest eternity;
We'll unmolested e'er adore;
'Tis all we wish, to sin no more.

JAMES MILLER.

HUNDRED AND EIGHTEENTH SONG.
(TUNE, 'Hearts of Oak.')

REJOICE, all my friends, while to glory I steer,
My sails are all set, and I find the coast clear;
At the third commission, I'll anchor and stay,
From that peaceful harbour, I'll ne'er go away;
  True faith is my ship,
  Peace and love rules the helm,
  This union so pure
  Keeps my soul secure,
With brave Reeve and Muggleton's only true God.
  True faith, &c.

2.

On the ocean of peace I contentedly ride,
Now Reeve is my pilot, and Muggleton my guide;
Their coast I will follow, With heart and with voice,
Till my voyage is complete, that my soul may rejoice.
  True faith is my ship,
  Peace and love rules the helm,
  This union so pure
  Keeps my soul secure,

With brave Reeve and Muggleton's only true God.
    True faith, &c.

3.

Should you tempest break forth, that appease to my
    view,
Be it ever so violent, to my faith I'll stand true;
While envious thunder it threats and it roars,
Still my pilots will steer me safe on to the shore.
    True faith is my ship,
    Peace and love rules the helm,
    This union so pure
    Keeps my soul secure,
With brave Reeve and Muggleton's only true God.
    True faith, &c.

4.

Should Boreas of reason, blow up as mach strife,
As to burst her black clouds, to condemn my poor life,
I'll endanger the storm from her envious rod,
And find a protection in my infinite God.
    True faith is my ship,
    Peace and love rules the helm,
    This union so pure
    Keeps my soul secure,
With brave Reeve and Muggleton's only true God.
    True faith, &c.

5.

The olive and vine does afford me more shield,
Then the lofty tall cedar, that spreads o'er the field,
Tho' its knowledge is great, yet its fruit is not Good,
For the rot's at the root, which decays the whole wood.
    True faith is my ship,
    Peace and love rules the helm,
    This union so pure
    Keeps my soul secure,
With brave Reeve and Muggleton's only true God.
    True faith, &c.

6.

There's tempests at sea, and there's storms on the
    land,
But the worst of all storms, is by vile reason's hands,
Yet their words, nor their blows, nor their tortures
    likewise,

Shall e'er shake my faith, I so dearly do prize.
  True faith's is my soul,
  Peace and love's in my mind;
  I always am ready
  And willing to follow
My crucified Lord, with my cross, to the grave.
  True faith's, &c.

JAMES FROST, 1803.

HUNDRED AND NINETEENTH SONG.
(TUNE, 'Eternal life it is to me.')

Great Reeve and. Muggleton declare
 To me the living bread,
And said, I need not be afraid,
 For God for me had bled;
And when I had drank a sup
 Of the blood of God divine,
My fears were then all dried up,
 And with praises my soul did shine.
  And when, &c.

2.

When in the wilderness I cried
 To God, that he pity would show;
The law is then unsatisfied,
 For my God I did not know;
And when that the water did rise,
 Jordan did ebb and flow;
This gave my soul a great surprise,
 Till I into Canaan did go.
  And when, &c.

3.

And in that land great peace I found,
 When I drank of the spiritual wine;
This did my reason quite confound,
 And my faith did abundantly shine;
Like the widow that gave the mite,
 My living I all give up,
When of my God I had a sight,
 For to drink of his glorious cup.
  Like the, &c.

4.

Elijah did the water smite,
 When he pass'd over Jordan, I see;

And often men he did delight,
  When from fear he set them free;
But when he to heaven did go,
  He did more, I am satisfied;
He smote the sorrow in God below,
  And then God grim death defied.
      But when, &c.

5.

For God then said, 'I'll freely give
  My soul as a ransom to death,
That my elect with me may live,
  When I give them immortal breath,
And now I will freely drink up,
  The cup my father gave;
The cup of death, that bitter cup,
  For to save my elect from the grave.'
      And now, &c.

                    BOYER GLOVER.

HUNDRED AND TWENTIETH SONG.
(TUNE, 'A rose tree in full bearing.')

THE truth in all its splendour,
  By faith I clearly see,
That God, the great Jehovah,
  Died here to ransom me.
The storms they are all over
  And the work is wholly done;
In this truth I'm well assured,
  By Reeve and Muggleton.
      The storms, &c.

2.

They are the Lord's last prophets
  That he will ever send,
Or any inspiration,
  Till time is at an end.
      The storms, &c.

3.

God's myst'ry they have finish'd,
  And the work made quite complete;
They left us bread and wine enough,
  For all true saints to eat.
      The storms, &c.

4.

Now I'm logging for that morning,
When my God will call me home;
It will be a glorious dawning
Unto true faith alone.
The clouds will disappear,
The sun will in full splendour shine,
And I shall meet my God above.
To sing new songs of praise divine.
    The clouds, &c.

MARGARET FROST.

HUNDRED AND TWENTY-FIRST SONG.

GOD of glory, great Redeemer,
Spring of joy and source of love,
Faith's true object, and saints treasure,
Christ eternal God above;
O thy love will ever be
Our praise to all eternity;
None but faith these joys can see
Or comprehend this mystery,
How the eternal God alone.
Is one in three, and three in one.

2.

There's none but Muggletonians only,
That this secret can define;
Thanks to God his prophets told us,
Shew'd this mystery divine;
Reeve his mission knew full well,
And Muggleton the same did tell;
They both upon this earth did dwell,
To let saints know both heaven and hell;
How the eternal God alone
Is one in three, and three in one.

3.

The glorious news those days commenc'd,
Happy those who can believe,
Salvation's offered in the doctrine
Of great Muggleton and Reeve;
No other church there is that can
Know what God is, for God was man;
No other system truth can scan,
But the Muggletonians can,
How the eternal God alone

Is one in three, and three in one.

4.

All glory then and praise be given
To our God of glory high,
Who dwells above the starry heavens,
Reigns in immortality;
Oh! glorious God, redeeming king,
Thy matchless love we'll ever sing,
And strive thy praise now to begin,
Who did salvation to us bring;
And let us know that thou alone,
Art one in three, and three in one.

JAMES MILLER.

HUNDRED AND TWENTY-SECOND SONG.

WHAT love, O God, can equal thine
   To mortals here below!
Who can thy glary here define,
   Or who thy brightness show?
By faith we see, as thro' a glass,
   Refulgent rays divine;
But what is this to that, alas!
   When we in glory shine.

2.

Oh! Christ, thy love will ever be
   My lasting theme and praise;
To time's last date we'll all agree
   To celebrate those days;
But, oh! eternity wo'nt be
   Sufficient to declare,
The riches of thy love to me,
   They so exceeding are.

3.

Redeeming love, Redeemer dear,
   Our grateful souls adore;
True faith employs a heart sincere
   In praise, till time's no more;
With patience waiting for our change,
   Would willingly resign
Our souls in death, for death's a friend,
   The way to joys divine.

4.

Welcome, my soul, this glorious morn,
  In songs your praise proclaim,
And let the morrow be adorn'd
  With anthems of the same;
The third, which did our joys complete,
  Alike commemorate;
And every year those days we'll meet,
  The same to celebrate.

5.

The glorious mission of our Lord,
  These three days did employ,
And from his high divine abode,
  Sent sweet salvation joy;
Which Reeve and Muggleton declar'd,
  True prophets from on high;
Eternal joys God has prepar'd
  For us eternally.

6.

Then, saints, in transports let us sing,
  Since we have such joys in store,
To Jesus Christ, the king of kings,
  Elective love adore;
With hearts united all combine,
  Sweet hallelujahs raise;
And let us all in praises join,
  To crown those happy days.

                                JAMES MILLER.

HUNDRED AND TWENTY-THIRD SONG.

HAPPY mortals, filled with praises,
  On these blessed glorious days,
To that mighty rock of ages,
  Sound your sweet and tuneful lays.
      To that, &c.

2.

See, my friends, your God from heaven,
  Born a creature here on earth;
For to faith alone 'tis given,
  To behold his wondrous birth.
      For to, &c.

3.
Upon the cross, when just expiring,
  How his blood in streams did flow,
True saints will ever be admiring,
  What their God did undergo.
    True saints, &c.

4.
Resigning there his sacred breath,
  Now he's ascended far on high,
By conquering sin, death and hell,
  Rose again victoriously.
    By conquering, &c.

5.
Upon his precious blood depending,
  Faithful souls an earnest have,
Of their pleasures never ending,
  Which do lie beyond the grave.
    Of their, &c.

6.
COME, sweet Jesus, end our sorrows,
  We are willing to resign
Our souls in death, for joy it follows,
  Endless joys and all divine.
    Our souls, &c.

7.
Center'd in that blessed kingdom,
  Where the spring of love we see,
Happy in our glorious freedom,
  Unto all eternity.
    Happy in, &c.

BOYER GLOVER.

HUNDRED AND TWENTY-FOURTH SONG.
(TUNE, 'Haste, Phillis, haste.')

WHEN my sins did accuse me,
  And justice me bound,
I cried for mercy,
  But no mercy I found;
While I was in false worship,
  In Egypt's dark land,
God's law did inform me,

I in justice must stand.

2.

From God's infinite justice
How fain would I fly,
When the law it condemn'd me
For ever to die;
But no place to hide me,
Could by me be found,
So I lay down at justice
Till mercy I found.

3.

Now the way I found mercy,
To you I will show;
'Twas by the third commission,
By which I do know,
That God that created
As Father on high,
To satisfy justice,
In mercy did die.

4.

If God had all power,
  What could him impede;
Or why must he die,
  To redeem his lost seed?
Was his hand ever shortened
  Since he formed on high;
Or why to save sinners,
  Must the soul of God die?

5.

To this curious question,
  I make this reply;
That for breaking God's law,
  It is just all should die;
And to manifest justice,
  Grim death did succeed;
And to manifest mercy,
  In love God did bleed.

6.

Pray, where is God's justice,
  If all are set free?
Or, where is his mercy,
  If none saved me?

And if God aton'd justice
  In mercy and love,
He has purchas'd a power
  To call us above.

7.

It was love was the motive
  Which caus'd God to die,
And to manifest power,
  He formed on high;
But, oh! what a power
  In God did appear,
When he died as a ransom
  For his elect so dear.

8.

Thus justice offended,
  All creatures must die,
And nought could atone it
  But infinity:
Thus justice eternal
  To Cain and his seed,
And mercy for ever
  To the faithful indeed.

BOYER GLOVER.

HUNDRED AND TWENTY-FIFTH SONG

WHEN I praise the God of Jacob,
In my soul what joys do flow,
For to see, by his last prophets,
We this mighty God do know.
Now will I praise this Lord of life,
That in my soul has banished strife.

2.

The law of God, me sore opprest,
Till by his prophets I found rest;
For now by faith, I clearly see,
This mighty God has died for me.
       Now will, &c.

3.

Mighty Jesus, Lord above,
How shall we speak thy boundless love,
Who, to poor sinners here below,

Does give thy mighty self to know.
>   Now will, &c.

4.

Now, my dear friends, let us all agree
To live in peace and unity,
And ever praise his holy name,
Who once for us a son became.
>   Now will, &c.

5.

A Son, a Saviour, and our God,
As we are taught by this record;
For here we sinners see indeed,
Our mighty God for us did bleed.
>   Now will, &c.

6.

So let us all together join
To praise this God that is so divine;
For by his witnesses we see,
One mighty God, with titles three.
>   Now will, &c.

7.

Now I will joyfully make known,
His prophets Reeve and Muggleton;
That all my friends may plainly see,
What my great God has done for me.
>   Now will, &c.

REBECCA BURTON.

HUNDRED AND TWENTY-SIXTH SONG.
(TUNE, 'Pretty Polly say.')

HARK, hark, ye sons of faith,
What bold reason saith,
How he boasts of mighty arms,
In hopes thereby to conquer;
>   With sword and shield,
>   Reaps the field,
>   Captives yield,

With thundering smoking cannon;
While the saints in love combine,
And with faithful hearts do join
Great Reeve sad Muggleton.
>   While the, &c.

2.

Then let true saints adore
Those blessings in great store,
And praise that God that shed his blood,
To save us evermore;
   Let us sing
   To that king,
   That doth us bring
To a throne that's never undone,
Where we ever shall accord
With the prophets of the Lord,
Great Reeve and Muggleton.
      Where we, &c.

3.

One glance from heaven's throne
Into the soul of man,
Doth so much joy and comfort bring,
It fills his heart with pleasure;
   It takes off fears,
   Wipes off tears,
   And appears
Surpassing earthly mammon;
True faith it is we now retain,
The declaration of two men,
Great Reeve and Muggleton.
      True faith, &c.

4.

Let reason plunder still,
And his own nature kill,
Since that he no other light
Never must discover;
   Blest are we,
   Who do see,
   Ourselves free,
And heirs to a commission,
By the words that we have read,
In the writings of the dead,
Great Reeve and Muggleton.
      By the, &c.

5.

All honor thanks and praise,
Be given all our days,
To the fountain of all faith,

From whence all joys proceedeth;
  And as before,
  Sing once more,
  And adore
The glorious God of heaven,
That a commission great did give,
To his prophets while they lived,
Great Reeve and Muggleton.
    That a, &c.

6.

Now they are gone to sleep,
Let us take care and keep
Those prophets they have left behind,
And we shall live for ever,
  To behold
  Crowns of gold
  Uncontroul'd,
In the presence of our Saviour;
Where we ever shall remain,
And in hallelujahs join
Great Reeve and Muggleton.
    While we, &c.

                    WILLIAM WOOD, *Joiner.*

HUNDRED AND TWENTYSEVENTH SONG.
(TUNE, 'Ye Gentlemen of England.')

You faithful Muggletonians who truly do believe
The doctrine of Muggleton to be the same as Reeve;
Let no wise anti-followers infuse into your ear,
That a prayer, Christ does hear, from us mortals here
    below.

2.

Great Reeve, God gave him power his secret to declare,
With Muggleton, two champions, this world can ne'er
    compare;
Great Muggleton declar'd the truth for us to know,
That the law condemns all whate'er from reason flow.

3.

Our prophets tell us plainly, God of them notice took,
And from no other power for notice we must look,
Excepting from our conscience, in which God's law do
    grow;
This I know, Reeve says so, and in our souls does flow.

4.

It's by our faith in Muggleton and Reeve that gives us
    peace,
And elevates our souls with joy that daily do increase;
The motions do immediate all thro' our conscience
    move,
Where it grows, there it flows, not direct from God
    above.

5.

Our prophets they did both agree; God did ordain it so;
And none in faith will e'er assume beyond the truth to
    go;
But justify our works by faith, seal'd by God's law in
    love;
Then in peace, joys increase, and thro' our souls do
    move.

6.

We must go unto Muggleton and Reeve's fountain of
    love,
It is the very fountain that flows in God above,
And there all wants will be supplied to all who do them
    own;
This we're sure, and as pure, as if come from God
    alone.

                        JAMES FROST, 1809.

HUNDRED AND TWENTY-EIGHTH SONG.

OH! how happy's my condition,
    From false worship am set free,
And have store of ammunition,
    For to face the enemy;
Of the comforts of salvation,
    Sure there is no joy like this.
Springs of water ever flowing,
    And I am for ever blest.

2.

When read the prophets' writings,
    It doth so my soul revive,
Reason it becomes a captive,
    And my faith doth daily thrive;
In a desert I was wandering,
    Musing by myself alone,

But I could not find my way out,
　　　　Till I came to Muggleton.

3.
Then I saw the secret mysteries,
　　Which the world could not unfold,
And I stood like one amazed,
　　For to see the serpent's roll;
For they often are professing
　　Of a God, but know him not;
For in sins they are all drunken.
　　And they stagger like a sot.

4.
But my God will love and pity,
　　Set me in the promis'd land,
Giving me great store of riches,
　　That I evermore might stand,
And plac'd me in a commission,
　　That he gave to prophet Reeve;
Oh my soul be ever thankful
　　That such blessings I receive.

5.
Hallelujah sing for ever
　　To our glorious God above;
In his wisdom us created,
　　And redeem'd us with his blood:
The Jews, full of spite and envy,
　　Nail'd our Saviour to the cross;
Unto us it is salvation.
　　But to them it is a curse.

6.
Tho' his precious blood they spilled,
　　'Twas to wash our sins away,
That the scriptures might be fulfilled,
　　For they speak of that dreadful day;
If the Jews could have kept him under,
　　Then the day had been their own;
But it was beyond their power,
　　For he is ascended unto his throne.

7.
But the Jews were all amazed,
　　When the stone was rolled away,
And their hearts ware sorely pricked,

Divine Songs

For they knew not what to say;
But the rulers they consulted
  With the soldiers this to say;
'His disciples, while we sleeping,
  Came and stole his corpse away.'

8.

But we know he is ascended,
  Tho' it is to their disgrace;
When all time is gone and ended,
  We shall see him face to face;
Hallelujah sing for ever,
  And for over praise his name;
Let all saints now join together,
  And for ever praise his name.

JOHANNA STRAGHT.

HUNDRED AND TWENTY-NINTH SONG.

How sweet and pleasant are those days,
  Now I my God can see,
His precious blood my soul has freed
  From death eternally;
  From death eternally;
The fears of death will ne'er surprise,
  Salvation's wrought in me;
Now I redeeming love shall sing,
  To all eternity.
    To all, &c.

2.

When that our God was under death,
  How vain did reason boost;
Not thinking he had power then,
  Those fetters to unloose;
    Those fetters, &c.
But David's root salvation brought,
  Unto the royal seed;
Damnation unto root and branch,
  Of those that made him bleed.
    Of those, &c.

3.

Now reason in their vaunted pride,

Salvation would obtain
By outward form, but faith doth know
  Their prayers are in vain;
    Their prayers, &c.
For God's rejection's on them sure,
  No favor can they gain;
When we to glory all arise,
  In hell they'll all remain.
    In hell, &c.

4.

Come Zion's sons, rejoice with me,
  To see the work is done;
We nothing else have for to do,
  But praise that glorious one;
    But praise, &c.
While thro this mortal life we pass,
  Our praises we will sing;
Till rais'd to realms of lasting bliss,
  With an immortal king
    With an, &c.

THOMAS MUDFORD.

HUNDRED AND THIRTIETH SONG.

HAPPY ye above all mankind,
Who from an inward light can see,
With a pure unclouded mind,
The long unravell'd mystery,
Can behold that only good,
And get from thence celestial food.
    Can behold, &c.

2.

Tyrant boast thyself in power,
Go, pride thee in thy rigid sway,
Joy thee in thy golden store,
Vain glories that must soon decay;
Tyrannize o'er all thy land,
And lord thyself in wide command.
    Tyrannize o'er, &c.

3.

Happy he who can despise
Thy power, thy sway, thy store and land;
Whilst more glorious objects rise,
And make him scorn thy wide command,

He from thence may dig such ore,
As is not in thy golden store.
    He from, &c.

4.

Happy he, thrice happy he,
Who plainly see with sacred eyes,
Christ in one, that glorious three,
In whom alone the Godhead lies;
May from thence such wealth receive,
As pompous empire ne'er can give.
    May from, &c.

THOMAS COOK.

HUNDRED AND THIRTY-FIRST SONG.

OH! Lord, my God and king,
All praise to thee will I sing;
Jesus, my king,
Oh! thou ancient of days,
Worthy art thou of praise;
Unto the end of days
  We will adore.

2.

'Worthy the Lamb,' they cried,
Sweet Jesus who for us died,
Oh! king of saints;
For thy elect alone,
Thy blood it did atone;
Thou art my God alone,
  And no one else.

3.

Tho' the world worships three,
They're blind and can't see,
Nor know the true God;
His blood they do despise,
And say, we believe in lies:
Because they do despise,
  They will be damn'd.

4.

This is their sentence sure,
Which they cannot endure,
But true it is,

Their God cannot them save,
From torments they will have,
When they're raised from the grave.
For evermore.

THOMAS LUTHER.

HUNDRED AND THIRTY-SECOND SONG.

OH! happy elect, ye elect that believe
In the principles that are laid down
In the commission great of the great prophet Reeve,
And likewise of great Muggleton;
Most heavenly truths in their doctrine we find.
And we heavenly manna feed on,
Makes new revelation arise in our minds,
And we bless the day that we were born,
That we were born, that we were born.
    And we, &c.

2.

Curst reason doth hate us, and that we do know,
For they oftimes do us persecute;
Such spiritual trials, adds strength to our bow,
Then we see both the seed and the fruit;
If once we our arrows upon them let fly,
How dreadful their state, and forlorn;
Then we know they are damn'd to eternity,
And they'll curse the day that they were born,
That they were born, that they were born.
    And they'll, &c.

3.

The nature of reason, of reason so blind,
It cannot see that which is good;
For the imagination of its own dark mind,
It worships, and thinks it is God;
The true God and his prophets, their fathers did kill,
And God's children they now hold in scorn;
Were it not for the law, our blood they would spill,
But the law hath stunted their horn,
It hath stunted their horn, it hath stunted their horn.
    But the, &c.

4.

How blessed it is, it is for to see,
The distinction between the two seeds.

The knowledge of which gives true liberty,
And shows as how from bondage we are freed;
The mystery of God is finished, I see,
And his love is so to made us known,
That we are sure to live with him to eternity,
And praise him with all the new-born,
With all the new-born, with all the new-born.
      And praise, &c.
                                  REBECCA BATT.

HUNDRED AND THIRTY-THIRD SONG

I do believe in God alone,
Likewise in Reeve and Muggleton,
And that true witnesses they be,
Which sets me in sweet liberty.

2.

There was none alive on this earth could tell,
What was heaven, or what was hell;
Nor yet the soul's mortality,
Which sets me in sweet liberty.

3.

Angels in heaven too there be,
Subject to pure reason and mutability;
The rise and fall of the two seeds, I see,
Which sets me in sweet liberty.

4.

Our God was on his heavenly throne,
And from that throne descended down,
A time in the virgin's womb to be,
To set his own at liberty.

5.

Then a sore journey he did go,
And on this earth walk'd to and fro;
At length he died upon a tree,
To set his own at liberty.

6.

Oh! then they buried him in a tomb,
In hopes he would not rise again;
But the all quick'ning power was free,
To set him in sweet liberty.

7.
Then he ascended the heavens high,
And there to reign eternally;
Where I am sure, my God I shall see,
When I am in sweet liberty.

8.
So now, my soul, look back and see,
What thy dear God has done for thee;
His electing love it has been free,
To set thee in sweet liberty.

9.
So now, my friends, let's all agree,
In love and peace and unity;
Since we are sure our God we will see,
When we are in perfect liberty.

MARTHA CARTER.

HUNDRED AND THIRTY-FORTH SONG.
(TUNE, 'Bishop of Hereford and Robin Hood.')

IN the days of my ignorance I worshipp'd a God,
  Without form, call'd persons three;
But since that I came to the knowledge of truth,
  One God is enough for me.
    But since, &c.

2.
When the law did accuse me, I fear'd to die,
  I wept most bitterly;
But the God that I pray'd to, was not to be found,
  He could neither hear nor see.
    But the, &c.

3.
The woful condition my soul it was in,
  All you that have felt can see;
With the damn'd in hell, I fear'd I should remain.
  Unto all eternity.
    With the, &c.

4.
But when that I unto true prophets did come,
  This thing they show'd unto me;
That if I could believe in this third record,
  I should live eternally.

That if, &c.

5.
This thing I pondered in my soul,
  For it seem'd strange to me;
Till I saw by the blood of a crucified God,
  I should live eternally.
    Till I, &c.

6.
Oh! then, how I lift up my voice and wept
  For joy, when I could see,
That I was by the blood of a crucified God,
  From eternal death set free.
    That I, &c.

7.
When Christ he here was crucified,
  From death to set us free;
Then the Father, Son and Holy Ghost,
  All died upon a tree.
    Then the, &c.

8.
And tho' he here as a creature died,
  What a glorious sight to see;
He was Father, Son and Holy Ghost,
  One God, but titles three.
    He was, &c.

9.
His glorious spirit the Father was,
  His body was the Son,
And the Holy Ghost his power was,
  All centering in one.
    And the, &c.

10.
All you that to these truths do come,
  If you by faith them see;
Then go, wash in the blood of a crucified God,
  And you'll live eternally.
    Then go, &c.

BOYER GLOVER.

HUNDRED AND THIRTY-FIFTH SONG.

DEAR friends in truth, that in your youth,
   So happy are with me,
To know that our eternal God,
   Did die to set us free.

2.

Oh! blest Jehovah, that has given
   To us the seed of faith,
To eat thy flesh and drink thy blood,
   For so the scripture saith.

3.

The mighty Jesus doth invite
   Us to the blessed feast;
Lord, we will come, Lord, we are come,
   Since we are welcome guests.

4.

Come, loving brethren, let us drink,
   For that will make us sing,
Continual praises unto him,
   That's our immortal king.

5.

O, dear Redeemer, we have drank,
   And we are satisfied;
Our sins are washed all away,
   As filth before the tide.

6.

Thy flesh we find is meat indeed,
   Thy blood doth satisfy,
Each thirsty soul that unto those
   Celestial streams do fly.

7.

Both old and young, both rich and poor,
   Thou sayest shall welcome be;
The chains of sin thou'll take away,
   If they have faith in thee.

8.

Oh! blessed be thy holy name,
   That by this third record,
Our faith revived, and we can see

The goodness of the Lord.

9.

The mysteries of thy holy word,
   Abundantly we know,
The golden oil into our souls,
   Continually doth flow.

10.

And we will let the people know,
   What blessings we enjoy;
We'd have them not to take our words,
   But come, and taste and try.

11.

But you, dear brethren, that have tried,
   With me can truly say,
We have the blood of God to drink,
   Which many cast away.

12.

Oh! let us love this mighty God,
   With love that's pure and free;
For we shall live and reign with him
   To all eternity.

13.

And let's each other dearly love,
   Nor can it otherwise be;
For that's the precious fruit of faith,
   That cometh from that tree.

14.

The world will hate us, that we know,
   Against us they'll combine;
O, let us lovingly agree,
   That so our faith may shine.

15.

Should persecution flow amain,
   Our God, our Strength will be;
For should the serpent bruise our heel,
   His head shall broken be.

16.

Our joyful sufferings they will bring,

Unto the serpent's seed;
That envy, horror, shame and grief,
  That for them was decreed.

17.

What, if they send us to the grave,
  A poor revenge indeed;
A glorious day will quickly come,
  And we shall all be freed.

18.

And then, dear brethren, you and I,
  And all the seed of faith,
Shall hear the joyful trumpet sound,
  Fur so the scripture saith.

19.

O come, ye blessed, come with me,
  The mansions are prepar'd;
Then all shall know that it was truth,
  His prophets have declar'd.

ROBERT GREGORY.

HUNDRED AND THIRTY-SIXTH SONG.
(TUNE, 'Darby and Joan.')

JEHOVAH, that infinite God,
Came down from his kingdom on high;
A creature he here did become,
And for to redeem us did die;
But, oh! what a change did he make,
From glories that did him surround,
When he here mortal became,
And for us with thorns he was crown'd.

2.

Oh! think of his wonderful love,
Where you your salvation see clear;
'Twas none but the blood of a God,
Could purchase a ransom so dear;
It was none but an infinite God,
Here for to redeem us could die,
And live by the power of his word,
From death, unto eternity.

3.

Since God he had infinite power,

Divine Songs

What could his great word then impede?
What made him come down here to die;
Or for to redeem us, to bleed?
It was justice was made wroth with sin,
Which none e'er could satisfy;
This made God come down in his love,
And for to redeem us, did die.

4.

Since this was the love of our God,
That infinite pattern on high,
Let us his divine precepts keep,
Until that the day we do die;
And when we are center'd in death,
We there but a moment shall lie;
Till God he will come in his love,
To raise us to eternity.

5.

In love here now let us combine,
For to praise our alone God on high;
All you that have faith in his blood,
Your lost souls for to satisfy;
And when on his love you do feed,
Your souls it will here satisfy;
Like me, you will here be assur'd,
To live with God eternally.

6.

My soul doth live here in peace,
I praise my dear God night and day;
The faith that I have in his blood,
Hath taken all fears quite away;
While devils in envy here dwell,
The love of our God never can see,
And having no faith in their souls,
Are damn'd to eternity.

7.

Tho' we here in Egypt do live,
The true light of Goshen we see,
White reason quite blinded with folly,
The life of redemption can't see;
While we by the faith in God's blood,
Can soar to a kingdom on high;
There drink of the fountain of life,

And live unto eternity.

8.

The wilderness we have gone through,
And Jordan we have pass'd over;
In Canaan now we do live,
Where we have great plenty in store;
Great giants we saw slew by the way,
Whose envy to us it was great,
When we by the faith in our souls,
The wonders of God did relate.

BOYER GLOVER.

HUNDRED AND THIRTY-SEVENTH SONG.
(TUNE, 'An uncreated essence.')

GOD in bright burning glory,
  My soul does long to see;
My sins are gone before me,
  God's blood has set me free;
'Tis by the third commission,
  Salvation I do see,
And stand in a blest condition,
  An heir to God I be.
      'Tis by, &c.

2.

From Edom, with dyed garments,
  Our God came up so red,
And trod within the wine-press,
  Until his soul was dead;
His body was the wine-press,
  Wherein the spirit trod;
The law it was the fierceness
  And wrath of mighty God.
      His body, &c.

3.

His body was extended
  Upon a cursed tree.
And then his soul descended
  Into grim death, I see;
Although with thorns they crowned
  Heaven's immortal heir,
His glories now surrounded,
  He tripple crowns does wear.
      Although with, &c.

4.

They nail'd a superscription
  Above his head, I see;
And said, 'this great deceiver,
  The king of the Jews would be;'
And then they brought him vinegar,
  And mingled it with gall:
He who was deem'd a traitor,
  Is now the Lord of all.
    And then, &c.

5.

Death conquer'd as a creature,
  The soul of heaven's king;
Anil God the great Creator,
  Did down to silence bring;
But death for want of power,
  His chains too weak were found;
So God at his own hour,
  Did quicken from the ground.
    But death, &c.

6.

As Father, he created;
  As Son, he did redeem;
As Holy Ghost, he sanctifies
  Those that have faith in him;
And now like heaven's host,
  Christ's praises let us sing;
He's Father, Son and Holy Ghost,
  One God and glorious king.
    And now, &c.

BOYER GLOVER.

HUNDRED AND THIRTY-EIGHTH SONG.

How blest and how happy am I,
  My God he has honor'd me much,
He sent his two prophets to me,
  And I have receiv'd them as such;
Therefore I receive the reward,
  Which is an eternal blessing;
None other I'll ever regard;
  All praise to my glorious king.

2.
From whom flows all heavenly joy,
   That arises in the hearts of his saints,
Which reason can never enjoy,
   So they well may make heavy complaints;
But patiently here we do wait,
   The true Muggletonians king;
For being assure of our state,
   Our praises for ever we'll sing.

3.
My soul is refreshed with grace,
   All praised be thy holy name;
I soon shall see thee face to face,
   Then loud I'll thy praises proclaim,
Though now I will praise thee in time,
   For thou art the pattern of love;
How boundless my joys then will be,
   To see my Redeemer above.

4.
In motion that is swift as thought,
   Our bodies all glorious will be;
Our God has dearly us bought,
   For to live with him eternally,
Beholding this God-man divine;
   What a glorious object to see
Whose body transparent doth shine;
   This, this is the God that loves me.

5.
Oh! Jesus my God an my guide,
   My heavenly Father and king,
There never was any beside;
   Thou art the eternal seed-spring,
From whence flows all heavenly love,
   True peace and tranquility;
Our God he will of us approve,
   And we shall partake of his joy.

AVIES SARAH TOONE.
(Afterwards Mrs. WALLIS.)

HUNDRED AND THIRTY-NINTH SONG

GREAT Jesus, our Saviour and God of all might,
To sound forth thy praise, is our duty and right,
For sending his prophets, our souls to set free,
We'll sing and rejoice now for this liberty.

2.

They have brought us from bondage, from shadows
          and ties,
And from those formalities that have blinded our eyes;
Then this a day that merry we'll be,
And sing song of praises for this liberty.

3.

Rome, thou art in fetters, and we are at ease,
Religion hath freedom, but yet cannot please,
Because it is empty, but filled are we,
With joy and rejoicing for this liberty.

4.

A freedom observant to this do we mind,
Being healthful and good, and by law enjoin'd,
That no man, for his faith, now troubled may be,
Then we will rejoice now for this liberty.

5.

Our joy doth not come from the mighty rebound
Of preaching and teaching which makes such a sound;
Our joys spring from light that from sin is set free,
We'll rejoice and be glad now for this liberty.

                      THOMAS TOMKINSON.

HUNDRED AND FORTIETH SONG.

NOW the world are affrighted, and dread the last day,
All praise to my God, nothing does me dismay;
For to cheer my flag'd spirits, I drink my God's blood,
When I die, I shall live by his almighty word;
For the debt due to nature, I know I must pay,
And my soul is prepar'd to see the last day.
      For the, &c.

2.

Tho' the world worship nothing, it is very clear,
Tho' their Gad he is nothing, yet something they fear;
'Tis the law in their conscience which makes them to dread,
And they're always afraid when they think of being dead;
Tho' they sin and repent, yet their debt they pay;
So they are never prepar'd to see the last day.
    Tho' they, &c.

3.

But the sanctified sinner has nothing to fear,
For his God he died for him when Christ suffered here;
Loud thunder and earthquakes he need not to dread,
For his soul is prepar'd to sleep with the dead;
When time then is ended, his sleep then will cease;
At the sight of his God, then his joys will increase.
    When time, &c.

4.

In the great day of judgment, the world then will fear,
And the priest like the people, in shame will appear;
But the sheep, which the true shepherd's voice once did hear,
In the form of their God, will in glory appear;
While the world, here in darkness for ever will be,
They'll be praising their God unto eternity.
    While the, &c.

BOYER GLOVER.

HUNDRED AND FORTY FIRST SONG.

HONOR'D Sir, to whom honor doth belong,
  Whom God with true faith did inspire,
I received your lines, which to we were welcome,
  They have satisfied all my desire;
The true form and nature of God is made known,
  Set forth in a wonderful measure;
Which is life and salvation to all that do own;
  Then my soul is secured for ever.

2.

To me are made known the heavens above,
  And the heavenly food to feed on,
And how God redeemed his own seed in love,
  And quite banish'd mason his kingdom;

Divine Songs

The knowledge of God, in my heart it is writ,
   Which is that most secret treasure,
That worldlings can never attain by their wit,
   But my soul is secured for ever.

3.

My soul it hath eaten of the tree of life,
   Which is the sacrament that is commanded;
My thirst it is quench'd with the water of life,
   Thus with heavenly food I am maintained;
God in the beginning gave reason a law,
   Which was placed in the angels' nature;
When, by faith, myself free from it, I saw,
   Then my soul was secured for ever.

4.

For, by true faith in the prophets of God,
   Knowledge of the two seeds, me is given;
Which is the very key spoke of in his word,
   That unlocketh the kingdom of heaven
To the seed of faith, when they are call'd forth
   Out of grave, by a word of his pleasure;
Persecutors are left on earth in the dark,
   Then my soul is secured for ever.

5.

Then now I'll rejoice with heart and with voice,
   So long as this world I do live in;
To me it is made now a paradise,
   In three heavenly paths to walk in;
On my heed, a helmet of salvation,
   And the shield of faith to secure,
The two-edged sword upon occasion,
   Then my soul is secured for ever.

6.

Then now welcome death, whensoever you come,
   To embrace your power, I am willing;
I shall have a kingdom of glory in the room,
   For my sins they are all now forgiven;
The white stone in my heart is plac'd by his word,
   And a new name written there to my pleasure,
Which makes me an heir with the Son of God,
   Then my soul is secured for ever.

THOMAS LADD.

HUNDRED AND FORTY-SECOND SONG.

LOVE, what art thou that art divinely bent?
And how cam'st thou into this continent?
What is thy birth, and where can divines tell?
Yes, but not such as in Cambridge do dwell.
      What is, &c.

2.

Yet Cambridge schools know thy bare name of love,
But not the nature that comes from above;
For tho' love there was born and born again,
Yet divine breath's not known by learned men.
      For tho' &c.

3.

But love, I know thee in thy parts divine,
Being of thy lineage, and thy lineage mine;
Therefore I will describe thy pedigree,
And speak the praise that doth belong to thee.
      Therefore I, &c.

4.

Love is the daughter of dame faith divine,
Love is the queen of virtues in faith's line;
Love is the princeliest grace of faith that's given,
Love is faith's life, and faith's love lives from heaven.
      Love is, &c.

5.

Love is a star of the first magnitude,
Love shines so bright as blinds the owlish brood;
Love is the pearl of paradise therefore,
Love is our glory, but the world's no more.
      Love is, &c.

6.

Love is that balsam which heals all our wounds,
Love is the circuit of the churches bounds,
Love is the load-stone that doth draw to life,
Love is the empress to defend from strife.
      Love is, &c.

7.

Love is the fiery chariot sent from on high,
Love mounts the saints into eternal joy,
Love being such as I've describ'd to be,

Love I will love, and love, do thou love me.
> Love being, &c.
>
> THOMAS TOMKINSON.

HUNDRED AND FORTY-THIRD SONG.

HOW happy is Britain's fair isle,
  Which is blest with such transcendant light;
Surpassing all kingdoms does smile,
  To be honored with truth that's so bright.

2.
But, alas! how few have believed
  In the record that's now upon earth;
With falsehood' the world is deceived,
  For they know not this truth, nor its worth.

3.
Let us welcome this jubilee day,
  When this mission became first to dawn:
Our Lord did in a divine ray,
  Usher in this most glorious morn.

4.
Adorn'd with two prophets sublime,
  As St. John's revelation relates,
Endued both with power divine,
  To determine men's eternal state.

5.
Many reprobates they've seal'd up,
  Those that truly believed them they blest,
Proud reason must fill up his cup,
  While the saints here enjoy certain rest.

6.
As an earnest of heavenly joys,
  True believers shall shortly possess,
In those mansions which never will cloy,
  No nor mortal can never express.

7.
Whilst rebels remain here below,
  In this tophet of darkness to dwell,
What torments they must undergo,

For their heaven now then will be hell.

8.
On earth where they acted all sin,
  There in horror eternal they'll moan;
This state will the devil be in,
  Who for ever and ever shall groan.

9.
My brethren dear, let's rejoice,
  And praise our Redeemer's great love,
Since we are his elected choice,
  And shall surely reign with him above.

10.
Where pleasures on pleasures do roll,
  There his mercy and love shall we sing,
In springs that will flow from full souls,
  To that infinite king of all kings.

WILLIAM MILLER, 1737.

HUNDRED AND FORTY-FOURTH SONG.
(TUNE, 'Black eyed Susan.')

MY swelling heart now leaps with joy,
And Christ does all my thoughts employ;
The veil is taken from mine eyes,
All other gods I do despise;
For that eternal rock shall be
A sure foundation unto me;
    A sure, &c.
No more dare I say, there is three.

2.
'Twas he alone that did create,
Then in a fatherly estate;
'Twas he also that did transmute,
When divine wisdom mov'd him to it,
Into a virgin's womb that he,
From power of death to set me free;
    From power, &c.
This is a glorious sight to see.

3.
Here David's Lord became his son,
Eternal God manifest in man;
Then in condition for to die,

For he was in mortality;
Cover'd with flesh as with a robe,
External man, internal God;
    External man, &c.
Praise him ye saints with one accord.

4.

His righteous law he walked through,
Which none of Adam's sons could do;
When by curs'd hands betray'd and sold,
Worthy of death they did him hold,
Prefer'd a robber by their choice,
And crucified the Lord of life;
    And crucified, &c.
This was the devils curst device.

5.

Immediate from that deadly wound,
Water and blood came to the ground;
The water it did signify,
A righteous man it was did die;
And blood that after water came,
Was From the Son of God by name,
    Was from, &c.
And to their everlasting shame.

6.

By faith I see my Lord was dead,
And in the earth was buried;
By his own power himself he rais'd,
Conquering death, hell and the grave!
Above the stars he now does live,
And led captivity captive;
    And led, &c.
Then gifts unto men he did give.

7.

Upon the day of Penticost,
My God sent forth the Holy Ghost;
His choice disciples to inspire,
Appear'd like cloven tongues of fire,
From Jesus Christ, Father and Son,
And sanctifier all in one;
    And sanctifier, &c.
The trinity of Muggleton.

THOMAS PERRY.

HUNDRED AND FORTY-FIFTH SONG.
(TUNE, 'Too mean's this world, with all its splendor.')

ONCE I was with darkness blinded,
   Seeking for the living bread,
With the world confusion minded,
   With the world appear'd as dead;
Often did I read the letter,
   Which my reason would confound;
Still, by reading ne'er the better,
   Till the living bread I found.
      Often did, &c.

2.

When I heard truth first declared,
   Faith my reason did withstand;
Yet, still the toad will be prepared,
   Willing still to bear command;
Exerting all his skill each hour,
   Would objecting questions raise;
But by faith he has lost his power,
   To my dear Redeemer's praise.
      Exerting all, &c.

3.

Then did I reflect and ponder,
   Living in so choice a land,
Where the Almighty had with wonder
   Acted with a mighty hand;
Where his prophets did appear,
   And where thousand saints did dwell
How ignorant I was while there,
   Of these truths 'tis strange to tell.
      Where his, &c.

4.

But my God, the man Christ Jesus,
   Blessed be his holy name;
By this third record has eas'd us,
   Put an end to reason's reign,
By faith, which is his divine nature
   Operating forth does fly,
And upon substantial matter,
   Feasts itself continually.
      By faith, &c.

Divine Songs

5.
His great providence did guide me,
  Where I my salvation found;
Let me know what would betide me,
  And with joy my wishes crown'd;
How shall my full soul declare
  His great benefits to me;
Lord!, thou knowest, my soul's sincere,
  Oh! that it was but full of thee.
    How shall, &c.

6.
Then should I exalted raising,
  Swift as thought ascend above;
Ever singing, ever praising,
  Feasting on this God of love;
If one glimpse can't be related,
  So exceeding the delight,
What shall we enjoy translated
  Into realms of light and life!
    If one, &c.

7.
Thro' the mighty seas I've travell'd,
  Seen the wonders of the deep,
And with perils often grappled,
  Both awaking and asleep;
But the Lord being my protector,
  Helping with his unseen hand,
As a merciful director,
  Brought me to my native land.
    But the, &c.

8.
When in dangers great surrounded,
  Nothing but despair took place,
Aching hearts, and hopes confounded,
  And death star'd me in the face;
Then thou didst thy love declare,
  Unexpected gave relief;
Then thy goodness did appear,
  Mitigating all my grief.
    Then thou, &c.

9.
Christ, O God of my salvation,
　Thanks to thee I'll ever pay;
Since thy prophets' declaration,
　Assures me of eternal day:
Saints, partake with me in praises,
　And in joyful anthems join;
For such joys as those 'tis raises
　Mortal souls to joys divine.
　　　Saints, partake, &c.

　　　　　　　　　　　JAMES MILLER.

HUNDRED AND FORTY-SIXTH SONG.

O wondrous great, amazing!
It sets my soul a gazing,
And I my God am praising,
For his great love to me;
His promise is so sure,
For ever will endure.
Until time is no more,
To all eternity.
　　　His promise, &c.

2.
He has great joys in treasure,
His love's beyond all measure;
It was his royal pleasure,
To make it known to me;
All them that firmly believe,
He never will deceive,
But he will them relieve
From death eternally.
　　　All them, &c.

3.
John Reeve I plainly see,
Was chose by God's decree,
His messenger to be,
His mind for to declare;
And Muggleton his mouth;
All you that see them both,
True messengers sent forth
You need no foe to fear.
　　　And Muggleton, &c.

4.
I'll not so much as fear death,
When I resign my last breath;
Because my God he now saith,
From death you shall be free,
If you will me regard,
And believe my prophets' word,
You shall have a prophet's reward,
Which is life eternally.
    If you, &c.

5.
This I believe sincerely,
And likewise see most clearly,
My soul was bought full dearly,
With my Redeemer's blood;
The flesh of God I see,
Was nail'd upon a tree,
His blood was shed for me,
And all believer's good.
    The flesh, &c.

6.
In this world we are but strangers,
Exposed to all dangers;
Like pilgrims we are rangers,
To our heavenly country,
And when time is no more,
There we shall go, I am sure,
For ever to endure,
To all eternity.
    And when, &c.

7.
And leave the seed of reason,
For their rebellious treason,
Not only for a season,
But to all eternity;
In hell for to remain,
With their cursed father Cain;
The Lord of life they've slain,
So they're damn'd eternally.
    In hell, &c.

WILLIAM SEDGWICK.

HUNDRED AND FORTY-SEVENTH SONG.

OH! what a glorious sight it is,
   Salvation to behold;
It is more precious unto me,
   Than silver and fine gold;
For silver and gold perish,
   Heaven and earth will pass away;
But one word of my dear God,
   Never, never will decay.
      For silver, &c.

2.

A glorious promise he has made,
   Which is a firm decree;
To know the true and living God,
   'Tis eternal life to see;
Now by faith I plainly see,
   And likewise know full well,
The eternal Father died for me,
   To redeem my soul from hell.
      Now by, &c.

3.

There's a curse lays on the serpent's seed,
   And will for ever be;
'I'll render vengeance,' saith the Lord,
   'On them that know not me;'
Their hire they will certainly have,
   And that I plainly see;
With cursed Cain they will remain,
   In hell to all eternity.
      Their hire, &c.

4.

God sent two prophets great to me,
   These wondrous truths to tell;
That he did die upon a tree,
   To save my soul from hell;
All praise and glory be to God,
   Who shed his blood for me;
His Godhead life did surely die,
   Eternal life this is to see.
      All praise, &c.

5.

The blood of God has quench'd my soul,

So now I'll take my rest;
Christ Jesus is the very God,
  In this truth I am well versed;
And now my God I plainly see,
  In peace I'll sit and sing;
All praise and glory be to him,
  He is my everlasting king.
    And now, &c.

6.

You firm believers every one,
  In love sit down by me,
Beneath this pleasant shady vine,
  And there your God you'll see;
His body is the bread of life,
  And his blood the water I see;
Come, eat his flesh and drink his blood,
  And you'll live eternally.
    His body, &c.

7.

The eternal Spirit the Father is,
His body is the Son;
His blessed word's the Holy Ghost,
Three titles, person one;
All you that can this truth believe,
In love sit down with me;
And honor Muggleton and Reeve,
Turn praise to Christ's majesty.
    All you, &c.

WILLIAM SEDGWICK.

HUNDRED AND FORTY-EIGHTH SONG.

These verses were made by JOHN LADD, and sung before the prophet Muggleton, on the 19th day of July 1681, old style; being kept as a day of Jubilee for his happy deliverance out of Prison, &c.

(TUNE, "Is there a charm, ye powers above.")

OH! God how wondrous are thy works,
  Who can thy power know,

That with one touch so elevates,
   Poor mortals here below;
The works of thy creation doth
   Great wonders plainly tell;
But our redemption truly doth
   Those wonders far excel.
        Those wonders, &c.

2.

Such are thy sacred mysteries,
   When thou dost them unfold;
It operates by miracles,
   As in the days of old;
It takes the scales from off our eyes,
   That we can plainly see;
It opens all the prison doors,
   And sets the prisoners free.
        And sets, &c.

3.

It's a strong tower of defence
Against our enemy;
And doth our warfare recompense,
With victim victory;
Its pools are also virtuous,
That being wash'd, we can
With great delight both leap and skip,
That ne'er before could stand.
        That ne'er, &c.

4.

Its language is a parable,
   Both life and death sets free;
It bindeth some in chains,
   And sets the rest at liberty;
A jubilee let's ever keep,
   And make our souls right glad,
We were in bonds, but now by faith,
   A liberty is had.
        A liberty, &c.

5.

And you, great Sir, who bonds for truth
So lately did retain;
Rejoice with us, at being set
At liberty again;
With dangers and such perils we

Poor mortals are oppress'd;
But death at last will set us free,
With an eternal rest.
    With an, &c.

JOHN LADD.

HUNDRED AND FORTY-NINTH SONG.

(TUNE, 'The Woodpecker.')

I KNOW by the third, which is the last record,
  Where the truth of all truths so plainly appear;
And know if there's peace to be found in God's word,
  The heart that is humble may hope for it there;
All my fears were expell'd, when by faith I could see
  And believe all those truths the prophets declare.

2.

That Jehovah in whom our forefathers did trust,
  The same did the promise in his seed confide;
To come down here in flesh, they saw that he must,
  To work that redemption on which they relied;
All my fears were expell'd when by faith I could see,
  It was Jacob's mighty God wrought redemption for me.

3.

When Abraham went to obey his God's command,
  He took a knife to slay his dear and only son;
Then God knew he fear'd him, he bid him stay his hand,
  By faith then he saw what his God would become,
All my rears were expell'd when by faith I could see,
  Their forms did typify the immaculate Lamb.

4.

On that dear Lamb alone, the apostles did rely,
  It was Jesus Christ the Lord our God from above;
Who was then come on earth for his own seed to die,
  To fulfil that promise he made us in love;
All my fears were expell'd when by faith I could see,
  He died and rose again by his own firm decree.

5.

Now Cain's cursed seed by faith they could not see,
  So crucified our God and pierc'd his precious side;

But little did they think it was God's firm decree,
   And by the same law they themselves should be tried;
All my fears were expell'd when by faith I could see
   A cleft in that rock was a refuge for me.

6.

Justification by faith I clearly can see,
   The law in my conscience condemns me no more,
For by faith in Jesus from sin I'm set free,
   My God he has wash'd me in his purple gore;
All my fears use expell'd, now by faith I can see,
   Being wash'd in God's blood there's no blemish in me.

7.

Praises due to my God I never can sing,
   For dying to save us and raise us above;
Permitting me to taste of that eternal spring,
   Which only could be tasted thro' his boundless love;
By Christ's resurrection I plainly can see,
   We must all pass thro' death to live eternally.

8.

Then we with new garments, not old ones repair'd,
   With our faithful fathers, God again will us raise
Unto those blest mansions which he has prepared,
   Where we shall sing new songs of eternal praise;
Then no longer will we on earthly things dwell,
   Since by faith we've escaped the torments of hell.

ELIZABETH CLAY, 1824.

HUNDRED AND FIFTIETH SONG.

GREAT God, thy people always did rejoice,
When as from thee they heard thy heavenly voice,
We have more cause than any heretofore,
For thou hast set us on the spiritual shore;
Where safe we are landed by thy prophets' word,
With joy now in this third and last record.
Then come all saints now, and rejoice with me,
For we shall ever be blest eternally.
      Then come, &c.

2.

This is the last record, therefore let us rejoice,
No more shall any hear thy heavenly voice,

Until thou come to raise us unto glory,
Where we shall remain in heaven's highest story,
Far above angels that in presence be,
We shall remain to all eternity.
      Then come, &c.

3.
Now let our love to each other still abound,
Until we hear that sweet and heavenly sound,
Which then will say, 'Come, blessed, come with me,
You shall enjoy a happy eternity;
Until which time, let us rest satisfied,
Because for us our God and Saviour died.
      Then come, &c.

4.
The very God from heaven did descend,
And did eat and drink with sinners as a friend;
And now to us thy love is freely given,
By voice of words, even from the throne of heaven;
And blessed are thy prophets that brought to us this
      peace,
That from all outward worship hath caused us to
      cease.
      Then come, &c.
                    MARTHA JENKINS.

HUNDRED AND FIFTY FIRST SONG.
(TUNE, 'Oh! where will you hurry, my dearest.')

WHEN Jesus our God had descended,
  And lived here with reason a time;
From earth he to heaven ascended,
  And now enjoys pleasures divine.
      From earth, &c.

2.
Though cruelly here they have us'd him,
  And nail'd our dear God to the cross;
They all will be damn'd that refuse him,
  We joy in their eternal loss.
      They all, &c.

3.
No other there is we desire,
For he has redeem'd all who fell;

Though reason may heaven require,
Mistake not, they'll all be to hell.
  Though reason, &c.

JAMES MILLER.

HUNDRED AND FIFTY-SECOND SONG.

ONCE reason and folly strong hold did maintain,
O'er my ignorant heart their ascendance to gain;
For many long years they play'd me their tricks,
And thought in my heart they for ever were fix'd;
Too strong for my weakness with them to contest,
While oceans of trouble did hourly infest,
Infest, did hourly infest.

2.

But wisdom long slighted in beauty complete,
Step'd to my relief and discover'd the cheat;
This friend unexpected I gladly embrac'd,
Proud reason and folly gave over the chase;
Those thieves that had robb'd me of all my sweet rest,
And with darkness obscur'd the fair gem in my breast.
My breast, the fair gem in my breast.

3.

I was wounded and maul'd, I was sorely disguis'd,
My jewel they hid, and they blinded my eyes;
But wisdom appearing, reliev'd all my pain,
Restor'd my lost eyes and my jewel again;
With the garment of truth my redemption doth shine,
And I am wash'd with God's blood in bright crimson
  divine,
Divine, in bright crimson divine.

4.

Sweet jewel, fair gem it is thou that I prize,
The crown of rejoicing, the joy of my eyes,
Thou art a pearl of great price, and sent to restore
My Maker's lost image, thou'lt leave me no more;
Truth's girdle shall bind thee so fast to my heart,
Cold death can't dissolve thee thou'lt conquer his dart.
His dart, thou'lt conquer his dart.

5.

Kind wisdom advis'd me and bid me to live,
And all my past slights he'd forget and forgive;
My heart then resolv'd his sweet counsel to take,

The jewel he polish'd I'll wear for his sake;
'Twill defend me from harm, while time is no more;
Proud reason and folly 'twill turn out of doors,
Of doors, 'twill turn out of doors.

6.

It will fight all my battles and victory gain,
Assist me in trouble, in sickness and pain;
'Twill catch my last breath in the arms of its love,
And wake me with music of angles above;
With cheerful delight it will waft me to heaven,
And praise its kind Lord for its victory given,
Given, for its victory given.

7.

I oft times reflect on the joys I shall see,
My glorious dear Saviour that suffer'd for me;
I shall see all the redeem'd, a numerous throng,
Three glorious armies, to one I belong;
In the first resurrection our prophets we'll join,
We believe their commission is truly divine,
Divine, is truly divine.

ANN WARD, 1797.

HUNDRED AND FIFTY-THIRD SONG.

IN the year fifty-one, in the month February,
A commission was given, which none can contrary;
Two prophets were sent by our heavenly king,
Glad tidings of joy to the elect they did bring;
Therefore, for that cause, when together you are met,
Be sure that happy day you never forget.

2.

The true God was pleas'd to them to make known,
Both his form and nature, which the world doth
    disown,
With the form of heaven, hell, angels and devil,
Who was that tree of knowledge, both of good and evil;
With many more things which come from above,
To the elect, as a token of his eternal love.

3.

As the soul being mortal, with the body doth die;
Being void of all motion, as a tree dead they must lie,
Till the God of all glory creates all things new,

And life out of death, which is certainly true;
Rejoice therefore, saints, and with cheerfulness sing.
That are children and heirs to an immortal king.

4.

But on the contrary, unto the seed of season,
Who against the king of kings hath spoken high treason;
Which unpardonable is, and ever will be,
Both in this world and to all eternity
Therefore, endless pain it is their just due,
Became these two prophets they have counted untrue.

5.

Who for their unbelief, and their great blasphemy,
Shall prevent them from ascending to heaven so high;
Where saints, fill'd with glory, hallelujah shall sing
Unto their Redeemer and king of all kings.
With him to remain, and to depart never,
Who is above all Gods, blessed for ever.

6.

Lot those that are elected, be faithful with zeal,
Unto this commission we have set our seal,
Because adulterers, idolaters and hypocrites too,
In hell must have their portion which is to them due,
With their father, the devil, to lament, howl and weep,
And to be as dust under the soles of our feet.

7.

And so I will end with my brotherly advice,
Hoping you'll contend For him, who of you hath made choice
His soldiers to be, to fight under his banner,
By faith and true reason, as may be for the honor
Of the last true prophets that ever will be,
Till time is swallow'd up in eternity.

ROBERT TYRER.

HUNDRED AND FIFTY-FOURTH SONG

O, HAPPY's the man that has got a friend,
Who, in time of need, him a penny will lend,
To free him from gaol; but there's great love, I see,
When God's blood was spill'd, my soul to set free.
    To free, &c.

2.

It's from the gaol of the grave,
What though I must die,
I shall not lay there unto eternity;
God did make a promise, and has it fulfill'd,
In becoming man, his blood has been spill'd.
    God did, &c.

3.

Then, oh! what a glorious sight do I see,
The immortal God was in mortality,
For to break death's fetters, his bonds to make free,
That I should praise him in eternity.
    For to, &c.

4.

Then how now enough can I praise such a friend,
Who from his heavenly throne did descend,
In a virgin's womb some time for to lay,
And so became mortal, my debt for to pay.
    In a, &c.

5.

That's to take upon him the burden of sin,
And in the grave to lay it down again;
There to conquer death, hell and devil, I see,
Then return again into eternity.
    There to, &c.

6.

So now all my joy shall be in my friend,
Since he to me such a penny did lend;
Nay, not only lend, but freely did give,
For which I will love him as long as I live.
    Nay, not, &c.

MATTHEW HAGUE.

HUNDRED AND FIFTY-FIFTH SONG.

My father me my portion gave,
  Upon a certain day,
And like a wild ungrateful son,
  I fool'd it all away;
But God became my fatted calf,
  And for me he did die;
I have eat his flesh, and drank his blood,

And shall live eternally.
    But God, &c.

2.

I travell'd into countries far,
    On husks I could not feed;
I knew not at that very time
    My God for me did bleed,
But now by faith I clearly see,
    My God for me did die;
I have eat his flesh, and drank his blood,
    And shall live eternally.
        But now, &c.

3.

My faith hath wash'd my soul quite clean,
    Within Bethsadia's pool;
It was the very blood of God,
    Which did the law quite cool;
The water that was troubled,
    It was my peace of soul;
But I've eat God's flesh, and drank his blood,
    And my soul is made quite whole.
        The water, &c.

4.

God sent two prophets great to me,
    This wondrous truth to tell,
That he did die upon a tree,
    To save my soul front hell;
This glorious truth they shew'd to me,
    And unto me did cry,
Come eat God's flesh and drink his blood,
    And live eternally.
        This glorious, &c.

5.

These glorious truths I feed upon,
    They never will me cloy;
I none of them can give away,
    Can neither sell nor buy;
But in the morning when I awake,
    At night when down I lie,
I eat God's flesh and drink his blood,
    And shall live eternally.
        But in, &c.

6.

Oh! what a glorious sight it is,
  To see that God did die,
For to redeem our souls from sin
  And death eternally;
All you that can this truth believe,
  In love sit down with me,
And eat God's flesh and drink his blood,
  And live eternally.
     All you, &c.

7.

What tho' I here on earth must die,
  And turn to silent dust;
My God he will me raise again,
  Because in him I trust;
And in that morning when I awake,
  I'll fly to God on high,
And eat his flesh and drink his blood,
  And live eternally.
     And in, &c.

HUNDRED AND FIFTY-SIXTH SONG.

OH! God, the true centre of life,
The true fountain whence life doth proceed,
Whose person to know doth extirpate all woe,
And is life everlasting indeed;
What God can you find like this,
Amongst all your idolatrous crew,
That is able to save from hell and the grave,
And can make to himself all things new?

2.

Then all you that are sealed to his grace,
Come forth, and rejoice now with me,
And let's sing forth all praise to the ancient of days,
Whose grace now hath set us all free;
He hath bought us with his divine blood,
Which his pilot is here to maintain;
And ye need not to fear, but he's able to steer,
And to carry us all over the main.

3.

Tho' once by a den of foul beasts,
Our pilot for truth was confin'd;
In their hearts they did say, 'let us block up their way,
And hinder their voyage designed;
But, alas! they but kick against pricks,
Tho' the mark of the beast they adore;
There's a power too high for blind serpents to spy,
That hath turn'd them all quite out of door.

4.

What power is in heaven or in earth,
Like this, which is power indeed!
He refus'd not to die, to get victory
Over those who'd destroy his own seed;
Then rejoice, and let's hoist up our sail,
And Jehovah for ever adore;
For tho' here we live hard, we doubt not a reward,
When we come to the celestial shore.

WILLIAM WOOD.

HUNDRED AND FIFTY-SEVENTH SONG.

OH! what joy my soul will see,
When I'm from the grave set free,
And the face of God can see
In his blest eternity.

2.

Saints and angels will behold
Prophets crown'd with crowns of gold,
Praising of their God they'll see,
In his blest eternity.

3.

That which will us most delight,
When of God we have a sight,
Is in harmony to join,
To raise the God of Gods divine.

4.

Here will end our sad distress,
There begins our happiness;
Praises in our souls will shine
To the God of Gods divine.

Divine Songs

5.
Fill'd with joy when here we think,
That we have God's blood to drink,
Cry by faith, when love does shine,
Oh! the love of God divine.

6.
Tho' we sinners all here be,
And are justly damn'd, I see;
Mercy in our souls does shine;
Oh! the love of God divine.

7.
When to justice I resign'd,
I was cloth'd in my right mind,
And the flesh of God did eat,
When I fell at mercy's feet.

8.
Who the friend could ever see.
That would die to set him free?
This was done by God divine;
Oh! how mercy then did shine.

9.
See God in his sad distress,
When he left his happiness;
Moses made the face to shine
Of the God of Gods divine.

10.
Tho' Elias sat on high,
While the very God did die;
Yet no creature e'er could shine
Like the God of Gods divine.

11.
Tho' they acted here in time
By a power pure divine,
Yet they ne'er men's thoughts could know,
Like the God of Gods below.

12.
Though, as creature, here I see,
Christ he died upon a tree;
Yet according to record,

He was perfect man and Lord.

13.
Lord above and here below,
As the scriptures they do show;
Now with praises here let's sing,
Oh! the love of heaven's king.

14.
Forms are all now done away;
Keep the law, you need not pray,
Praises in your soul will shine,
To praise the God of Gods divine.

15.
When the soldier pierc'd the side
Of our Saviour when he died,
Blood and water then did flow,
From the God of Gods below.

16.
When they pierc'd his spotless side,
That Christ was dead, it certified;
And the blood that did then flow,
Cleans'd my soul from sin and woe.

17.
You that can this rock once smite
By your faith, 'twill give delight;
With grateful love your souls will shine,
To praise the God of Gods divine.

BOYER GLOVER.

HUNDRED AND FIFTY-EIGHTH SONG.

OH! wondrous great, amazing strange,
Man sat as God, while God did change,
From a bright glorious God above,
To a pure creature; oh! what love.
    From a, &c.

2.
And of this love how few can find
The blood of God to ease their mind;
Oh! happy state, where'er I be,
I know my God has died for me.
    Oh! happy, &c.

Divine Songs

3.
The thief upon the cross did say,
'Remember me O Lord I pray,
When thou dost to thy kingdom come,
Forgive the sins that I have done.'
    When thou, &c.

4.
Then unto him our God did say,
'Your soul with me this very day,
In paradise shall surely see
An earnest of eternity.'
    In paradise, &c.

5.
What joy and peace those words did give
To a lost soul who then did live,
The power of his great God to see,
Altho' in shame and misery.
    The power, &c.

6.
Submissively his life laid down,
Assur'd he was to wear a crown;
For tho' a sinner great was he,
The blood of God had set him free.
    For tho', &c.

7.
Altho' our sins are manifold,
If we by faith can God behold,
When in his bitter agony,
From death eternal we are free.
    When in, &c.

8.
For when that Christ was crucified,
The Almighty languish'd, God wholly died,
And rose according to decree,
Eternal life this is to see.
    And rose, &c.

9.
When Christ he in the wine-press trod,
His vesture that was dipp'd in blood;

It was the flesh the Godhead wore,
When died for sin in purple gore.
    It was, &c.

10.

And true it was without a seam,
For none are sav'd by part of him;
For none can e'er be sanctified,
But those that see God wholly died.
    For none, &c.

11.

God's justice, God aton'd alone,
Ha cried for help, but he found none;
For tho' Elias sat on high,
He left our glorious God to die.
    For tho', &c.

12.

And when Christ was in silent death,
The whole Godhead was void of breath;
But death with him no union found,
So God he quicken'd from the ground.
    But death, &c.

13.

And when be soar'd up on high,
And resum'd all majesty;
Elias then with joy laid down,
At his God's feet, his ruling crown.
    Elias then, &c.

14.

And now our God he sits on high,
In power and glorious majesty;
In Christ alone all power doth dwell,
To raise us all from death and hell.
    In Christ, &c.

                BOYER GLOVER.

HUNDRED AND FIFTY-NINTH SONG.

OH! how my soul does soar above,
To praise my God for his great love;
Now I, by faith can see,
That God that died for me,
Was Jesus Christ, that God on high.

2.

His name I ever will adore,
He is my God, and I'll have no more;
He is a glorious king;
I will for ever sing,
Lord Jesus Christ is God on high.

3.

When envious reason does deny,
That to redeem 'me my God did die;
In my soul there's a spring,
Which flows up to that king,
Dear Jesus Christ that God on high.

4.

There I find my peace and lasting joy,
Which envious reason can't destroy,
By faith in my God's blood,
Gave by the royal word
Of Jesus Christ that God on high.

5.

Kings by their riches ne'er can find
This glorious treasure of the mind;
I'm richer than a king,
Now I by faith can sing,
Praise to my glorious God on high.

6.

Come now your tuneful voices raise,
Your dear Redeemer for to praise,
You that by faith can see,
None died to set you free,
But Jesus Christ, that God on high.

BOYER GLOVER.

HUNDRED AND SIXTIETH SONG.

SWEET is the love to those that sympathize
With grace and truth, a pleasant sacrifice;
But those that with a mask do vail their faces,
Stand against truth with all its gifts and graces.

2.

Who seek their own destruction without care,
Of feeble saints running into a snare;

But when love's present in the sacrifice,
It consecrates the temple of the wise.
                              JOHN NICHOLS.

HUNDRED AND SIXTY-FIRST SONG.
(TUNE, 'Guardian angels.')

SAINTS, behold your great Creator,
Who did leave divine abode,
And became a spotless creature,
Tho' he was the very God;
My soul with wonder was surprized,
At his great stupendous love;
But 'tis by faith, I see,
My God he died for me,
And left his glorious throne above.

2.

Guardian angels did protect him,
In his journey here on earth;
Eastern wise-men they beheld him,
In a manger at his birth;
Then their offerings they presented,
And their adoration paid,
To him who was their God,
Now in this vile abode,
Tho' by his power the world was made.

3.

See, my friends, your dear Redeemer
Nail'd unto a cursed tree,
To redeem his seed for ever,
And fulfil his own decree;
Voluntarily he resign'd
His most precious sacred breath;
The very God did die,
And in the grave did lie,
But rose again and conquer'd death.

4.

Believers, now raise all your voices,
See the mighty God ascend,
Descending angels, sweet rejoicing,
Round their absent God attend;
His stewards then with joys surrender,
Glory, power and majesty;

His glories brighter shine
Transcendant more sublime,
And will to all eternity.

MARTHA MILLER.

HUNDRED AND SIXTY-SECOND SONG.

SEE this happy day, which with cheerful ray,
Once more is allow'd us our souls to excite;
This, this was the morning and glorious dawning,
   Which brought truth to light,
   By Christ, God alone;
   In distinct words from heaven,
   This commission was given,
   In a divine ray,
   To Reeve 'twas made known,
   Which Muggleton own'd;
What one had receiv'd, the other believ'd,
   His words did obey;
Thus both were ordain'd, both power obtain'd
   On this glorious day.

2.

True believers, then raise your voices in praise
To Christ, our redeemer, our father, and king;
His love we'll adore now and evermore;
   To him we will sing,
   Since he has made known
   By his last commission,
   We all have remission
   Of our former crimes;
   Then, saints, this faith own,
   There's no doubt of a crown,
Which will be enjoy'd when the devil's destroy'd;
   We in glory shall shine,
For for us it's declar'd to be only prepar'd,
   By these prophets divine.

JAMES MILLER.

HUNDRED AND SIXTY-THIRD SONG.

TRUE saints, come rejoice,
With heart and with voice,
To Christ our Redeemer and king;
Who from heaven's throne,

This commission sent down,
Which joy and salvation does bring,
  To all poor lost souls,
  Whom reason controuls,
But by faith now the tyrants are bound;
  For a stronger than he,
  Will a conqueror be,
That he never again will be found.

2.

While here he will grieve
Poor souls who believe;
But when faith is active he's dead,
But, oh! what sad cares,
What anguish and fears,
Are we under, while by him we're led;
Yet unless he had been,
We had never known sin,
Or the mercy of God could we see;
Then let us all sing,
To our heavenly king,
Since we all shall by faith be made free.

3.

This day did John Reeve;
This commission receive,
From the God all glory above;
These days did he chuse,
To send joyful news,
Glad tidings of mercy and love;
  Then saints, let us raise
  Our voices with praise,
To Christ who hath been such a friend,
  By his prophets below,
  To let us all know,
We have joys that will never have end.

4.

Though they are asleep,
Those days we will keep,
A jubilee to our great king,
In anthems divine,
With thanksgiving we'll join,
To Christ will we evermore sing;
  For salvation we have,
  Which he freely gave;
Come saints, now let us adore,

Remembering these days
  Are the subjects of praise,
An earnest of praise evermore.

5.

In the prophet John Reeve,
We all do believe
And great Muggleton's doctrine we own,
What they did declare,
Sure witnesses are,
They were sent from God's heavenly throne,
  For the secrets they told,
  There was none could unfold,
Such infallible truths there doth shine;
  How the Father and Son
  Are united in one,
And found in Christ Jesus divine.

6.

There was none but them two
The form of God knew,
Or his nature could ever make known;
There was no one could tell
What place would be hell,
Where the damn'd for ever will groan;
  Nor none could relate
  The mystery great
Of the nature of angels on high.
  But those who believe
  In the great prophet Reeve,
And with Muggleton's doctrine comply.

7.

The nature of heaven,
Was never yet given
To any so fully before;
And tho' most men deny
That the souls of men die,
They have prov'd it till time is no more;
  And as for the devil,
  That acteth all evil,
John Reeve and his writings doth show,
  And Muggleton plain
  Says, 'there's none but in man,
For man is the devil below.'

8.

These six sacred things,
Unknown pleasures will bring
To all who true faith do embrace;
These mysteries divine,
Assurance will find,
Of seeing their God face to face;
  On those do depend,
  True joys without end,
Which the tongue of no mortal can tell;
  But those who despise,
  Will in torments arise,
And for over be left here in hell.

9.

Oh! glorious God,
Christ Jesus our Lord,
Who's an inaccessible light,
Transparent divine,
Transcendant sublime,
Too great for frail weak mortal's sight;
But when he will raise
Our souls from the grave,
In spiritual glory shall shine;
See the abject above,
Who's God of all love,
In mansions of transport divine.

JAMES MILLER.

HUNDRED AND SIXTY-FOURTH SONG

THE first created blessed pair,
The Lord made perfect pure and fair;
Planted a garden, placed them there,
  As lords of this creation;
The devil here seduced Eve,
By which two seeds we do perceive
Were introduced here to live,
  Until time's last duration.

2.

Then all true saints, come sing with me,
In praises to Christ's majesty;
Whose precious blood by faith I see,
  In this his last commission;
Wherein they clearly have made known,

That Christ is God, in him alone
The everlasting Father alone,
   As by his prophets' mission.

3.

I mean John Rom and Muggleton,
Prophets from God's imperial throne;
Who joyful news brought every one,
   That can believe their power;
Happy the soul that comes to see,
That Christ is God and only he,
Who chose to die and set us free,
   His death did death devour.

4.

The last great prophet of the Lord,
Who witness'd to the third record,
At him the devils draw'd their swords,
And punishments assign'd;
When he appear'd within their court,
The great ones they begun to sport;
But God their power did cut short,
Their hellish wrath confin'd.

5.

Now his greet foe in judgment sat,
An hundred pounds* they priz'd him at;
'Twas more than their forefathers set
   Upon the Lord of glory;
The fine was paid, the prophet clear'd,
Their malice now need not be fear'd;
Rouse up, my friends, and let's be cheer'd,
   To hear this welcome story.

6.

This nineteenth day of July, my friends,
Our thanks and praises shall ascend;
This jubilee we'll yearly spend
To Christ the God of power;
For this day Muggleton the great,
Was freed from the cursed hate,
And devilish fury of the great,
Who fain would him devour.

---

* The fine of five hundred pounds was mitigated to one hundred pounds by the sheriff's Sir JOHN PEAK, Sheriff of London, and Sir THOMAS STAMP, Sheriff of Middlesex.

7.
Both prophets now are in the dust,
Their writings are both true and just,
In which we put our only trust,
That we might live for ever,
In realms of light and bliss above,
Where God does reign in peace and love;
The devils never shall remove,
But live in hell for ever.

WILLIAM MILLER.

HUNDRED AND SIXTY-FIFTH SONG.
A Kingdom of Love, and of lovely Songs.

DOCTRINE.

THIS kingdom of eternal glory is a kingdom of love; there is not one spark of anger there; for there is love without opposition. As this place is a vale of tears, so it is of love and anger; each runs its round, and we cannot help it.

ILLUSTRATED.

IF we were not angry in sin, but unto sin, it were well; but affections ore sometimes so pressing, that we are not only unjustly angry, but are ready to justify unjust anger. But, oh! happy country, where love is all in all; because no sorrow is there, so no anger. Hero we are pettish and foolish, and ready' to fall out with our best friends, and after, we relent, and are troubled at our unbridled anger. Love is now the comfort our life, but then it will be the crown of our life; and there shall we love and be loved, and loaded with love, as the bee is with honey, and God will set his love on us all; and this his love shall rest on us.

APPLIED.

THERE is a sweet saying by the prophet Zephaniah, 'The Lord thy God saith, the prophet shall save us; he will rejoice over thee with joy; he will rest in his love; he will joy over thee with singing.' Here is love indeed; this makes glad the city of God; for this city rests in the arms of his love, he rejoicing over them with singing: this will ravish the hearts of the elect too with astonished joy; not only to hear the songs of your love and sorrow, but to hear the songs of praises and love, and dear you are to him. Will not this now strike the flints of the heart, and make the fire to ascend to heaven in praises here? How much more will it do it there, where the holy love fire is ever burring? No heart can now conceive, nor tongue can utter, what joy and love, and songs of joy and love, will be between the Redeemer and redeemed. And as the saints do all join together, singing songs Of praise unto their good God, even so likewise they, as children of one father, and heirs of one kingdom, do all mutually embrace each other and kiss each other, with lovely songs, as they meet, they sweetly greet in this wise.

HAIL! my dear brother, have l met with thee!
Oh ! welcome into this felicity,
Where perfect love and concord doth abound,
No strife or discord in it can be found.

2.
Come, let us love, and in love let us greet
Our bless'd God, when we with him do meet;
Oh! sovereign sweetness, our joy, and eke our crown,
What thou hast given us, at thy feet we cast down.

3.
For thou hast redeem'd us with thy precious blood
Of Godhead life, laid down in thy manhood;
Our faith, in which was made the seal of heaven,
And now the glory of it thou hast given.

4.
'You are my jewels,' will our Lord reply,
'And welcome now into your master's joy;
For I joy in you, as well as you in me,
And take you for my sweet society.

5.
'All my delight on earth was amongst you,
You had my promise, and now you find it true;
You did believe me, now shall joys abound,
Possess all joys that in my courts are found.'

THOMAS TOMKINSON.

HUNDRED AND SIXTY-SIXTH SONG.
(TUNE, 'Down in a meadow,' and "Stern winter hasten.')

THIS day great Reeve and Muggleton,
Receiv'd from God's imperial throne,
This last commission, pure, divine,
Which will remain as long as time.

2.
Oh! glorious day that has reveal'd
Those sacred truths that lay conceal'd,
From earth's foundation never known,
That God was Christ, and Christ is one.

3.
One essential, glorious Lord,
Who has appear'd in three records,
Unto his chosen here below;
But for the devils overthrow.

4.
First, as Father, full of power;
Next, as Son, did death devour;
And in this last, as Holy Ghost,
Believed by few, denied by most.

5.
Come, true believers, let's rejoice
In Jesus Christ, with heart and voice,
For he is God, and only he
By suffering death could set us free.

6.
Free from death's tyrannic power,
Which reign'd o'er all, until that hour,
In which his Godhead spirit died;
Swifter than thought again revived.

7.
And now's ascended far on high,
Leading captive captivity;
Seated on his imperial throne,
And crowned with a triple crown.

8.
Refulgent glories round him shine,

From his redeeming love in time,
Unto poor Adam's seed alone;
Come, let's rejoice, for heaven's our own.

9.
Happy's the soul that can believe,
And own the mission of John Reeve;
Eternal life's the sure reward
Of those that seal this third record.

10.
Those that despise it, ne'er will know
Nothing but pain and endless woe,
In utter darkness as decreed,
Both for the serpent and his seed.

11.
The seed of faith shall all arise,
Ascending far above the skies,
Into that blest divine abode,
Where saints and angels see the Lord.

12.
Come quickly, Christ our God and king,
Finish our faith that we may sing
Our deer Redeemer's matchless love,
In those eternal realms above.

WILLIAM MILLER.

HUNDRED AND SIXTY-SEVENTH SONG.

WHEN first the truth I came to know,
Great joy therein my soul did flow;
The third record I do behold,
Purer to me than crowns of gold.

2.
It show me those sweet joys in love,
By faith my God that is above,
'Twas him in time that did come down,
Cloth'd himself with flesh, blood and bone.

3.
He in a virgin's womb did lie,
There the immortal seed did die,

For to fulfil his own decree,
Quicken'd in pure mortality.

4.

The virgin's seed then did unite
With the eternal seed of light,
Thro' union was instantly
Quicken'd in pure mortality.

5.

Then unto us a child is born,
Lord Jesus Christ, the holy one;
Who liv'd and died, now lives again,
In glorious heavens ever reign.

6.

Now under Reeve and Muggleton,
I write these you may muse upon;
All glory to my God, I see,
I am assured of eternity.

THOMAS PICKERSGILL.

HUNDRED AND SIXTY-EIGHTH SONG
(TUNE, 'The malice of reason.')

To God, our creator, redeemer and king,
All in one true concert, hallelujahs we'll sing,
For his infinite love, that all love doth exceed;
Who for us sinful mortal was pleased to bleed.
    For his, &c.

2.

Unto death to secure us from death's tyranny,
And thereby to procure us true felicity,
In those blessed mansions that for ever remain,
Expressless in joy, and free from all pain.
    In those, &c.

3.

Where nothing for ever shall ever be found,
To disturb our enjoyments, but to make them abound;
There openly we face to face shall behold
Our God in his glory, with the prophets of old.
    There openly, &c.

4.
Apostles and witnesses who have run their race,
And finish'd their courses thro' faith by his grace;
Undaunted then we with them shall appear,
With high praises before him, when horror and fear.
    Undaunted then, &c.

5.
And amazement shall seize on the devils our foes,
Who would not believe them, but still did oppose,
Deride and afflict, and at last crucify
Our sovereign Lord, now ascended on high.
    Deride and, &c.

6.
By his own power alone, when in clouds he shall come,
With his saints and blest angels to give them their doom;
In black dismal darkness they then must be penn'd,
Where worm never die, nor pain never end.
    In black, &c.

7.
Tho' on earth whilst they dwell, as monarchs they reign,
Surrounded with pleasures and fill'd with disdain
Of the saints, who as bond-slaves and vassals they use.
And void of all mercy as tyrants they abuse.
    Of the, &c.

8.
For refusing to worship those shadows which they
From their own brains extracted, in distraction obey;
And adoring Christ Jesus, who is God over all,
By the breath of whose mouth they and their God both must fall.
    And adoring, &c.

9.
By their reason's blind zeal they vainly suppose,
What they do to the saints they do to God's foes;
And by their false worship, the devils persuade
Them, in heaven a purchase secure they have made.
    And by, &c.

10.
Thus fed with vain fancies, in heaven they seem,
But at last their enjoyment will prove but a dream;
When the trump shall awake them and make them arise,
Then upon them confusion and terror shall seize.
    When the, &c.

11.
Their good deeds, whereby they expected to be
Install'd in glory, quite from them shall flee,
And no more be found, but their bad deeds appear,
To witness against them and fill them with fear.
    And no, &c.

12.
And the false gods they worshipp'd no help shall extend,
Nor from the vengeance of the true God defend;
Thus the God they disown'd and whose messengers dear,
They despis'd and afflicted, in glory appear.
    Thus they, &c.

13.
In judgment against them, to doom them to hell,
There for ever and ever in torment to dwell;
By the thought of those glories that by faith we have felt,
Tho' in part and distance, our senses all melt.
    By the, &c.

14.
Into raptures celestial that makes our souls fly,
With contempt to the world, to the region, on high,
To the throne of our Saviour, where we may behold,
By his infinite love, our names are enroll'd.
    To the, &c.

15.
In his sacred decrees that are seal'd with the blood
Of no less than himself who is our only God;
Our faith in that title shall ever expel,
Tho' we dwell among devils the terror of hell.
    Our faith, &c.

16.

Tho' they gnash, foam and rage, and devour us would
     fain,
Still their venom retorts, and their labour is vain;
Let them foam and swell then with malice accurst,
Until with their poison their bellied do burst;
We will laugh them to scorn with a holy disdain,
For we know they are kept within length of their chain.

ELIZABETH HENN.

HUNDRED AND SIXTY-NINTH SONG.

ONCE more this day of great joy and pleasure,
   Time swift revolving again has brought round;
On this day both prophets and saints joy in measure,
   Where in true liberty free did abound;
The high power of fines and devils and law,
   Nor sly lying preachers, they could not prevail;
His faith it was sound, in his case was no flaw,
   The power of his mission made his enemies fail.
          The high, &c.

2.

What manifold sufferings our God and his prophets,
   Without cause, have received from the bastard seed;
But they shall loud roar, when they find themselves
     Tophet's,
   Who made great Jehovah's eternal soul bleed;
In the Son, they the Godhead kill'd on a curst tree,
   Infinity dead, when the Son lost his breath,
They have beaten his friends here in mortality,
   Both master and servant they've laid low in death.
          In the, &c.

3.

But long-look'd for doomsday will make the scale turn;
   All nature will tremble, the sun down will fall;
Their heavens once vanish'd, lost souls hot will burn,
   And earthquakes will shake all this ponderous ball;
The fat-gutted priest will roar for assistance;
   The lawyer may say, he did plead for a fee;
But unto our God they have both shewn resistance,
   They are damn'd without mercy to eternity.
          The fat gutted, &c.

4.

The fate of the cloth in the end most disgraceful,
  They who with kings and with rulers could dine,
Will, by their own clan, be found out deceitful;
  The bishops will then lodge with devils and swine,
Instead of a silk gown to clothe the false rubbish,
  Or bottle of claret to please his proud heart,
Or fine high cock'd mitre, to make him look bobbish,
  The waters of death will new torments impart.
      Instead of, &c.

5.

Instead of his palace, a dry burning sand
He'll lay on, with body more heavy than lead;
There he'll lay in anguish, he's lost his command,
He'll blaspheme afresh, and would gladly be dead;
His dust-licking friend will be his companion,
Who loved his money more dear than God's seed;
He thought self and offspring on it might depend on,
Not caring how the friend of God here did bleed.
      His dust, &c.

6.

How happy are we who have laid up such treasure,
  As makes God his banker, he calls man, his friend;
His love he has made manifest in a great measure,
  By sending an ambassador, who was detain'd
Within a dark cell of reason's invention;
  For reason with God's friend is at enmity;
But that could not hinder Jehovah's intention,
  For this day his messenger great was set free.
      Within a, &c.

7.

Then since he delights to give peace to his creature,
  Let us love each other, if it's but for his sake;
We know that his seed must be of his own nature;
  So to comfort each other Let us measures take,
And rejoice on this day for our prophet's deliverance;
  Let all wrath and malice be quite laid aside,
If any has sinn'd, let us hope for repentance,
  And pray that the prophets be ever our guide.
      And rejoice, &c.

8.

For love to each other brings pence and contentment,

It causes the soul to sing sweet to its king,
It causes the heart to forget all resentment,
   Makes knowledge and pleasure in me for to spring;
Wine that's celestial gives peace to my soul,
   My faith it doth drink of a fountain that's free;
For the blood of God has wash'd me quite whole,
   And now I am longing for eternity.
       Wine that's, &c.

JOHN PEAT

HUNDRED AND SEVENTIETH SONG.
(TUNE, 'Old iron to find.')

'TIS true I can't worship now as the world doth,
Because their false God and false doctrine I loathe;
Yet I am true hearted unto Christ, my king,
I am a true Muggletonian, with clear conscience can
      sing;
I can pass to and fro, and fear no deadly foe,
Since that the true God and right devil I know.
      I can pass, &c.

2.

I fear not proud reason, I break not his law,
Their scoffs, nor their jeers, I don't value one straw,
And their persecutions I patiently bear,
It is a crown of thorns which I know I must wear;
I can pass to and fro, and fear no deadly foe,
Since that the true God and right devil I know.
      I can, &c.

3.

The true God is my friend, I can plainly see,
He pour'd forth his soul unto death on a tree;
His eternal spirit for me here did die,
That I might live with hits to eternity.
I can pass to and fro, and fear no deadly foe,
Since that the true God and right devil I know.
      I can, &c.

4.

When reason in fear on their death-bed do lay,
They must have their false ministers for them to pray,
Their false sacrament receive, in a false God believe,
And with false hopes they their own souls deceive;
I can pass to and fro and fear no deadly foe,

Since that the true God and right devil I know.
    I can, &c.

5.

The sting of sin's took from me, I've no need to prepare,
God did the work for me, when he suffered here,
There need no amendment to Gods work, I am sure;
Nor none can be made by us mortals so poor;
I can pass to and fro, and fear no deadly foe,
And praise my dear God, who by faith now I know.
    I can, &c.

6.

God laid down his glory in a virgin's womb,
That God pure man for us might become,
From his spirituality there did he die,
And quicken'd himself in pure mortality.
I can pass to and fro, and fear no deadly foe,
And praise my dear God, who by faith now I know.
    I can, &c.

7.

God's precious blood was shed on across for me,
It hath wash'd my soul from all sin I can see;
In the first resurrection I have my part, I see,
Therefore the second death can have no power over me;
I can pass to and fro and fear no deadly foe,
And praise my dear God, who by faith now I know.
    I can, &c.

8.

Three days and three nights in the grave God did lie,
Then rais'd himself and ascended on high;
And his blessed person the heavens will contain,
Till to raise us in glory he cometh again:
I can pass to and fro and fear no deadly foe,
And praise my dear God, who by faith now I know.
    I can, &c.

9.

When reason is rais'd in eternity,
Then their place of hell on this earth here will be,
One and other's dreadful face they never will see,
But in blackness of darkness for ever they'll be:
I can pass to and fro and fear no deadly foe,
And praise my dear God, who by faith now I know.
    I can, &c.

10.

When time's at an end, we the faithful shall be,
With our glorious God unto eternity;
Then instead of thorns, a bright crown we shall wear,
In the heavenly mansions, our God will prepare:
We shall pass to and fro and fear no deadly foe,
And see God face to face, who by faith now we know,
      We shall, &c.

11.

Tears will he wip'd away, and all sorrows will cease,
Then springs of new joy in our souls will increase;
A new song of praise to the Lamb, we shall sing,
To our Lord Jesus Christ, our alone God and king:
We shall pass to and fro, and fear no deadly foe,
And see God face to face, who by faith we now know.
      We shall, &c.

12.

In the glorious kingdom no bounds we shall see,
Their bodies in motion, swift as thought will be;
Shall see all such creatures on this earth here,
But in spiritual glory like crystal so clear:
We shall pass to and fro, and fear no deadly foe,
And see God face to face, who by faith now we know.
      We shall, &c.

13.

There Adam and Eve will in glory be seen,
And all their righteous seed whom our God did redeem;
There'll be prophets and apostles in glory divine,
And the two last great prophets will gloriously shine:
We shall pass to and fro, and fear no deadly foe,
And see God face to face, who by faith now we know.
      We shall, &c.

14.

There Moses and Elias will in glory appear;
But our God will exceed all in brightness so clear,
Seated on his throne of divine majesty,
In the midst of all crowns of bright burning glory;
We shall pass to and fro, and fear no deadly foe,
And see God face to face, who by faith now we know.
      We shall, &c.

15.
Our blest bodies as a robe of righteousness divine,
Is that heavenly garment in which we shall shine;
And the spiritual food which our souls shall suffice,
In a never failing fountain out of our spirits will arise.
We shall pass to and fro, and fear no deadly foe,
And see God face to face, who by faith now we know.
    We shall, &c.

16.
We shall feed on the remembrance of Christ's
    righteousness,
And his suffering for us in the days of his flesh,
Or else on the grace, in which here we did grow,
Or on the persecutions we suffer'd below.
We shall pass to and fro, and fear no deadly foe,
And see God face to face, who by faith now we
    know.
    We shall, &c.

17.
The spiritual motion that in us now rise,
We shall sensibly feed on with Godlike new joys;
And the heavenly communion with each other so
    sweet,
We had in mortality- when we did meet.
We shall pass to and fro, and fear no deadly foe,
And see God face to face, who by faith now we know.
    We shall, &c.

18.
There, for our creation, our God we shall praise,
For our glorious redemption, shall chant divine lays;
The angels will praise God for creation too;
But from us double praises, glory and honour is due.
We shall pass to and fro, and fear no deadly foe,
And praise our dear God, who by faith now we know.
    We shall, &c.

19.
There in loud hosannas our voices will ring,
And in sweet hallelujahs to Zion's great king,
The Lamb on Mount Zion, we shall joyfully praise,
Who is creator, redeemer, and ancient of days.
We shall pass to and fro, and fear no deadly foe,
And praise our dear God, who by faith now we know.

We shall, &c.

REBECCA BATT.

HUNDRED AND SEVENTY-FIRST SONG.
(TUNE, 'Galley slave.')

OH! think on my state I now freedom enjoy,
  I am as happy as happy can be;
What pleasure I have now death's sting is destroy'd.
  I am no longer a captive to be;
I fear not that foe, I know it's my fate,
  To be taken from this world evermore;
When thought brings to mind my future happy state,
  I die, I die, sure to live evermore.
    When thought, &c.

2.

How kind is my fate, I am free from reason's chains,
  And my life steers by faith's balmy chart:
Tho' devils against me may sorely complain,
  I ne'er from true faith will depart;
When Jehovah does come, I know its my fate,
  To glory to go, I am sure;
When time brings my end from this mortal state,
  I'll die, I'll die, sure to live evermore.
    When time, &c.

3.

With great Muggleton and Reeve I am sure I shall go
  To that place where there's bliss ever new;
That wish'd happy morn will bring many their woe,
  While, my Saviour, I ascend to you;
So come, welcome death, and finish this state,
  Then depart hence from me evermore;
For whenever I end this my pilgrim state,
  I'll die, I'll die, assur'd to live evermore.
    For whenever, &c.

GEORGE ROBINSON.

HUNDRED AND SEVENTY-SECOND SONG.

OH! cease, vain man, for to declare
That your frail souls immortal are;
This finite state cannot compare
With infinite condition;
If they immortal were, they'd be

Of uncorrupted purity,
Not subject to mortality;
But would be ever free,
And flee into eternity,
To perfect full fruition.

2.

How can the soul immortal be,
In man while in mortality;
When none can tell haw soon it may be,
Ere life becomes inactive;
Who can one moment here insure?
Or who can escape a dying hour?
Or pray, what does grim death devour
Without strife, nought but life?
If life's the soul, then soul's the life,
To him becomes a captive.

3.

Besides don't beast to beast below,
Give life as nature here doth show,
And vegetables likewise so;
Yet man's the noblest creature,
He who was made the lord of all,
Within this fair terrestrial ball,
Must he inferior be to all?
Don't he convey, as well as they,
Life to his issue, and obey
The first great law of nature?

4.

Whatever man may here pretend,
From his imaginary friend,
I know full well what does attend
Mankind in this creation;
For God has no execution made,
But life is in the seed convey'd,
This law must ever be obey'd,
Man and all within this ball,
Do souls beget, and ever shall
While time has here duration.

5.

There was no more than two, we find,
At first to propagate mankind,
Adam and Eve, the two design'd,
Plac'd here by the Creator;

Or how could Eve the mother be
Of all living posterity,
Unless life, by divine decree,
Was design'd through her loins,
By almighty power divine,
To make a perfect creature.

6.

Besides did not almighty God
In six days time complete this orb,
By virtue of his royal word,
Then rested from creation;
And when he had the whole survey'd,
Even every thing that he had made;
'Behold it's good,' the Lord he said,
Then how can we think it can be
Imperfect, since it doth agree
With his divine relation.

7.

If souls are not generated then,
Falsehood unerring truth attend,
And God a liar made by man,
Who still must he creating,
And wont, while time does last, have done,
If souls, do still from heaven come,
In mortal flesh to be entomb'd;
If from God all are good,
No bad ones can be understood,
Since unto him related.

8.

What is the soul, can any tell?
Or, where without the body dwell?
Does it exist in heaven or hell,
Is what I now require?
Or, does a purgatory hold
The false conceiv'd departed soul?
Or, what place else can you unfold,
From whence it can return again,
To re-unite a lifeless thing;
This question I require?

9.

Both states eternal all agree,
Either of bliss or misery;

No middle state there cannot be
For a departed spirit;
If such a thing as that could be,
When freed from this mortality,
It must be in eternity;
Why, then 'tis strange how it can change
From its eternal state again,
And yet the same inherit.

10.

But since no man I yet could hear,
That could by scripture make appear,
That any souls immortal are
While in this finite station;
Then all are mortal here below,
And generated too also,
All into senseless dust must go,
Till Christ descends to put end
To time, and recreate again,
Or make a new creation.

11.

Then death, life's enemy, will die,
Life in eternal death will lie,
Add dying, live eternally,
From torments never ceasing;
While crowns of uncorrupted gold,
Too great for me now to unfold,
Will grace each beatific soul,
In joys sublime, pure, divine;
Each happy soul will ever shine,
Christ Jesus ever praising.

12.

Then will our new created spring
Flow over to the king of kings;
How sweetly shall we ever sing,
In extacies of pleasure;
Oh! come, sweet Jesus, come away,
I long to see that glorious day,
When thou wilt to thine own seed say,
'Come, my dove, ascend above,
Enjoy with me eternal love,
For thou art mine only treasure.

JAMES MILLER.

HUNDRED AND SEVENTY-THIRD SONG.
(TUNE, 'What beauteous scenes doth charm.')

ALL glory to my gracious God,
Who his condition chang'd,
For to redeem Adam's lost seed,
He David's son became;
For when his image was overcome,
He did the promise make,
That the seed of the woman,
The serpent's head should break.
   The serpent's, &c.

2.

A virgin then, of David's seed,
The Lord God did prepare,
Him to receive, because that she
Of fallen nature were;
But when the blessed tidings came,
All reason passive lay,
She dictated by faith alone,
Which only could obey.
   Which only, &c.

3.

Swifter than thought the Lord descends,
Or she had been consum'd
His Godhead glory he laid down,
In the pure virgin's womb;
His Godhead spirit he cloth'd
With Abraham's pure seed,
He by her side was David's son,
Yet very God indeed.
   Yet very, &c.

4.

There the eternal Spirit died,
Condition for to change,
Quicken'd in pure mortality;
Oh! wonderfully strange!
One divine essence with nature,
The Godhead spirit were,
Subject to hunger, thirst and cold,
As Adam's children are.
   As Adam's, &c.

5.
Behold your God a perfect child,
In spotless pure nature,
Though very God, he knew it not,
Till he became mature;
Then his commission he received
From Elias on high;
That he was God, he then did know,
In pure mortality.
      In pure, &c.

6.
As man, the law he walk'd through,
No guile was found in him;
As God, miracles he wrought,
As God, he forgave sin,
As God, he them permission gave
His precious life to take,
As God, he said he'd rise again,
By virtue of his faith.
      By virtue, &c.

7.
As man, he to the garden came,
His pure nature fears death,
He prays the cup might pass from him,
Which caused that bloody sweat;
But, when as God, his spirit mov'd,
He saw his own decree;
All fears were gone, then he as man,
That it fulfill'd might be.
      That it, &c.

8.
Heaven's kingdom was by violence seiz'd,
And before Pilate brought;
False witnesses, him to accuse,
With diligence they sought;
The witnesses they against him brought,
Was from his own decree,
That they that temple should destroy,
Which now fulfill'd must be.
      Which now, &c.

9.
'His blood on us,' they did cry,

'If that Gods son he be;'
Then they did doom my God to die,
And let a thief go free;
Then like a Lamb they did him lead,
He his own cross did bear,
In derision his divine head
A crown of thorns did wear.
        A crown, &c.

          10.
When he was come unto the place,
They him did crucify,
Between two thieves his blood they spill'd,
Which caused his soul to die;
In bitterness and in anguish
Of soul, the Lord did cry,
He looked all around—help there was none'
Compell'd he was to die.
        Compell'd, &c.

          11.
One thief revil'd, the other cried,
'O Lord, remember me
When thou into thy kingdom come;'
'Tis plain his God he see,
And then, as God, his spirit mov'd,
And he his sins forgave;
Power then became all passive,
That death might conquest have.
        That death, &c.

          12.
In the condition of a son,
''Tis finished,' he cried;
By loss of blood, anguish and pain,
The Godhead spirit died,
Death manifested first on him,
For divine order sake,
That scripture might be fulfilled,
A bone they should not break.
        A bone, &c.

          13.
The wine-press of God's wrath he trod
Alone, and all fulfill'd,
Which would not have been done by him,

Had his soul not been kill'd;
Sin brought God's wrath, its wages death;
The Lord God no sin hath,
Permits death's conquest---rose again,
And so became death's death.
      And so, &c.

14.

When the decreed time was fulfill'd,
He naturally arose;
Salvation wrought for the elect,
Damnation to his foes;
Death had no power to detain,
For why? no sin was there;
He burst death's bands triumphantly,
The very God appear'd.
      The very, &c.

15.

With his right hand and holy arm,
The victory he gain'd,
A double glory to himself
The Lord God hath attain'd,
Now he's ascended far on high,
From whence he did descend,
Where he will reign eternally,
When time is at an end.
      When time, &c.

16.

Come, brothers all, with joyful hearts,
Your thankful praises join,
Patiently waiting for your God
To pat an end to time;
Oh! come, my dear Redeemer, come,
I long thy face to see,
That in thy blessed mansion, I
May praise eternally.
      May praise, &c.

                                        THOMAS PERRY.

HUNDRED AND SEVENTY-FOURTH SONG.

OH! liberty, where shall I find
   Thee, in this orb below;
I know that here thou art confin'd,

And so am I also;
For if my body like my faith,
  As swift as thought could be;
Then no restraint should me controul,
  Then no, &c.
  From perfect liberty.

2.

'True liberty,' the world does cry,
  'Within our church is found;'
But oh! how falsely they do lie,
  And liberty confound;
For how can liberty appear
  In ignorance below;
Or who true liberty can share;
  Or who, &c.
  That liberty don't know?

3.

It's true the devils think they are blest,
  But they are much deceiv'd;
God's sacred truths they ne'er possest,
  Nor his prophets e'er believ'd;
And tho' in darkness they oft weep,
  And in distress oft cry,
Yet in their travels they do sleep,
  Yet in, &c.
  And find not liberty.

4.

O liberty, thy place so great,
  My tuneful theme shall tell,
The way to thee's through heaven's gate,
  The way to that's through hell;
And when our God calls all from rest,
  All Adam's seed will fly
To praise their God in endless rest,
  To praise, &c.
  In perfect liberty.

5.

For from that seed spontaneously
  All praises then will flow,
When they are left at liberty,
  Their gratitude to shew;

Not like that angel which once fell
  When he was left on high,
His cursed spirit did rebel,
  His cursed, &c.
  And died in liberty.

6.

And all that nature which live on high,
  By God's dear boundless love,
From life to death would quickly fly,
  If left alone above;
For as that spirit came from death,
  They to that centre fly;
But God gave us an heavenly breath,
  But God, &c.
  Which leads to liberty.

7.

That breath it was the breath of life,
  Which God to Adam gave,
Free from all envy, care and strife,
  It wanted none to save;
But when he sinn'd, he quickly fell,
  And for his sin did die;
But God himself went down to hell,
  But God, &c.
  And purchas'd liberty.

8.

O liberty, thy glorious crown
  My soul is sure to wear,
With mighty men of high renown,
  Who see thy shining star;
That star it was Elias great,
  In power and majesty;
Who did thy wonders great relate,
  Who did, &c.
  When you came down to die.

9.

He did them to the stable bring,
  Where yon in peace did lay,
And show'd them their redeeming king,
  Here cloth'd with spotless clay;
'For in the inn no room,' they said,
  So shut you out of door;
And in a manger you was laid,

And in, &c.
  Where none had lain before.

10.
And when that you grew up mature,
  And died for Adam's sin;
Against them all you shut the door,
  And let none of them in,
To see the greatest mystery,
  That ever here was done;
Your very soul in flesh did die,
  Your very, &c.
  And bled here as a son.

11.
That great and mighty rock was rent,
  When they did pierce Christ's side,
Both blood and water did descend,
  And flesh and blood divide;
And when Christ did to death descend,
  Wise men of reason cried,
'Surely the world is at an end,
  Surely the, &c.
  Or nature's God has died.

12.
But if the world had ended then,
  I never God had known;
Nor never liv'd to guide my pen,
  Or praises ever shown;
But now I'm here, I'll patient wait,
  Until my soul does die;
Then fly from death to heaven's gate,
  Then fly, &c.
  To endless liberty.

BOYER GLOVER.

HUNDRED AND SEVENTY-FIFTH SONG.

How happy's that mortal who by faith can see,
That Christ he is God, and only he,
And in his blest body the Godhead did lie,
When he was in time and in eternity.

2.

Ev'ry virtue in him was infinite, I see,
When he was existing in eternity,
Ev'ry property in him sweetly did shine;
Who can but adore a God of divine!

3.

From the crown of his head to the soles of feet,
In form of a man so sweet and complete,
The sun in his strength he far did outshine;
Oh! let us all join for to praise him in time.

4.

His immortal soul was his nature divine,
In quantity like to a mustard grain;
Its quality is so infinite, I see,
Like a fountain it flow'd from eternity.

5.

His bright burning glory it did him surround,
In his presence no creature there was to be found,
A kingdom of pleasure he is all within,
Which did arise in him from his eternal spring.

6.

Oh! this is my God that by faith I can see,
And thus he existed in eternity;
Tho' titles he had three, persons had but one,
In which blessed person all myst'ry is done.

WILLIAM CURTOYSE.

HUNDRED AND SEVENTY-SIXTH SONG.
(TUNE, 'Who has e'er been at Baldock.')

Whene'er my faith it soars above,
It instantly thinks of God's love,
How he did die upon a cross,
To save his seed in Adam lost.
    How he, &c.

2.

His glorious head he did recline,
His heavenly breath he did resign,
His precious blood the ground bespread,
And then the whole Godhead was dead.
    His precious, &c.

3.
My soul it doth rejoice to think,
That it his precious blood can drink;
His body too I eat likewise;
Oh! how glorious is the prize.
  His body, &c.

4.
Oh! still my soul it doth rejoice,
To know it was God's holy voice,
Upon the cross, aloud did cry,
In bitter pangs of death, 'Eli!'
  Upon a, &c.

5.
But, how these truths should I have known,
Had not the Almighty, from his throne,
Sent two prophets for to tell,
That he redeem'd my soul from hell.
  Sent two, &c.

6.
These great prophets I receive,
For they have brought the grand reprieve;
From death to life we are set free,
And we shall live eternally.
  From death, &c.

7.
Then, loving friends, let us all sing
Our songs of praise to Christ our king,
The king of kings and lord of lords,
Who hath strewn to us the three records.
  The king, &c.

       RICHARD WYNNE, 1757.

HUNDRED AND SEVENTY-SEVENTH SONG.

THOUGH I a captive slave have been
 In Babylon's city great,
Where many a tower high is rais'd,
 Poor souls to captivate;
Where many silver merchants dwell,
 Who make an hideous noise;
They are like their gilded organ pipes,
 They know not whom they praise.

2.

Or, like the barren heath that grows
  On a burning sandy soil,
That never any fruit doth bare,
  To suffice an hungry soul;
What mortal man could think to find
  On a burning sandy soil,
Any thing that would any comfort bring,
  To heal a wounded soul.

3.

Long on this barren plain I've been,
  And there must have remain'd,
Had I not known two golden pipes
  From a true fountain came,
Which did convey the golden oil
  Into my wounded soul;
A sovereign balm it is I'm sure,
  Unto a wounded soul.

JAMES CULLAM.

HUNDRED AND SEVENTY-EIGHTH SONG.

OH! how happy are we whose thirst is quench'd
In our Redeemer's blood, which hath prevented
The sting of death, which would have kept us under;
But through Christ's precious blood, the bond's
        asunder;
Therefore all praises be to him ascrib'd,
That so hath set us free and us reviv'd,
For the yokes of our necks that made us weary,
And our dim eyes are wash'd, now we see clearly.
    For the, &c.

2.

'Tis not the strength of sin that e'er shall storm us,
Since we have faith and truth that will inform us;
Which truth declar'd is by the true prophets
Of our almighty God whose divine office
We give all reverence to, as is our duty,
Embracing charity, which is faith's beauty,
Which effects brings us to sweet contemplation,
Opening the springs of faith with elevation.
    Which effects, &c.

3.

And now, my brethren dear, let's love sincerely,
Since we are all one flock, and bought so dearly,
Valiantly standing up all for the honor
Of our eternal God, under whose banner
We bravely will maintain truth in its centre,
Knowing by faith that we ere long shall enter
Into a place of bliss with joys surrounded,
Leaving our foes behind to be confounded.
    Into a, &c.

JOHN NICHOLS, SEN.

HUNDRED AND SEVENTY-NINTH SONG.

WHEN I saw my great Creator,
  Oh! what joy my soul did see;
Could I but shake off human nature,
  I'd fly into eternity.

2.

There no envy e'er can reach me,
  There curst reason ne'er can roar,
All in obedience, faith doth teach me,
  When our God we do adore.

3.

There's that crystal glorious fountain,
  Darting forth his streams of love,
When on the wings of faith we're mounting
  In his bless'd abode above.

4.

How the sun when in his splendour,
  Does the soul of man delight;
But when the grave doth us surrender;
  How far surprizing is the sight!

5.

All amaz'd and struck with wonder,
  Praises to our God we'll sing,
In a shrill voice, more loud than thunder,
  Hosanna to our glorious king.

6.
Then we'll gaze upon our treasure,
  Which our souls did long to see;
Faith in our souls will flow in measure,
  With Godlike joys eternally.

7.
Then our souls free from desire,
  Will burn in praise to God above;
Faith in our souls will be that fire,
  Returning praise in love for love.

8.
Then our candle will be lighted,
  And will burn eternally;
When the curst devils are benighted,
  And the light will never see.

9.
Now the state of two conditions,
  In my soul I clearly see;
Faith will be blest with full fruition,
  Reason damn'd eternally.

10.
Now we see by this commission,
Who came up grom Bozrah red,
That it was God's in man's condition,
When for his lost elect he bled.

11.
This is call'd the hidden manna,
Which God gives to his saints to eat,
When in their souls they cry, hosanna,
And bow down at his royal feet.

12.
How the Son of glory shineth,
  In a soul once sanctified,
When that his faith to him defineth,
  That God in flesh here for him died.

BOYER GLOVER.

Divine Songs

HUNDRED AND EIGHTIETH SONG.

PROUD reason does pretend for to interpret the letter,
But all the doctrine they do teach is like the troubled
           water;
False guides they be, I plainly see, that wander to and
           fro,
Then how shall they the truth declare, when it they do
           not know,

2.

The mysteries that do belong unto a God divine,
But as so many herdsmen that a feeding are of swine;
Just so they be when they expound and harp upon the
           letter;
This is a just comparison, I cannot make a better.

3.

All you that do profess in love this third and last
           commission,
Which does declare, that Christ above, he is the only
           Lord;
In the belief of this alone, salvation does depend,
'Tis promised to every one that holds out to the end.

4.

Blessed are those that can behold, and see the
           transmutation
Of the Creator, who did die for ownseed's salvation;
This mystery is very great, and much to be admir'd,
But never could have been declar'd, except by those
           inspir'd.

5.

Great Reeve and Muggleton are those that have
           declar'd the same,
They are true prophets of the Lord, prais'd be his holy
           name;
What tho' extinct by death they be, the promise is
           made sure,
'Twill stand to all eternity, when time shall be no more.

6.

They are the last God e'er will send, while time it does
           endure,
Their commission does infull force stand, and will till

time's no more;
For whilst there is believers here below upon this earth,
It will not loose its virtual power, tho' they're extinct in death.

7.

Now, my friends rejoice and sing, and praise the glorious One,
For there is nothing else to do, we see the work is done;
But to stand firm unto the faith, so then we may depend
For to enjoy eternal life, when time is at an end.

8.

For then the Lord, who did create man of this earth below,
For to fulfil his royal will, he'll make all things anew;
The saints to enjoy eternal bliss, with all the elect likewise,
But reason ne'er will have the power above this earth to rise.

9.

But doom'd in darkness here below for ever for to dwell,
And this that is their heaven now, will be their only hell;
Whilst we enjoy eternal bliss, with all the elect likewise,
Proud reason ne'er will have the power above this earth to rise.

WILLIAM SEDGWICK.

HUNDRED AND EIGHTY-FIRST SONG.
(TUNE, 'Hearts of oak.')

HOW happy the soul that's possess'd with true love,
The love of pure faith which can soar up above;
Such enjoy a true peace which doth grow and increase,
Though the malice of reason would fain it remove;
  Such are precious saints,
  Who need make no complaints,
  For they enjoy a pleasure,
  To know they have a treasure
For them laid up in store, in a kingdom above.
    Such are, &c.

2.

Come, my dear faithful friends, let us nothing fear,
For we are the elect whom our God loves so dear,
To leave his throne on high, and come down here to
        die,
That we may live with him to eternity.
  Since my soul this did see,
  That my God died for me
  Oh! what a pleasure
  I have enjoy'd in great measure,
Now I know I am redeem'd from death's captivity.
     Since my, &c.

3.

Oh! what a happy state those believers are in,
Who know they are new-born, and have pardon of sin;
Whose experience doth prove their God doth love,
And are sure they shall see him in glory above;
  Free from malice and spite,
  They should truly unite
  In love to each other;
  True faith loves his brother,
And all reason's malice cannot them affright.
     Free from, &c.

REBECCA BATT.

HUNDRED AND EIGHTY-SECOND SONG.
(TUNE, 'Dearest Daphne, turn thy eyes.')

OH! what joys there doth arise
In my soul above the skies;
Oh! the raptures I possess,
I cannot with my tongue express,
When by faith I view my God
Open'd by the third record,
By two prophets that were sent,
Glorious tidings to present.

2.

First, they do declare to be,
One God from all eternity;
His form it is a man all o'er,
His nature is pure faith, I am sure;
The angel's nature likewise tell,
It is pure reason in them dwell,
According to his grand decree,

They in obedience are to be.

3.
The devils nature they tell plain,
At first it aid arise from Cain,
The father of all mischief, who
His brother righteous Abel slew;
With all the rest of his curst seed,
From earth's foundation lay conceal'd,
Will here on earth for ever lie
In hell to all eternity.

4.
To conquer death, our God came down,
And did leave his glorious throne,
For to save all Adam's seed,
Upon a cross our God did bleed,
Both soul and body dead, I see,
When Christ he died upon a tree;
Three days he in this earth did lie,
Then rose again victoriously.

5.
By that same power himself he rais'd,
By that same power we shall arise;
In fullness then of faith shall we
Praise God to all eternity;
If in our souls such raptures flow,
While we are in this world below,
How greater far our joys will be,
When we the face of God do see.

CATHARINE PEERS.

HUNDRED AND EIGHTY-THIRD SONG.
(TUNE, Queen of the May.')

SEE, see, our Creator, Redeemer, and King,
Came down from his kingdom, salvation to bring,
His bright burning glory with him he brought down,
And vail'd in flash his bright glorious crown.

2.
When he call'd us to life, he was Father on high,
And when be redeem'd us, he for us did die,
And in him the Godhead it wholly did dwell,
No part of a God could redeem us from hell.

3.

When Christ he was dead, and in silence did lie,
There lay the whole source of great infinity;
He, when in his glory, bright light did surround,
Now center'd in darkness was there to be found.

4.

But long in that centre he could not remain,
To fulfil his promise he rose up again;
Or else for redemption he need not to die,
If he could not live unto eternity.

5.

Now the waters of peace glide over my soul,
Like a ship in a tempest, my reason does roll;
While my faith sits in quiet fruition to see,
When God he will call me to eternity.

BOYER GLOVER.

HUNDRED AND EIGHTY-FOURTH SONG.
(TUNE, 'Swift on the wings of faith let's fly.')

WHEN my faith soars up on high,
I see the great Eternity,
And I know when I do die,
I shall have joy for ever.
  And I, &c.

2.

From the fall of Adam, God decreed,
That here on earth should reign two seeds,
Which made God to come down to bleed,
That we might have joys for ever.
  Which made, &c.

3.

Oh! the love of God on high,
That did here come down to die,
For to raise his seed on high,
To live in joys for ever.
  For to, &c.

4.

When I think of the bitter cup,

That my God he did drink up;
But on these devils we shall sup,
When we are in joys for ever.
    But on, &c.

5.

Oh! what horror they did see,
When they nail'd Christ unto the tree;
A type of future misery,
To live in hell for ever.
    A type, &c.

6.

But their power did decline,
For God they could not confine,
For his person was divine,
And now he lives for ever.
    For his, &c.

7.

How should we those truths have known,
If God in his love had not made known
To two prophets of renown,
The joys we shall have for ever.
    To two, &c.

8.

Now the time it doth draw near,
Great Jehovah will appear
With his host of angels fair,
To call us home for ever.
    With his, &c.

9.

When his glorious voice we hear,
Our faith will quicken without fear,
And swift attend him in the air,
To live in joys for ever.
    And swift, &c.

10.

Oh! how sweet our faith will rise,
As we move above the skies,
To the fountain of all joys,
To praise his name for ever.
    To the, &c.

CATHERINE PEERS.

HUNDRED AND EIGHTY-FIFTH SONG.
(TUNE, 'Old Oxford.')

SWIFT on the wings of faith let's fly
To God in eternity,
Whose blood was shed when he did die,
That we might live for ever.
    Whose blood, &c.

2.

When in his bitter agony,
God on the cross for aid did cry,
He by decree was compell'd to die,
That we might live for ever.
    He by, &c.

3.

When that the streams of blood did flow,
Oh! what God did undergo;
Pains that no mortal ne'er can know,
That we might live for ever.
    Pains that, &c.

4.

God died fully satisfied,
'Now all is finish'd,' he cried,
And bow'd his glorious head and died,
Assur'd to live for ever.
    And bow'd, &c.

5.

Tho' God was a glorious fountain bright,
When he with flesh did here unite,
He was compell'd to pass thro' night,
That we might live for ever.
    He was, &c.

6.

He that to beings all gave breath,
Senseless lay upon this earth;
But rose again and conquer'd death,
That we might live for ever.
    But rose, &c.

7.

When that the blood from God did flow,

And brought him down to death so low,
Oh! what a power God did show,
To rise and live for ever.
    Oh! what, &c.

8.

None such a power e'er could show,
None but a God when by death slew,
Could create his life anew
When dead, and live for ever.
    Could create, &c.

9.

For in the body that he died,
He quicken'd, I am satisfied,
And heal'd the wound they had made in his side,
That we might live for ever.
    And heard, &c.

10.

His body was the altar pure,
His Spirit was the offering sure,
Which makes us here sit down secure,
Assur'd to live for ever.
    Which makes, &c.

11.

When in his burning glory bright,
God comes and calls us all from night;
We shall be ravish'd at the sight,
And praise his name for ever.
    We shall, &c.

12.

Come in love, now let us sing,
To our dear redeeming king,
Who has shorten'd grim death's sting,
That we might live for ever.
    Who has, &c.

13.

Oh! what a joy there did appear,
When God's prophets I did hear
Cry, 'drink God's blood, your soul to cheer,
And you shall live for ever.'
    Cry, drink, &c.

14.
Darkness did oppress my mind,
When in Egypt I was blind;
But mow to the truth I am resign'd,
My soul is blest for ever.
      But now, &c.

15.
When I come to the fountain brink,
Fain my thirsty soul would drink;
But God's law made me to think,
Ere I could live for ever.
      But God's, &c.

16.
When I believ'd the prophet's word,
Soon it devour'd Moses's rod;
And when I drank the blood of God,
My soul was blest for ever.
      And when, &c.

                                    BOYER GLOVER.

HUNDRED AND EIGHTY-SIXTH SONG.

ARISE, 'Tis morn, my soul, arise,
And with great joy and great surprise,
Think of the works of our great God,
Who in the three commissions stood.

2.
First, as a Father to create,
And all things for his pleasure make;
That to his glorious will redound,
Where saints for e'er his praise shall sound.

3.
Next, as a Son, suffer'd severe,
For lost elect he lov'd so dear,
By taking of that dreadful cup,
For our salvation he has drank up.

4.
Next, as a Spirit pure divine,
Sent forth those two prophets in his due time,

That they to us the truth might reveal;
Now nothing from us can be conceal'd.

5.

Then happy, ever happy are we,
Who do those three commissions see,
One only God, with titles, three;
His name we'll praise eternally.

PHILIP LATHORP.

HUNDRED AND EIGHTY-SEVENTH SONG.

WHILE my treasures I'm surveying,
  In my heart laid up in store,
Joy and pleasure I can't measure,
  When my God I do adore;
I have gold tried in the fire,
  In a limbeck---precious ore!
Which makes me my God admire,
  And his boundless love adore.
      I have, &c.

2.

In my heart the joys that's flowing,
  Men nor angels ne'er can tell,
My salvation always knowing,
  God has me redeem'd from hell;
See God in bright burning glory
  Leaves the lofty heavens high,
And for Adam's seed's redemption,
  In a virgin's womb did lie.
      See God, &c.

3.

In a manger mean was lying
  Heaven's great imperial king;
He did differ from all mortals,
  He was not conceiv'd in sin;
His great angels did protect him,
  When in his minority;
Devils great they did reject him,
  Caus'd his glorious soul to die.
      His great, &c.

4.

See the blood that there was flowing
  When a soldier pierc'd his side;

By that witness we are knowing,
  That for us our God he died;
And the water that was flowing,
  When that devil pierc'd his side,
By that witness we are knowing,
  That his spirit there did die.
        And the, &c.

           5.
These are joys that far surpasses
  Reason's false deluding gold,
And of that I am not wanting;
  Oh! what joys for to behold;
Kings would give their golden scepters,
  Earthly treasures all lay down,
If like me they were assured
  For to wear a glorious crown.
        Kings would, &c.
                            BOYER GLOVER.

       HUNDRED AND EIGHTY-EIGHTH SONG.

ROUSE, rouse up, awake,
My senses and speak
Of the mysteries God has made known
To all Adam's seed,
That on them they may feed,
Being sent from God's heavenly throne,
By the great prophet Reeve
And Muggleton too;
Whom God has been pleas'd to inspire,
His will to make known
To his elect alone;
So his free grace we'll ever admire.
        His will, &c.

           2.
How great and how wise,
Is the God of all joys,
Who saw all things naked and bare,
In root and in fruit,
So without all dispute,
With his wisdom there's none can compare;
His prerogative royal

Was the glorious wheel,
That mov'd him at first to create
The angels above,
To admire his love,
And the man in his innocent state.
       The angels, &c.

3.

Now the prophets of old,
With Isaiah foretold,
That their God would in time become flesh;
And now its fulfill'd,
For his blood has been spill'd,
Which for ever my soul doth refresh;
Oh! wonder of wonders,
The soul of God died,
Or else we for ever must lie
Void of motion or breath,
In the fetters of death,
Like a captive in captivity.
       Void of, &c.

4.

In vain, all in vain,
Doth the devils complain,
For this secret they never shall know,
How the streams of God's blood
Was pour'd forth like a flood,
To redeem his elect from all woe;
Nor how that the Father
Became a Son,
This secret they can't comprehend;
But in chains they are bound,
Never lost, never found;
So their torments shall never have end.
       But in, &c.

5.

They will not believe
In the prophet John Reeve,
And great Muggleton's doctrine they scorn;
Like wolves they would rend us,
Did the law not defend us;
It had been better they ne'er had been born;
When the divine rock of all ages,
Descends from his throne,
Then the devils shall certainly know,

That our God has decreed,
That both Cain and his seed,
Shall for ever remain here below.
    That our, &c.

6.

But those who are true saints,
Never make such complaints,
For a pardon they have got ready seal'd;
True balm they have found,
That has cur'd all their wounds,
And for ever, for ever, they're heal'd;
No power on such,
Can the second death have,
For faith's of the nature divine,
Which will pierce through the skies,
Into ravishing joys,
Where we ever in glory shall shine.
    Which will, &c.

7.

I wish the elect,
Whom my God doth protect,
Were from all false worship set free;
Who in thraldom are bound,
For the lack of truth's sound,
Being kept still in captivity;
Oh! there is good ground,
If the truth was but known,
No doubt of a glorious increase
Of heavenly joys
In their hearts would arise,
Which never---no, never would cease.
    Of heavenly, &c.

8.

Like the troubled seas,
They are never at ease,
Who in false worship are tumbled and tost
With care and with strife,
Seeking eternal life,
But in fruitless forms they are lost,
Until the true shepherd's voice
Sounds in their ears;
Then faith which before lay as dead,
Rises up out of bond,

And doth reason command,
Which before in their souls rul'd as head.
      Rises up, &c.

9.

Now too all the elect,
Whom my soul doth respect,
Who were lost, but by faith have been found,
Who patiently wait
For the change of their state,
Not doubting at last to be crown'd;
Oh! God then come quickly,
And finish our faith,
That thy glorious face we may see,
Who was dead and alive,
And doth ever survive,
Yea, unto all eternity.
      Who was, &c.

                                ROBERT PICKARD.

HUNDRED AND EIGHTY-NINTH SONG.

WHEN God he descended,
Redemption intended,
His glory surpassing,
The sun did outshine;
Oh! what can be greater
Than for the Creator,
To clothe with pure nature
His Godhead divine?
      Oh! what, &c.

2.

It makes men to wonder,
When God was brought under,
Death conquer'd the soul
Of the eternal God;
But what was still greater,
Our God, the Creator,
He died and he liv'd
By his almighty word.
      But what, &c.

3.

The body dissolved,
When he was resolved,
To clothe with pure nature

His Godhead divine;
And there did inherit
The infinite spirit,
Which makes him pure creature,
Or God-man divine.
  And there, &c.

4.

When they had him killed;
Theo all was fulfilled
Which had been foretold
Of the death of our God;
And when he ascended,
Redemption then ended,
And glories surrounded
This crucified God.
  And when, &c.

5.

Arriv'd at fruition,
There was no addition
Could ever be made
To his Godhead divine;
The spirit inherent
Did shine so transparent,
It made human nature
All glorious divine.
  The spirit, &c.

6.

And that which is whiter
Than snow, and shone brighter,
Did shine from his
Infinite spirit divine;
This none put upon him,
For that which shone from him,
The sun in his splendour
By far did outshine,
  This none, &c.

7.

The angels adore him,
Elias before him,
His power and glory
Did freely resign;
Thus God the Creator

Does surpass his creature,
With immortal crowns
Of bright glories divine.
    Thus God& &c.

BOYER GLOVER.

HUNDRED AND NINETIETH SONG.
(TUNE, 'Dying swain.')

WHEN shall I see that happy hour,
  When death shall set me free,
And I releas'd from these complaints,
  Whilst here are plagues to me?

2.

When shall I see that glorious day,
  That long and wish'd for hour,
When I shall see thy glorious face
  Descend in thy great power?

3.

Then shall my ravish'd soul in joy,
  Spring from his dusty bed,
Rejoicing at that glorious sound,
  'Arise! come forth, ye dead!'

4.

I, in the air, amongst the saints,
  Shall meet with Christ, my king,
Where angels and archangels both,
  Thy conquering trophies sing.

5.

Then come, dear Lord, this work fulfil,
  And let thy kingdom come;
Thus I resign, and wrought my will,
  Till thou shall call me home.

6.

No more, bold tyrant, dare to boast
  With pains to torture me;
Thy power, beyond the grave, is lost;
  No more thy prisoner be.

MRS. THOMAS.

Divine Songs

HUNDRED AND NINETY-FIRST SONG.
(TUNE, 'Black ey'd Susan.')

WHAT dreadful horror I did see,
When that God's laws condemn'd me;
No hiding place I then could find,
Which then could ease my troubled mind;
For in my blood I loud did cry,
To have some comfort from on high,
For in that state I fear'd to die.

2.

Oh! what a dreadful sight I see,
Nothing but death eternally;
Egypt's chains so fast me bound,
There was no balsam for my wound,
Till God's true prophets said to me,
Although a sinner, great you be,
Wash in God's blood, and you'll be free.

3.

This thing I often strove to do,
Ere I my punishment went through,
The law then in my soul did cry,
'You justly do deserve to die;'
But when my faith soar'd up on high,
And saw God in eternity,
This my lost soul did satisfy.

4.

The tree or life I saw there stand,
And touch'd it with my purest hand,
The hand of faith, by which I see
My glorious God did die for me;
When in the wine-press he was red
With blood, to break the serpent's head,
I know my God for me there bled.

5.

This is a glorious sight indeed,
Unto all Adam's faithful seed,
Who from false worship are set free,
And know they'll live eternally,
They have the flesh of God to eat,
His blood to drink, that is se sweet,
In love each other now let's greet.

BOYER GLOVER.

HUNDRED AND NINETY-SECOND SONG.
(TUNE, 'The Miller.')

SINCE I am enlighten'd once more,
And can see my dear Saviour and king,
His free grace I'll ever adore,
To him I will evermore sing.
Tho' by reason I've captive been led,
And by sin have in darkness been bound;
By faith now I see the true bread,
And those joys which I've heretofore found.

2.

No darkness there is upon earth,
Can compare with the darkness of mind;
But he that is blind from his birth,
Cannot know what the seeing do find;
This, this is the state of the world,
Thus reason is lock'd up in sin,
With pleasure asleep fast are lull'd,
Knows not the condition they're in.

3.

What horrors, what fear, and what dread,
Was I under while servant to sin;
Like reason both senseless and dead,
Forgot almost what I had been;
For guilt reign'd sole lord of my soul,
And darkness spread over my mind,
No light could I see, for the whole
Of faith which I had, was confin'd.

4.

My sin I continually saw,
Which augmented my punishment more,
My mind with the breach of the law
Tormented was greviously sore;
Thus lifeless, bereav'd of all joy,
I mourning went day after day,
Till faith did my fears all destroy,
And wip'd all my sorrows away.

5.

Now my dear God I can see,
Who was nail'd to a cross for my sin,

All Adam's lost seed to set free,
Who have faith to believe it was him;
From his precious blood that was shed,
A remedy sure I have found;
His death raises me from the dead,
And his sufferings cures all my wounds.

6.

He that believes that the flesh
Of our Lord Jesus Christ that did die,
Was verily very God's flesh,
Shall reign with him eternally;
And he that believes that the blood
That Christ pour'd forth from the cross,
Was verily very God's blood,
That soul it can never he lost.

7.

On his flesh by true faith if you feed,
Your hungry souls 'twill suffice;
One draught of his blood will indeed,
Occasion new springs to arise
In your souls, that you'll never thirst more;
For then your salvation you'll see,
His free grace with me you'll adore,
In time and in eternity.

JAMES MILLER.

HUNDRED AND NINETY-THIRD SONG.

WELCOME day of great joyful news,
  Come, saints, with voices raise,
For this, while here, we'll ever choose
  An annual jubilee of praise.

2.

In anthems then divine begin,
  Eternal love let us proclaim,
To Christ our God alone we'll sing,
  And magnify his holy name.

3.

What mortals here below can tell
  The sweet enjoyments we possess;

That happy soul that knows full well,
   Raptur'd in bliss cannot express.

4.

If faith the only earnest here
   Of those eternal joys above,
Does so exceedingly appear,
   What then must be eternal love?

5.

Come, poor despis'd brethren all,
   Who do among proud reason dwell;
Take care to live, but not enthral,
   For riches only lead to hell.

6.

He who enjoys the most below,
   Is as a steward put in trust;
Who always mercy ought to show,
   Lest he should find his Maker just.

7.

But so bewitching is the dross,
   Those who possess it shall want more;
And tho' in faith, can't bear the loss
   Of what their reason so adore.

8.

From those incumbrances free,
   Our souls can with our God converse;
And tho' press'd with necessity,
   His love and mercy still rehearse.

9.

Why should we then for riches crave,
   Since we do all of faith receive,
Sufficient, 'tis enough to have,
   Unless poor brethren to relieve.

10.

How surprising 'tis to see
   Some, tho' possessing riches store,
Strangers almost to charity,
   No bowels have to those that's poor.

11.

What, can they carry them away,

Or with them bribe impartial death?
Why then, I have no more to say,
   If riches will reclaim their breath.

12.
But the pale victor soon will come,
   And rob them of their earthly joys;
Confine them in a stinking tomb,
   For all their transitory joys.

13.
What difference then pray will be seen,
   When we are all levell'd in the ground,
Betwixt the beggar and the king,
   Or mighty heroes of renown?

14.
True heirs then of immortal crowns,
   Who can your own salvation see,
Contemn the dust and this world's frowns,
   Since sure of immortality.

15.
'Tis you alone can soar above,
   And by faith view eternity,
Know the immortal God of love,
   Center'd in immortality.

16.
Oh! that more love was more shown
   By those who know a second birth;
By this God's belov'd are known,
   That they each other love on earth.

17.
And how can we our love declare,
   But when a brother's in distress,
Rejoice, we have enough to spare,
   His indigency to redress.

18.
What's the commission grown deprav'd?
   No, God forbid that cannot be;
But some who own it are enslav'd
   With reason's damn'd depravity.

19.

Come, poor believers, don't repine,
  Heaven's our own, then be content;
Where we shall glorious saints all shine,
  Enrich'd with treasures permanent.

20.

Now, to the king of kings on high,
  Round whom ten thousand do adore,
Christ, God alone, eternally,
  Be glory now and evermore.

JAMES MILLER.

HUNDRED AND NINETY-FOURTH SONG.
(TUNE, 'To arms, to arms, my jolly granidiers.')

To praise, to praise the glorious King of heaven,
Help me, dear saints, in raptures join;
That unto us such knowledge is given,
In this third and last record which is so divine,
His mind in the scriptures is fully made known,
By his blessed prophets, great Reeve and Muggleton.
    His mind, &c.

2.

Behold our God, a spotless infant here,
Come to fulfil his own decree,
For his own seed whom he lov'd so dear,
That by his blood he might set them free;
Oh! boundless love it was Indeed, God did come down
      to die,
He left his glorious kingdom above the starry sky.
    Oh! boundless, &c.

3.

Among curst devils dwelt the Lord of life,
While he walk'd his journey here,
With him continually they were at strife,
But he never did them spare;
Those that would not believe in him, they in their sins
      must die,
But those that have no other God, are blest eternally.
    Those that, &c.

4.

Behold him stretch'd upon a cross,

Nail'd unto that cursed tree,
His precious life soon he lost,
'Twas then my God he ransom'd me;
His flesh I daily feed upon, his blood I drink likewise,
Those that eat and drink as I, can sound forth his
      praise.
    His flesh, &c.

5.

Our blessed prophets they have declar'd,
And by their commission have fully made known,
The Father and Son inseparable were,
Before, as well as after he left his throne;
'He is in me, and I in him,' our glorious God did say;
Oh! who can hear those blessed truths, and not them
      obey!
    He is, &c.

6.

No other God the Muggletonians own,
No other majesty adore,
Our praise we'll sing to Jesus Christ alone,
And so we will continue till time is no more,
For we are all well satisfied by him the work was done,
And we know how to honor the Father in the Son.
    For we, &c.

                AVIS SARAH TOONE.
                (Afterwards MRS. WALLIS.)

HUNDRED AND NINETY-FIFTH SONG.

WELCOME, are those happy days,
To all true saints who do believe;
For our prayers are turn'd to praise,
By this great mission of John Reeve;
Here we find that only good,
And feed by faith on spiritual food.

2.

Sacred are the truths we know,
The Lord's last prophets have made known
Unto mortals here below,
Who are of the royal seed alone;
Earnest of eternal bliss,
The sons of faith can never miss.

3.
Come, my friends, and let's rejoice,
To celebrate this jubilee,
Unto Christ, with heart and voice,
Our only God whom now we see
In this third and last record,
Blest tidings from our heavenly Lord.

4.
Reason here may vainly boast,
And pride them in their headless thing;
While they scorn the Lord of hosts,
Heaven's great imperial king,
Ever banish'd from his face,
In lasting pain---oh! dire disgrace.

5.
We shall then in glory shine,
Immortal crowns our heads adorn,
Adoring him that's so divine;
In that thrice happy glorious morn,
Eternal anthems shall resound,
Where endless pleasures will abound.

WILLIAM MILLER.

HUNDRED AND NINETY-SIXTH SONG.

Too mean's this world with all its splendor,
  Pomps and false alluring toys,
To make my soul to look behind her,
  And to lose eternal joys;
Tho' we in Sodom for a season,
  In our pilgrimage remain,
No gilded baits of leprous reason,
  Shall our cleansed garments stain.
    Tho' we, &c.

2.
But, strait our leaders we will follow
  To the mansions of the just,
And leave the Sodomites to wallow
  In the mite of brutish lust;
The beauty of all gaudy glory
  Is but like a fleeting shade,
All their grandeur's transitory,
  And in an instant falling fades.
    The beauty, &c.

3.
Kings' crowns and sceptres are but baubles,
  Vain is all supremacy,
Gay flattering titles are but fables
  To please the children when they cry;
Their pompous state and proud attendance,
  And their idolized gold,
On which they place their chief dependance,
  And that doth their lust uphold.
      Their pompous, &c.

4.
Like smoke shall vanish in a moment,
  And their enjoyments all expire,
And leave them in eternal torments,
  When this world's destroy'd by fire;
Their sumptuous glittering habitations,
  And their temples so adorn'd,
Shall be reduced to desolation,
  And for ever be forlorn.
      Their sumptuous, &c.

5.
Their well tun'd instruments and voices,
  That did their souls so sweetly charm,
Shall cease with all their sounding noises,
  Stunn'd by dreadful death's alarm;
No more shall pleasures then delight them,
  Nor their wealth, nor friends avail,
But tortures and terrors will affright them,
  And conscience make them weep and wail.
      No more, &c.

6.
Their non commissionated preachers,
  That did them long with fancies feed,
Will then, too late, be found false teachers,
  And their doctrine's a broken reed;
The two first records they depend on,
  And whereby they get great gain,
Shall not one drop of comfort lend them,
  To assuage their burning pain.
      The two, &c.

7.
But shall increase their condemnation,

And multiply their misery;
This last most glorious dispensation,
   In judgment shall against them arise,
Since this third record they've rejected,
   And God's message vilified,
His representatives have afflicted,
   They Christ afresh have crucified.
         Since this, &c.

8.

Salvation they have banish'd from them,
   And God's messengers have slain,
And brought their fathers' guilt upon them,
   Damnation only now remains;
Their curst contempt shall make their anguish
   Beyond all measure to increase;
Nor can their gods their flame extinguish,
   Nor give to them one moment's ease.
         Their curst, &c.

9.

But like to Sodom and Gomorrah,
   Their smoke shall evermore ascend,
Nor will the flames of wreaking sorrow
   Ever cease, world without end:
Then flee, my soul, flee from the ruin,
   Haste with blessed Lot to Zoar,
For there's true pleasure still renewing,
   That will last for evermore.
         Then flee, &c.

                              ELIZABETH HENN.

HUNDRED AND NINETY-SEVENTH SONG.
(TUNE, 'Dearest Daphne.')

WHEN into silent sleep from all
Distracting thoughts my soul did fall,
Reason in chains of darkness lay,
And faith dispell'd the fogs away;
God did by holy prophets speak,
And did my slumbering soul awake;
Faith then arose whilst reason slept,
Thus one was taken, the other left.

2.

Said he, 'arise, draw near, I'll show
The secret ne'er reveal'd till now,

The time is come, so long foretold
To finish prophecy of old;
All types and shadows are fled and gone,
The substance now remains alone,
All mysteries unveil'd lie,
To faith's all penetrating eye.

3.

Mount, mount, draw near, behold and see
The beauty of eternity;
Those words like flames of heavenly fire,
In raptures made my soul expire;
Swift film Elijah's horses they
Did in faith's chariot me convey,
From Sinai to Mount Zion, where
The anti type did soon appear.

4.

His thundering voice that rent the sky,
Makes the clouds before him fly;
When rending vengeance from above,
Is chang'd from anger into love;
The dispensation that did make
The heavens and the earth to quake,
And law that did our souls affright,
Is vanish'd in eternal night.

5.

Sin now has all his power lost,
And death and hell no more shall boast
For since to Zion we are come,
Sinai and all her shades are gone;
To Eden's paradise once more,
Our lapsed souls God does restore,
When we and all our posterity,
Shall rest unto eternity.

6.

The curse no longer shall remain,
But Eden now is blest again;
We thro' the guards may freely go,
Since God's broad seal we have to show;
By his soul's death our souls to save,
He has conquer'd death, hell and the grave,
And like the pelican for food,
To his elect he gave his blood.

7.

Curst death would our souls devour,
Being depriv'd of all its power,
We have free access unto the tree
Of life and immortality;
'Tis Jehovah did ordain,
Our hungry spirits to sustain;
He is the fountain, and his beams
Of revelation are his streams.

8.

That still our thirsty souls supply,
When nothing else can satisfy;
He is the tree that makes us wise,
Causing the springs of faith to rise,
Which mounteth God's elect on high,
When reprobates overwhelm'd lie
Under imagination's flood,
Whose notions only wise their food.

9.

'Tis he alone our souls can save
From hell's tempestuous tossing wave;
For in his ark salvation's found,
When fallen angels shall be drown'd;
Oh! then to him with speed let's go,
For a deluge does the world overflow.

ELIZABETH HENN.

HUNDRED AND NINETY-EIGHTH SONG.
(TUNE, 'The Billows.')

'Tis by the third commission
　　God gave forth from on high,
We here receive remission
　　Of sin before we die,
By the blood of our Saviour,
　　Who died upon a tree;
This is a matchless favor
　　For mortals here to see.
　　　　This is, &c.

2.

How the angel saluted
　　A spotless virgin fair,

Divine Songs

Her soul then unpolluted,
   To bring forth heaven's heir;
Her soul free from desire,
   Her virgin seed she shed
To clothe eternal fire,
   Or very God's Godhead.
      To clothe, &c.

3.

All glory that surrounded
   Eternal God on high,
Within her womb was bounded,
   When God he there did die;
The body with her nature
   Dissolv'd in seed to join,
But still the great Creator's
   Pure spirit was divine.
      But still, &c.

4.

Tho' in her womb she found him
   Convert to flesh and bone,
No evil did surround him,
   She had active reason none;
Which made her to admire
   The wonder great indeed,
How she without desire
   Should give forth mortal seed.
      How she, &c.

5.

And when nine months were over,
   The Lord of life she bore,
The son of rich Jehovah,
   By reason counted poor;
For in him lay that jewel,
   Which we should ne'er have found,
Unless by devils cruel,
   In death he had been bound.
      Unless by, &c.

6.

For he who ne'er offended,
   Was nail'd unto a tree,
And into death descended,
   From sin to set us free;

Here number'd with transgressors,
  In blood our God did die,
That we might be possessors
  Of bliss eternally.
    That we, &c.

7.

And when that we are raised,
  Such raptures then will move;
No saints in fallen nature,
  Can manifest such love,
Which will flow from our Saviour,
  When we are call'd from rest,
And have that happy favor,
  For ever to be blest.
    And have, &c.

BOYER GOLVER.

HUNDRED AND NINETY-NINTH SONG.
(TUNE, 'Welcome, brother debtor.')

WELCOME, welcome mighty Jesus,
  To old time to put an end,
And of cruel bondage ease us,
  And the power of reason rend;
Leave the curs'd leviathan,
  With his head broke on the ground,
And in eternal desolation,
  Let new sorrows fresh abound.

2.

Welcome, welcome, great deliverer,
  From eternal misery;
When I was in hell a prisoner,
  Thou the debt did pay for me;
Come then, oh! demand the debtor,
  Since for him thou didst suffice;
What could justice stern have greater,
  Than the Godhead sacrifice?

3.

Great havocs made by plague and pestilence,
  Sword and famine, thousands slay,
Earthquakes swallow without relentance,
  These presage that glorious day;
These aloud proclaim thy coming,

To cut short the thread of time;
Fulfil the promise, end our longing
　　To behold thy face divine.

4.

By the ephod faith divineth,
　　Some there is discern the time,
Nor at scoffs, nor scorn repineth,
　　Sure to share in joys divine;
While proud reason strives for mastery,
　　Faith with patience here below,
Sincerely looking at the mystery,
　　Sees proud reason's overthrow.

5.

Thou'st prepar'd me for the meeting
Of thee, with thy angels bright;
That will be a glorious greeting,
In the great eternity ;
Oh! let the groans of thy afflicted,
Centre in thy royal breast;
With briers and thorns they pricked are,
Longing for eternal rest.

6.

A bright lanthorn my feet adorneth,
　　Death I'm not afraid to see,
While the rich man howl and mourneth,
　　I shall joyfully sing to thee;
My loins are girded, my lamp is burning,
　　Ready at thy call to fly;
Oh! hear our cries and end our mourning,
　　With eternal liberty.

　　　　　　　　　　　　JOHN PEAT.

TWO HUNDREDTH SONG.
(TUNE, 'Uncreated essence.')

THE uncreated body of Christ our God alone,
More sweeter is than roses, and softer far than down,
In which his Godhead spirit eternally did shine;
Look, love, adore, admire a God that's so divine.
    In which, &c.

2.

His uncompounded texture so infinitely pure,
Was a substantial something, a form must have
    therefore;
Which form was man's similitude, where he did ever
    shine;
Look, love, adore, admire a God that's so divine.
    Which form, &c.

3.

Before there was creation, when all did hidden lie,
This was the tabernacle from all eternity,
Wherein bright burning glories eternally did shine;
Look, love, adore, admire a God that's so divine.
    Wherein bright, &c.

4.

His burning glorious majesty, refulgent glorious grace,
Ten thousand round adore him, and fall before his
    face,
For none there is in glory can equal with him shine;
Look, love, adore, admire a God that's so divine.
    For none, &c.

5.

He's purer far than gold, tho' e'er so much refin'd,
Swifter than thought in motion, and always unconfin'd,
And does the sun in strength exceedingly outshine;
Look, love, adore, admire a God that's so divine.
    And does, &c.

6.

So infinitely glorious his person now appears,
And such transcendent brightness as a Redeemer
    wears,
In spiritual flaming glory enthron'd above does shine;
Look, love, adore, admire a God that's so divine.
    In spiritual, &c.

7.

In that celestial kingdom where he does now reside,
Words are too weak to mention the joys that there
    abide,
Which we shall have beholding him, when we shall
    with him shine;
Look, love, adore, admire a God that's so divine.
    Which we, &c.

8.

Then, since such joys as these are for us laid up in
    store,
And mansions he's prepaid to be with him evermore;
What can we do while here, but all together join,
To praise, adore, admire a God that's so divine.
    What can, &c.

JAMES MILLER.

TWO HUNDRED AND FIRST SONG.

WHEN my soul it doth ponder,
On that great mystery
Of my God's incarnation,
Into which angels would pry,
How his Godhead glory
Was veil'd in the Son,
That the work of redemption
For us might be done;
His wondrous works and ways,
My admiration raise,
And fills my soul with praise
Of that glorious Son;
To know that my God
The wine-press hath trod,
And o'er death the victory won.

2.

Come, saints, let's rejoice,
For our God is ascended,
Redemption is finish'd,
That work God hath ended;
In that garment of flesh,
Which here he took on;
He now shines in glory,
Brighter than the sun;

That head which thorns one crown'd,
Bright glories now surround,
And wears that double crown,
He hath gloriously won;
He is our God and king,
The fountain and spring,
In that glorious and bright Son.

3.

Great joys to the faithful,
Our God will us raise
To a glorious kingdom;
To him be all praise;
We shall soar up above,
Where our God will be seen,
There feast of his love;
Praises will be the same;
Our joys will then abound,
When we our God surround,
And see him gloriously crown'd,
Who died to redeem;
How my soul longs to be
Christ Jesus with thee,
My glorious bright king.

REBECCA BATT.

TWO HUNDRED AND SECOND SONG.

WHAT glorious truths these are to see,
That the great Godhead died for me,
   Upon a cross below,
He pour'd his soul into the grave,
Alas! his life he could not save,
   He had decreed it so.

2.

But death could not his body keep,
For he did soon awake from sleep,
   For to ascend above;
Where he had left a glorious crown,
Which bless'd Elias did lay down,
   To him with joy and love.

3.

And now he reigns above the skies,
None can behold with mortal eyes,
   His majesty divine;

But time will come when we shall see,
The king of kings eternally,
  In praises then combine.

4.

To bless that Godhead who did send
These glorious truths unto the end,
  Which to us have been told,
By two sweet messengers of peace,
Which Christ did send for to give ease
  To the oppressed soul.

5.

And now these truths have set me free
From reason's bondage, I can see,
  Great Muggleton is true;
And praises I will ever give,
To think I am at last receiv'd
  Among such saints as you.

6.

Nor would I, were I assur'd to gain
Great reason's kingdom and to reign,
  Go back from whence I came;
But leave them to enjoy their feast,
Which many moments will not last,
  And then they'll know their doom.

                           ELIZABETH GLOVER.

TWO HUNDRED AND THIRD SONG.

WHEN Christ he here was crucified,
  The blood from God did flow ;
And then the eternal Spirit died
  To save lost souls from woe;
Eternal light which did surround
  God in eternity,
In darkness here in death was bound,
  When God, as man, did die.
      In darkness, &c.

2.

As God in man, Christ liv'd here'
  A creature seem'd to be,
And in his body liv'd, 'tis clear,
  The godhead bodily;

His attributes all infinite
  Alternately did flow,
His glorious spirit to delight,
  In his pure flesh below.
      His glorious, &c.

3.

For when that Christ came from above,
  Lost mankind to redeem,
His attributes, mercy and love,
  Inherent were in him;
And where must boundless power be,
  But here in him below;
His mercy it too weak would be,
  If power did not flow.
      His mercy, &c.

4.

Inherent power did create,
And inherent did redeem;
Infinitely in God so great,
Finite in all but him;
And which I see in silent death,
The sense of light and love,
All infiniteness was void of breath,
And finite all above.
      All infiniteness, &c.

5.

The spirit and its properties
  Essentially are one;
And when that God he wholly died,
  His properties had no one;
For there's no creature can retain,
  Thai in infinite state,
The properties of God, 'tis plain,
  For creatures were too great.
      The properties, &c.

6.

For tho' Elias sat above,
  And fill'd God's glorious throne,
Infinite power, glory and love,
  Center'd in God alone;
And when that Christ was crucified,
  Power it ceas'd to be,
The word he spoke before he died,

Became a firm decree.
  The word, &c.

7.

Behold our God was wholly dead,
  And virtually alive,
No power had to move his head,
  Or with grim death to strive;
For when Christ was in silent death,
  I see Infinity
Was wholly void of life and breath,
  While virtue liv'd on high.
    Was wholly, &c.

8.

For when that Christ rose from the grave,
  Oh! what a sight to see!
Said he, 'all power now I have;'
  Meaning infinity;
And where could boundless power flow
  But in infinite life,
Which wholly died in Christ below,
  And liv'd to conquer strife.
      Which wholly, &c.

BOYER GLOVER.

TWO HUNDRED AND FOURTH SONG.

WHEN that in Babel I did dwell,
I heard their priest strange stories tell;
But for a truth I now do know,
They know not where their souls must go.
      But for, &.

2.

There's some that do their audience tell
It's either to heaven or to hell;
Whilst some a middle state do find,
But they are all blind leaders of the blind.
      Whilst some, &c.

3.

Some say, 'that they do transmigrate
From their form, and take another shape;'
Whilst some by metamorphesy,
Think, 'their soul gets into a butterfly.'

Whilst some, &c.

4.
Some say, that they wander here and there,
And walk about they know not where;'
So in effect they do all agree,
That the soul of man cannot mortal be.
So in, &c.

5.
God sent two prophets great to me,
That the light from darkness I might see;
They told me, 'that my soul it must die,'
And in a silent grave must lie.
They told, &c.

6.
My soul it hath sinn'd grevious sore,
For which pale death it must endure;
What tho' it must lie in silent dust,
My God he is faithful, great and just.
What tho', &c.

7.
When he by his royal will doth choose,
The bands of death for to unloose,
All things he will then create anew,
He'll raise both soul and body too.
All things, &c.

8.
What joys will then to my sour appear,
When that his glorious voice it doth hear,
He speaking from his throne above,
'Come, enjoy the kingdom now, my love.'
He speaking, &c.

9.
I mean the Lamb that once was slain,
He'll cleanse my soul from every slain,
That it may dwell with him on high,
In endless pure eternity.
That it, &c.

10.
No other God then I believe,
But the God of Muggleton and Reeve;

That's the man Christ Jesus, the king of heaven,
All glory and praise to him be given.
    That's the, &c.
                            MATHEW HAGUE.

TWO HUNDRED AND FIFTH SONG.

An acrostic on the Names of JOHN REEVE and
LODOWICK MUGGLETON.

    Amiable and delightful are the ways of truth.

I N vain do anti-christian spirits strive,
O r think fallacious principles shall thrive;
H eaven disallows their tenets, and they fall,
N o less than damn'd pharasiacal.
R eeve rests in dust, who had commission given,
E ven from the eternal personal God of heaven;
E ternal is his power, his prophets can
V anquish whatever's anti-christian,
E ven all the devilish fallacies of man.

A nd tho' Reeve rests, yet this commission shall
N ever be vanquish'd , or be forc'd to fall;
D evils, do your worst, and for assistance call;

L o! here's a prophet still survives to be
O ur retain'd guide to true felicity;
D ivine expressions as e'er yet were taught,
O 'erflow in him, his mind's so richly wrought
W ith heavenly wisdom, that who e'er believes him,
I t surely from eternal death reprieves him;
C ome then, ye faithful ones, here's life's true spring.
K ept for your good, salvation to bring,
E ven blest messages from heaven's great king.

M ultitudes flock to hear men's false traditions,
V ain is their hope, and desperate their conditions,
G od's messengers are come to blast false teachers,
G reat power from them confounds all earthly
      preachers;
L et worldlings then admire their false devotion,
E nding their wretched lives in earthly notion;
T ruth to its centre drives and mounts on high,
O 'ertopping all this world's impiety,
N othing but faith will reach heaven's majesty.

TOBITT TERRY.

TWO HUNDRED AND SIXTH SONG.

Now sing unto the Lord on high,
   And glory give to his holy name,
He suffer'd for our sins to die,
   And now in heaven's ascended again,
And sitteth on a glorious throne;
   A place ordained there to be,
And angels waiting thereupon,
   Unto all eternity.

2.

Then he descended in a cloud,
And to John Reeve he spoke;
'Take Lodowick Muggleton for thy mouth,
And do you the scriptures ope';
I, you two therefore have chose
My last witnesses to be;
If you this strict command refuse,
Then damn'd are you to eternity.

3.

'Therefore, do you obey my voice,
And in my name prophesy,
For you two are my last choice,
And I'll be with you constantly;'
Then these two did prophesy,
And many devils did cast out,
They had the helmet of faith thereby,
And put the serpent to the rout.

WILLIAM TOMKINSON.

TWO HUNDRED AND SEVENTH SONG
(TUNE, 'Home, sweet home.')

IN celestial regions, eternal above.
In resplendent glory dwells Jesus our God,
Who descended transmuted, became his own son,
That his saints might inherit his glorious home.
   Home, home! Sweet, sweet home!
   Christ Jesus has purchas'd us a glorious home.

2.
This home was purchas'd at a price very dear,
By the blood of our God when he suffered here,
Since nothing but infinite life could atone,
And make his saints worthy his glorious home.
      Home, home, &c.

3.
The rock of all ages before this world took date,
Supremely crown'd in his bright eternal state,
Without any other, glories all his own,
Eternal inherited his glorious home.
      Home, home, &c.

4.
The Almighty Father, eternal divine,
Cloth'd with spirituality did e'er shine;
This spiritual form was the everlasting Son,
In which God inherited his ever sweet home.
      Home, home, &c.

5.
The powerful word of God is the Holy Ghost,
That produced the wondrous heavenly host
Of angels bright, in his all glorious throne,
Singing praise to their God in their new blessed home.
      Home, home, &c.

6.
The angels' persons, transcendant, bright and fair,
Their nature's not faith, of pure reason they are;
'They stand, upheld by God,' says Reeve and
      Muggleton,
Unupheld, they'd fall, expell'd God's glorious home.
      Home, home, &c.

7.
One angel God made, surpassing all the rest,
God left him alone, that he might try the test;
Now reason could not stand, in rebellion did roam,
For which he was then cast down from God's bright
      home.
      Home, home, &c.

8.
This angel cast down in Eden's garden fair,
With envy and malice beheld the blest pair,
Which God had there plac'd, pure faith their souls
      adorn'd,
Fill'd with sweet peace in their new and blessed home.
    Home, home, &c.

9.
This spiritual devil soon Eve ensnared,
By eating the fruit that God prohibited;
When Adam she had beguil'd, they wander'd forlorn,
Conscious of guilt, and lost their happy home.
    Home, home, &c.

10.
The offended God his creatures visited,
With benign sovereign grace their sins did forgive;
A promise God made, their sins he would atone,
By shedding his blood, then call his elect home.
    Home, home, &c.

11.
'Adam,' God did say, 'you punish'd must be,
Your souls were immortal, now mortality
Shall seize you and seed, with toil you'll sweat and moan,
When death's finish'd all, I'll call you to my home.
    Home, home, &c.

12.
So now, my friends, in sweet love and harmony,
We'll sing praise to our God since we redeem'd be,
By the blood of God, says Reeve and Muggleton,
Who, his seed to defend, left his blessed home.
  Home, home, &c.

13.
My Muggletonian friends, who faithful are,
Eat God's flesh and drink his blood, while devils war,
The curs'd seed of Cain all hate great Muggleton;
By whom we're assur'd of God's glorious home.
    Home, home, &c.

                ELIZABETH SUSAN WHITE.

Divine Songs

TWO HUNDRED AND EIGHTH SONG.

WHEN heaven's great God,
From his divine abode,
Did descend mortal flesh to assume;
The angels at his change,
Did think it very strange,
To see Moses and Elias in his room.
  The angels, &c.

2.

Admiring they gazed
Adoring they prais'd;
Knew not what of their God was become,
Till Moses from on high,
Did reveal it secretly,
He was here to be born a Son.
  Till Moses, &c.

3.

How much more cause have we,
To adore this mystery,
When God himself was entomb'd,
Whose glory was so bright,
None could behold the sight,
Yet the virgin remain'd unconsum'd.
  Whose glory, &c.

4.

When the God of all love,
Came down from above,
Sin, death and grave to o'ercome;
The eternal Father he,
Laid down divinity,
And his glory he veil'd the Son.
  The eternal, &c.

5.

And first without sin,
This great work did begin;
That infinite justice might be
Each way fully satisfied,
The eternal Spirit died,
In that spotless humanity.
  Each way, &c.

6.

The law he walked through,
Which we could not do,
And resign'd his sacred breath
  Upon a curs'd tree;
  He fulfil'd his own decree,
That for us he might conquer death.
     Upon a, &c.

7.

Thus heaven's great king,
For us satisfied sin,
And the power of death did destroy;
  Now in death we shall not remain,
  But till he comes again,
To raise us to eternal joys.
     Now in, &c.

8.

The grave will only' be,
A resting place for me,
And for all true believers likewise;
  But reason here below,
  Will find a hell of woe,
While we shall soar above the skies.
     But reason, &c.

9.

Father, Son and Spirit too,
By faith in Christ I view;
All praise to this glorious one,
  For in Christ the Godhead lies,
  And with Christ we shall arise,
Thus by Christ in this mystery done.
     For in, &c.

                    JAMES MILLER.

TWO HUNDRED AND NINTH SONG.
(TUNE, 'Rule Britannia.')

WHEN Reeve at first by God's command,
Receiv'd his royal power;
His God did charge him out of hand,
To tell his friend the choicest flower;
Christ Jehovah, Jehovah, God on high,
And Christ that God for man did die.
     Christ Jehovah, &c.

2.
When Reeve to Muggleton he came,
And his great secrets did reveal;
'Lord God I see thee very plain,'
Said Muggleton, 'my soul does heal,
Christ Jehovah, Jehovah, God on high,
And Christ that God for man did die.
   Christ Jehovah, &c.

3.
'Now we are chose by God,' says Reeve,
'His wondrous works for to expound;
All you that faithfully believe
In what we say, you will be crown'd,
By Jehovah, Jehovah God on high,
That very God that here did die.'
   By Jehovah, &c.

4.
Come, all true friends, and merry sing,
And fill your souls with pure divine,
From great Mount Zion's holy spring,
That flows with God's most sacred wine;
Praise Jehovah, Jehovah God on high,
For Christ your God for you did die.
   Praise Jehovah, &c.

5.
All reason's works throw at your feet,
And all their cunning knavery;
Avoid be sure and never greet,
So sure you do, true faith will fly,
See Jehovah, Jehovah God on high,
To save his faithful, God did die,
   See Jehovah, &c.

6.
Mount Sinai is the field of war,
Where all their wicked deeds do lay,
Murder and plunder in them are,
Who does obey what reason say;
Oh! vile dragon, vile dragon, here below,
Thy army will die living woes.
   Oh! vile, &c.

7.

Mount Zion is the field of peace,
True faith and love commandeth there;
All volunteers that enlist,
Fight firm for God while you are here;
For Jehovah, Jehovah God on high,
For me he died, for him will I.
    For Jehovah, &c.

8.

Our prophets bravely stood their ground,
And stood the test with great and small;
When that Christ Jesus, God they found,
They would not move, so let us all
Praise Jehovah, Jehovah God above,
Our God who died for us in love.
    Praise Jehovah, &c.

JAMES FROST, 1803.

TWO HUNDRED AND TENTH SONG.
(TUNE, 'Gramachree Molly.')

SAINTS, join with me to praise the God
  Of Reeve and Muggleton,
The king of heaven, the Lord of life,
  Christ the eternal one,
The great I AM who all things made
  In earth and heaven above,
Come, join in concert evermore,
  Returning praise for love.

2.

On viewing the creation round,
  Reason determin'd goes
To find out from whose attributes
  Such beauteous order flows;
But all in vain, their piercing wit
  Can't search the things of heaven;
None can by force obtain the prize,
  To faith it's only given.

3.

Well may the holy angels sing
  Their praises to our God,
Who of dead matter brought them forth,

By his all powerful word,
Into an endless life of joy,
  Where revelation do
Continually their souls supply,
  With transports sweet and new.

4.

Well might their joys and praise abound,
  When they beheld the fall
Of reason from its highest state,
  To this terrestrial ball;
Oh! how their joys most then increase,
  When they by reason saw
God's loving kindness to an end
  No nigher e'er would draw.

5.

Well may they sing creative love,
  For sin they never knew,
Had they remain'd in dreary death,
  No joys would e'er ensue;
Were all now left in darkness bound,
  No beauty could appear,
But love sent forth a fiery sound,
  That pierc'd dead nature's ear.

6.

Well may creative love demand
  From innocence great praise,
But when I found redeeming love,
  Myself was lost in maze;
Well might I strand as one that's dead
  To all things here below,
When faith did rise to heavenly joys,
  My soul once wrapt in woe.

7.

Who can devise words to express
  God's love to sinners shown,
When he resign'd his blessed state,
  His power, his heavenly throne,
And veil'd his glory here in seed,
  Within a virgin's womb;
There fed and nourish'd with her life,
  And thus became a Son?

8.
From seed his holy nature grew,
　　Nature brings its own form;
The virgin went her travail thro',
　　Sweet Jesus he was born,
Matur'd by years a perfect man,
　　With temper meek and mild,
Tho' tempted by bold reason, he
　　Could never be beguil'd.

9.
I need not sing his sufferings now,
So many and severe,
This will suffice, they crucified,
And goad him with a spear,
Until his precious life was spent,
His soul pour'd out to death;
They kill'd the Lord of heaven and earth,
Who gave them life and breath.

10.
Dry up your tears, dear saints, rejoice,
　　Death could not long detain;
A life so pure, in three days time
　　Our God arose again,
And did ascend his glorious throne,
　　His power took above,
But left his blood on earth to saints,
　　A token of his love.

11.
Impossible it is for love
Ever to exceed his,
Will any king thus suffer death,
To give a rebel bliss?
And if one suffer in his stead,
Why then without dispute,
The glory must on him attach,
Who is the substitute.

12.
But, oh! God's love was infinite,
　　The glory all his own,
Creation and redemption too,
　　He wrought himself alone;
The eternal Father wholly died,
　　When in the flesh a Son,

When Jesus Christ was crucified,
  Then died the eternal One.

13.

Redeeming love its pond'rous weight,
  I feel with pleasure sweet,
Bending beneath that mass so great,
  I bow at Jesus's feet;
Strain all your powers, oh! my soul,
  Pour forth an endless flood
Of adorative praise to Christ,
  My soul redeeming God.

                              JAMES DALE.

TWO HUNDRED AND ELEVENTH SONG.
(TUNE, 'Upon a summer's evening.')

WHEN first the third record I heard,
  It seem'd strange to me,
To venture there I was afraid,
  Till I could clearly see,
By faith which in my soul lay dead,
  By reason quite confin'd;
For reason rul'd as lord and head,
  For faith was born quite blind.

2.

I smote the rock of ages sure,
  And made the waters flow;
This water did my sold secure,
  And made my faith to grow;
From strength to strength on Zion's hill,
  My soul does swiftly fly,
And when grim death my soul does kill,
  I die to live on high.

3.

And when God calls us up from death,
  For to eat of his feast,
And gives us an immortal breath,
  How sweet that food will taste;
Come, eat the flesh of monarchs great,
  Our God to us will cry,
For they are those that did me hate,
  And caus'd my soul to die.

4.

Feed on the lying priests of Baal,
  For they are for your food;
Devour all, both great and small,
  Eat of that cursed brood;
Rejoice with me that they are damn'd,
  For they no pity shew'd;
They shew'd me none when I did stand
  Falsely condemn'd below.

5.

Eat of the devils, great and small,
  You need not for to spare;
My powerful word shall summons all
  In justice to appear;
Great popes and princes, high in power,
  And men of great renown,
I freely give you to devour,
  For none now wears a crown.

6.

When we are at this glorious feast,
  How we our God shall praise;
When we the flesh of devils taste,
  Our voices we shall raise
In praises to our glorious king,
  Redeeming God on high;
And with harmonious voices sing,
  Christ reigns eternally.

BOYER GLOVER.

TWO HUNDHED AND TWELFTH SONG.
(TUNE, 'If you mean to set sail for the land of delight.')

How blest is my time now,
  What days do I see,
Since Jesus my God
  Is revealed to me;
The blossoms of nature
  E'er beauteous appear,
And the odours of May
  Sheds perfumes thro' the year.

2.

When I wander'd about
 In the darkness of night,
And hell with its terrors,
 My soul did affright,
What beauty or fragrance
 Could long charm my soul,
When the waves of despondence
 So quickly did roll?

3.

But glory to God now,
 The horizon's clear,
The clouds are dispell'd,
 The bright sun doth appear,
By its light nature's seen
 In its bridal array,
Progressively moving,
 In harmonious play.

4.

Now delighted, the
 Meanders of scripture I trace,
Where God, as it were,
 Is beheld face to face;
The prophets there lead us,
 Thro' paths all divine,
Where the footsteps of God
 Doth transcendently shine.

5.

They lead through a series
 Of bliss here below,
A taste of delights
 That forever will grow,
A succession of transports
 That never will cloy,
From immensity springs
 In one eternal joy.

6.

Then you who have tasted
Those sweets that's so rare,
You know no delights on
This earth can compare;
Then what shall restrain us

That's favor'd so high,
From praising our God
Unto eternity.

JAMES DALE.

TWO HUNDRED AND THIRTEENTH SONG.
(TUNE, 'The Waterman,' and 'Gently touch the warbling lyre.')

WHILE thro' this wicked world I pass,
   Temptations shall I meet;
Which so alluring are, alas!
   So prevalent and sweet;
Nature and reason both combine,
   To lead my soul astray,
Unless my faith which is divine,
   And active doth obey.

2.

When by them both I'm overcome,
   And subject to their power,
The law awakens to confound,
   And my soul's peace devour,
My mind is sear'd with my guilt,
   What horror I endure,
Till I can see Christ's blood was spilt,
   Which doth my soul secure.

3.

What sad destructive thoughts arise,
   What darkness clouds my mind;
What fears and what anxieties,
   Rest no where can I find;
But like a ball tost to and fro,
   By reason I am hurl'd;
A hell in mind I undergo,
   Tho' fair unto the world.

4.

I self condemn'd to justice lay,
   Yet when it doth appear,
Fain would I escape, fain would I fly,
   But that I know not where;
No refuge is there to be found,
   For wheresoe'er I go,
God still is with me with his law,

His law condemns me so.

5.

If for the breach of moral acts,
   Such punishments ensue,
What must blaspheming cursed facts,
   Which reason daily do;
If such exceeding torments are
   By mortals felt below;
What must they be that are prepar'd
   For an eternal woe?

6.

Oh! Christ, for thy redeeming love,
   I'll ever homage pay,
And when from death I'm call'd above,
   Will praise thee eternally;
For thy electing love it is
   To my poor soul below,
Assur'd me of eternal bliss,
   A ransom from all woe.

7.

The sweet enjoyment I possess,
   When free from reason's reign,
The tongue of man cannot express,
   Or thought conceive my gain;
But when it doth with nature join,
   Doth my frail flesh subdue,
Guilt, fear and shame, my soul divide,
   I know not what to do.

8.

Guilt first for the offence I've done,
   In breaking of the law;
Fear of a tortur'd state to come,
   Next makes me stand in awe;
Shame charges me with ingratitude,
   To my great God on high,
Whose mercy I have much abus'd,
   Therefore deserve to die.

9.

But my dear Saviour's precious blood,
   That sovereign balsam sure,
Applied by faith, my wounded soul

No longer smart endures;
For it was for this he left his throne,
   Assum'd humanity,
To his own law became a Son,
   Walk'd thro' the law for me.

10.

Oh! wondrous works! stupendous love!
   That very God should come,
And leave his glorious throne above,
   And mortal flesh assume;
That he who made the worlds alone,
   Should leave divine abode,
And suffer death, to be death's death,
   While man, he's very God.

11.

Oh! how astonishing it is,
   To think Eternity,
Who was the immortal source of bliss
   In immortality,
Should heaven leave, for us come down,
   And Adam's race employ,
To be a God to him their God.
   Till he should death destroy.

12.

For Moses and Elias sat
   On heaven's imperial throne;
Till God begat himself a Son,
   In the chaste virgin's womb;
And they it were who from above,
   Protected him below,
From infancy to years mature,
   Till he himself did know.

13.

What cause of admiration here,
   To us who know his love,
Since 'twas for us he thus appear'd,
   And left those joys above;
Come, saints, with raptur'd joys like mine
   Your thankful voices raise,
For there's no joys like joys divine,
   No melody like praise.

14.
His matchless love, my friends, with me,
  Come, meditate upon;
The more I think, the more I am lost,
  In extacies o'ercome;
Yet tho' I can't my joys express,
  My soul does still adore,
An earnest which I here possess,
  Of praising evermore.

15.
By faith I saw him suffer death
  Upon a cursed tree;
By faith I saw him in the grave,
  Under captivity;
By faith I saw him rise again,
  By his own power on high;
And in triumphant manner, led
  Captive captivity.

16.
My faith then soar'd with him above,
  Into eternity,
And saw him resume his throne,
  Of immortality;
And as a Son the right hard took
  Of power and majesty;
Not from another, but himself,
  To all eternity.

17.
His faithful stewards did with joy,
  Surrender up their power,
Again as creatures homage paid,
  And did their God adore;
While the innumerable host
  Of angels round his throne,
Submissive at his royal feet,
  Laid their immortal crowns.

18.
The joy the eternal Spirit hath,
  The Father now on high,
With what he hath cloth'd himself withal,
  To all eternity;
That glorious garment of the flesh,

The joys that there do flow,
Not men nor angels can express,
The Father only knows.

19.

Christ Jesus, my redeemer dear,
   I still by faith can see,
Who was one undivided God,
   From all eternity;
Who's still the same, for in him dwells
   The godhead bodily:
God over all, none over him,
   To all eternity.

20.

He Father was, when made the world,
   And all therein contain'd;
And to redeem elect mankind,
   For them a Son became;
And now the Holy Ghost he is,
   By sanctifying those,
By faith in this commission, whim
   Before the world he chose.

21.

This is the very God, which is
   Eternal life to know;
Those that despise his real death,
   Their portion's endless woe;
By faith in him, I am assur'd,
   He has procured for me,
And all believers too, a crown
   Of immortality.

                                JAMES MILLER.

TWO HUNDRED AND FOURTEENTH SONG.

When darkness in her sable dress,
   This region overspread,
And reason as king did reign,
   The lambs with husks were fed,
They rang'd along o'er reason's plain,
   Some comfort for to find,
But all in vain, their hopes were dead,
      But all, &c.
Close in a restless mind.

2.
This darkness did such famine bring;
  The children cried for bread;
And those that did their fathers feed,
  Lay in their presence dead;
Great burthens did the children bear,
  With hunger, thirst and cold,
They wanted then their daily bread,
      They wanted, &c.
  More worth than the fairest gold.

3.
Then Shilo in his tender love,
  To immortals here below,
Sent forth a light which is divine,
  And marvellous to know;
Two shepherds then, he forth did send,
  The prisoners to relieve;
And eke to every thirsty soul,
      And eke, &c.
  Fresh waters they do give.

4.
The virtue of this water doth
  All poison soon expel;
It is a present antidote
  Against the fears of hell;
'Tis in the shepherds' hands alone,
  No man can them controul,
And of the same they freely give,
      And of, &c.
  To every thirsty soul.

5.
And he that drinks shall thirst no more,
  But still in streams will flow;
Each saint that tasteth of the same,
  Doth by experience know,
The streams thereof doth bear such force,
  The prisoners it sets free;
It converts foes to friends, and sets
      It converts, &c.
  The greatest friends at greatest enmity.

6.
In February, fifty and one, the grace it did abound,

And every saint that did it taste,
Their tears with joys are crown'd;
　Then let's lift up our hearts and souls,
To Shilo's name entire;
　If time could speak, then sure this month,
　　　If time, &c.
　Would join to make a choir.

7.

Oh! God whose love is pure divine,
　To us poor mortals here;
Whose heavenly light doth shine so bright,
　To those that do thee fear,
Our hearts and souls in raptures join,
　To praise thy holy name;
Let all the saints the world throughout,
　　　Let all, &c.
　For ever do the same.

WILLIAM WOOD, Painter.

TWO HUNDRED AND FIFTEENTH SONG.
On the Three Commissions.

Now to the scriptures I my mind will bend,
And to those writings pious men have penn'd;
For now by faith alone I'm come to see,
That here on earth have been commissions three;
First, Moses had his mission from the Lord,
The meekest man that is upon record,
From Egypt's darkness Israel's sons to free,
And from their bondage give them liberty ;
The next, was the commission of the blood,
Where persecution flow 'd like a flood,
'Twas brought by Jesus, call'd, the Son of God;
Who heal'd the lame, and made the blind to see,
The dumb to speak, the dead too rais'd he;
With whom curs'd priests and pharisees made strife,
And on a cross they nail'd the Lord of life;
But at his death what darkness did appear,
The sun was darken'd like sackcloth of hair;
Then did they tremble, quake and shake with fear,
Yet saints and apostles they us'd most severe,
And persecuted near three hundred year,
Till not a saint on earth was left behind,
But all men in religion were quite blind;
Then God by his most holy Spirit shone
Upon great Reeve and Muggleton,

That all men here should not in darknes be,
But some should praise their God continually;
The mysteries of the scriptures they reveal'd,
And nothing from God's prophets was conceal'd,
And they as freely gave as they receiv'd,
To those who in their record could believe;
And bless'd am I, to know I'm not deceiv'd,
For how should I have known that Christ was God,
If I had not in this commission trod;
The soul being mortal, or the place of hell,
Or heaven's throne where holy angels dwell;
For this my faith has made me rich indeed,
To know that I am of that bless'd seed;
When all the world will here in darkness be,
I shall ascend my glorious God to see,
Cloth'd with a white robe of my most holy faith,
Crown'd with a bright crown, for so the scripture saith.
WILLIAM CATES.

TWO HUNDRED AND SIXTEENTH SONG.
(TUNE, 'Kitty of the Clyde.')

MY soul glides on God's holy stream,
   In the third commission flowing,
Such beauteous treasures there are seen,
   God's prophets there are showing;
Great Reeve and Muggleton is there,
   As guardians of the tide;
They show'd me the fountain clear,
   Was Christ once crucified.

2.

God was from all eternity,
   His nature faith quite pure;
And so for ever will remain,
   This I by faith am sure;
And tho' a God, so great was he,
   Surpassing all beside,
I know it was God who died for me,
   When Christ was crucified.

3.

Death was from all eternity,
   His nature reason sure;
God did his angels bright create,

Their nature reason pure;
But one, more glorious than the rest,
   God's wisdom vilified;
God cast him down upon this earth,
   And woe doth him betide.

4.

God did create man in his form,
   Upon this earth, I am sure;
And when in his created state,
   His nature faith was pure;
But the lost angel him o'ercame,
   And so God's work destroy'd;
But God o'ercame this angel's power,
   When Christ was crucified.

5.

God sent his prophets unto men,
   His wondrous works to tell,
That he did die upon a tree,
   To redeem lost souls from hell;
Great Reeve and Muggleton declare,
   With them I am satisfied;
They show'd to me God suffer'd here,
   When Christ was crucified.

ISAAC FROST, 1829.

TWO HUNDRED AND SEVENTEENTH SONG.

YE faithful Muggletonians all,
Who are Muggletonians truly,
Let us with joy commemorate
This nineteenth day of July;
And let it ever be
A yearly jubilee
Of praise by us regarded;
When Muggleton the great,
Was set free from reason's hate,
And from prison was discharg'd.
         When Muggleton, &c.

2.

This was the joyful day indeed,
He was from goal releas'd;
Which bare remembrance fills my soul,
I find my joys increas'd;

The devils did combine,
For ever to confine
The Almighty's last annointed;
But what they thought to do,
Great Muggleton to you
This day were disappointed.
      But what, &c.

3.

Fain would their cursed malice do
By him, as the Messiah;
Destruction was their only view,
As 'twas to Jeremiah;
For they without dispute,
Had destroy'd tree and fruit,
Had their law but been provided,
For they did him despise,
And charge with writing lies,
And eternal truth derided.
      For they, &c.

4.

Their hellish rage was fully bent,
To finish his undoing;
The prophet they to prison sent,
To prove his utter ruin;
For since no way they saw,
They could touch his life by law,
Five hundred pounds they fin'd him;
But Muggleton this day,
The unjust fine did pay,
And left his foes behind him.
      But Muggleton, &c.

5.

Tho' they like kings in judgment sat,
Triumphing for a season,
Eternal death will be their lot,
With the rest of curs'd reason;
For when time comes that time
To eternity resign,
Their heaven then is ceased,
What they enjoy'd below,
Will be turned into woe,
And their torments ever increased.
      What they, &c.

6.
Then will great Muggleton and Reeve
Ascend with this commission,
And all who truly did believe
In this their sacred mission;
And we shall ever be
To all eternity,
With Christ our God receiving
New glorious crowns of praise;
Melodiously shall raise
Our voices, no longer believing.
    New glorious, &c.

7.
For faith which was an earnest here
Of that eternal treasure,
Will in enjoyment disappear,
Be swallow'd up in pleasure;
Hope will no longer then
Our longing souls attend,
In fruition it will be drowned;
But love, eternal love,
In eternity above,
Will with joys be forever surrounded.
    But love, &c.

8.
When time does come, that time must die,
That dreadful trump is sounded,
The dead in Christ will first arise,
To meet their God, surrounded
With hosts of angels bright,
Too great for reason's sight;
He'll open this creation,
Then we shall all repair
To attend him in the air,
Christ, God of our salvation,
    Then we, &c.

9.
Then will our foes, both great and small,
Be left in peak confusion,
Amidst the wreck of this fair ball,
Dame nature's last conclusion;
What dreadful horror then
Will seize the souls of men,

Who here are left confin'd,
When all will be on fire,
No place for to retire,
But to torments eternally join'd.
      When all, &c.

10.

Then come, my friends, their power scorn,
Since faith to us is given;
This world will quickly have an end,
Our hell, but reason's heaven;
Then, then the scale will turn,
They will for ever burn;
While we in joys are reigning
With Christ our God alone,
And Reeve and Muggleton,
In eternal bliss remaining.
      With Christ, &c.

11.

Those that proud reason did disdain,
Were favourites of heaven;
To whom by our dear Saviour Christ,
Eternal life is given;
Then let us ever praise
His mercy all our days,
And let this day be regarded,
When Muggleton the great,
Was set free from reason's hate,
And from prison was discharged.
      When Muggleton, &c.

                              WILLIAM MILLER.

TWO HUNDRED AND EIGHTEENTH SONG.
(TUNE, 'O God of all Gods and prince of all peace.')

OH! now, blessed saints, by divine revelation,
Sing praises to God for this his creation,
Considering well the works he hath done,
It's he was God the Father. and then God the Son,
And God the holy Ghost, as the scriptures show,
Or God the holy Spirit in these our days.
Then saints now on earth, his praises forth show,
By this third and last commission these secrets we
      know.

2.
As he was God the Father, he created on high
An host of holy angels for his society,
A glorious creation that were all elected
To fulfil his purpose, one only rejected;
His prerogative will compell'd him to create
That angelical serpent in reprobate state.
      Then saints, &c.

3.
This angel was created a glorious creature,
The image of God, but only his nature;
His nature pure reason remain'd in that station,
By being supplied by divine revelation,
Whom God did prefer to the highest degree,
All for his own glory, by a secret decree.
      Then saints, &c.

4.
Our glorious God his revelation withheld,
Which from his own nature, soon after rebell'd;
Then Jehovah was mov'd by his revelation,
To create here below another creation,
Representing the creation in heaven high,
In a blessed slate of innocency.
      Then saints, &c.

5.
Then he form'd man a wonderful creature,
The image of God, both in form and nature,
He made him the ruler of this creation to be,
And gave him a woman for his society;
And them in the garden of Eden put he,
In a blessed estate of immortality.
      Then saints, &c.

6.
This angel in heaven, he did so appear,
That God cast him down to the earth like fire,
He banish'd him out of his presence to be
Confin'd in this world to all eternity,
The prerogative power of God for to show,
To exalt some on high, and some to bring low.
      Then saints, &c.

7.
Then he had given by God, his creator,

The fruit of all trees to nourish his nature,
Except the tree of knowledge of good and evil,
Which afterwards known, a serpent, a devil,
Not for to eat by command from on high,
If that he did eat, he should surely die.
    Then saints, &c.

8.

When the angel once saw her, he did her admire,
She to taste of his fruit did much desire,
She, looking, beholding such a glorious person,
Forgot her command, and yielded her affection,
To come in unto her, in which act indeed,
He dissolved himself in her pure seed.
    Then saints, &c.

9.

Which she naturally conceived a serpent and devil,
That very man Cain, whose actions are evil;
His nature being in her, desire was so high,
That she did beguile her husband thereby,
Wherein they lost their bliss and satisfaction,
For a horrible fear of eternal separation.
    Then saints, &c.

10.

Then God gave promise, for the sake of his seed,
That the seed of the woman should break the serpent's
    head,
That his divine power became mortal to be,
To raise him again to immortality;
This promise to Adam it was his supply,
By faith he believ'd, and in peace he should die.
    Then saints, &c.

11.

Then Elijah and Moses, who were of his seed,
He took up to heaven, the angels to feed,
And them for to rule on his glorious throne,
And dissolv'd himself in the virgin's womb;
Thus the immortal God; of all things the creator,
He became a spotless babe, nurs'd up by his creatures.
    Then saints, &c.

12.

And as he grew up, did give a relation

Unto the seed of faith of the third commission,
That he was the Son of God, and came to relieve,
The sinners out of bondage, that by faith did believe;
This being so contrary for the world to know,
That they used him worse than a beast here below.
    Then saints, &c.

13.
They laid to his charge their high blasphemy,
For which they condemn'd him, and judg'd him to die;
They made him bear his cross to be crucified on,
And then a crown of thorns on his head they put on,
And scoffing Ishmael his nature did show,
And bid him help himself, if how he did know.
    Then saints, &c.

14.
To finish his work, as he was God the Son,
He gave up the ghost, for which he did come,
His Godhead life died in his body, I say,
And immortal he rose again the third day;
And now, daring devil, to thy coat thou shalt know,
Thou hast helped thyself to thy eternal woe.
    Then saints, &c.

15.
For now he is ascended to his glory on high,
And will execute justice for reason's cruelty;
Rejoice therefore, saints, he hath conquer'd all,
Death, hell and the grave for glory eternal;
A wonder of wonders, by faith the elect see,
His hell here below makes heaven to be.
    Then saints, &c.

16.
In the year fifty-one, by faith we believe,
That by voice of words God spoke to John Reeve,
And gave him a commission far passing the sun,
And gave, to be his mouth, Lodowick Muggleton,
Wherein the holy God, though titles are three,
Are plainly made appear one person to be.
    Then saints, &c.

17.
The knowledge of the scripture to them it was given,
With the knowledge of hell and the kingdom of heaven,
With the sword of the Spirit, God's battles to fight,

And to give saints and devils each nature their right,
As being chosen judges from a power on high,
And have power to judge all in mortality.
    Then saints, &c.

18.
The acceptable worship they have made known
        thereby,
And it was in old time, the world doth deny;
For which they have justl'd and abus'd him also,
And set him as a mark in the pillory too,
As did their forefathers in a most cursed mood,
They have shed again the blood of the prophet of God.
    Then saints, &c.

19.
It was always the actions of reason in hell,
To fight against faith with a sword of steel;
Bear up therefore, saints, in that you know well,
The pathway to heaven it is through hell;
When past, we have joy sod felicity,
With God, saints and angels to all eternity.
    Then saints, &c.
                        WILLIAM WOOD.

TWO HUNDRED AND NINETEENTH SONG.
(TUNE, 'Bonny Broom.')

WHEN first I saw how God came down,
    For his own seed to die;
How he did veil his Godhead crown,
    In pure mortality;
How he did die, lost knowledge great,
    What he did come to do;
His own decree's did him protect,
    Till man's estate he knew;
Oh! the blood, the precious blood,
    That from my God did flow,
It's heal'd my soul, and made it good,
    It's freed me from all woe.

2.
So exceeding well he lov'd his seed,
    He twice for them did die;
See on a cross his Godhead bleed,

Which in a womb did lie;
When I was prisoner confin'd,
  And in my blood must die,
He to be my ransom was inclin'd,
  And for his friend did die.
    Oh! the &c.

3.

Since he such wondrous works did do,
  For his belov'd elect;
Be, brethren, to each other true,
  Let none God's friends reject;
The man of war from death and hell,
  The victory regain'd;
Against such love let none rebel,
  He died to save his friend.
    Oh! the &c.

4.

His blood like Elisha's salt to me
  To cure my barren soul;
From bitterness it set me free,
  And made me perfect whole;
In peace I'll pass my pilgrimage,
  Waiting while God shall come,
To call me off this mortal stage,
  So come, sweet Jesus, come.
    Oh! the, &c.

                                    JOHN PEAT.

TWO HUNDRED AND TWENTIETH SONG.
(TUNE, 'Darby and Joan.')

WHEN God had left Jacob he halted,
When his reason it did interfere;
But oh! how his soul did rejoice,
When the Son of his God did appear,
In raptures of soul he then cried,
My God to redeem me will die;
And came from his kingdom above,
That I may live eternally.
    And came, &c.

2.

How grateful his soul it flow'd over,
For to praise his alone God divine;
Because in his soul he could see

The light of redemption did shine;
It quite him astonish'd with wonder,
To think that the Father on high,
Who caus'd us all for to live,
Should suffer so far as to die.
      Who caus'd, &c.

3.

These, these are God's reveal'd treasures,
Which he givers to us mortals below;
Rut when we do come up above,
We more of his secrets shall know;
There's a host of great angels so bright,
By the law they God's praises doth sing;
While we by the faith in our souls,
Shall adore our Redeemer and king.
      While we, &c.

4.

My soul has been wash'd in God's blood,
Not a spot or a stain can I see;
The law it me cannot accuse,
From all my past sins I am set free;
This, this is the state of the blest,
When by faith they can soar up on high,
They'll see God did die for their sins,
That they might live eternally.
      They'll see, &c.

5.

This, this is a beautiful treasure,
To the soul that has got it in store;
It makes him his God for to praise,
And his glorious person adore;
It makes him in peace here to dwell,
And his soul here in raptures to join;
It shows him there's no joys like faith,
No praises like praises divine.
      It shows, &c.

                              BOYER GLOVER.

TWO HUNDRED AND TWENTY-FIRST SONG.
    (TUNE, 'Scots wha hae wi' Wallace bled.')

COME, my friends, with me rejoice,
Sound forth your praise with heart and voice,

To our God who hath made choice,
   His messengers to be;
Of Muggleton and Reeve the great,
His profound secrets to relate,
Which from time's most early date,
   Had lain in mystery.
       Of Muggleton, &c.

2.

Now's declar'd the mind of God,
In the third and last record;
Believe, and sure is the reward
   Of bliss eternally;
If persecution, pain, or woe,
For our faith we undergo,
Patience will o'ercome the foe,
   And gain the victory.
       If persecution, &c.

3.

For our sins Christ Jesus bled
On the cross till he was dead,
In whom dwelt the whole Godhead
   This I by faith do see;
He rose again in mighty power,
At his own appointed hour,
Did sin, death and hell o'erpower,
   And reigns eternally.
       He rose, &c.

4.

In love and unity let's join,
To praise our God that's so divine;
With him in glory we shall shine,
   To all eternity;
And leave proud reason here below,
Their punishment to undergo,
To live an endless life of woe,
   In shame and misery.
       And leave, &c.

                        JOSEPH GANDAR, 1829.

TWO HUNDRED AND TWENTY-SECOND SONG.
(TUNE, 'Maid of Lodi.')

I AM did unto Moses make known,
   His people from bootleg he'd free;

Then his power in Egypt was shewn,
   As in Exodus you may see;
And those that did Moses believe,
   And the prophets under the law,
They all full assurance receiv'd,
   When they their ransom saw.

2.

I AM is the rock of all ages,
   On which my faith I'll build;
To him I'll sing all praises,
   For his promise he has fulfill'd;
The third record on earth he has sent,
   This mystery for to make known;
What God in man underwent,
   By his last prophets is shown.

3.

I AM, our glorious God and Creator,
   Came down from his kingdom above,
To take on himself human nature,
   And twice died for those he lov'd;
First, he died in the virgin's womb,
   Then quicken'd unto life again;
And pure mortal flesh did assume,
   Then was God a Son become.

4.

For unto us this Son was given,
   In brave Judah's royal line,
He was the very God from heaven,
   For eternity was become time;
Great I AM was then become Jesus,
   For all Adam's sons to die,
And from eternal death to release us,
   That we might live eternally.

5.

For on this earth Our God did dwell,
   And great miracles he did do;
But devils against him did rebel,
   Altho' his law he walk'd through;
They were fill'd with envy and strife
   Against Jesus Christ which we adore,
For they kill'd his Godhead life,
   When they shed the purple gore.

6.
For on a cross our God did die,
   And into the grave did descend,
Three days in the earth did lie,
   Until death's power did end;
Then the eternal God quicken'd again,
   And Christ from death did ascend;
Then time was eternity become,
   And their power was at an end.

7.
And now he sits upon his throne,
   In the boundless heavens high,
In that body of flesh and bone,
   Which the Father did glorify;
And he wears his royal crown,
   And his stewards do him greet,
For they gladly did lay down,
   All power at his royal feet.

8.
And suddenly there came a sound
   On the day of Penticost,
Which did man's reason confound,
   When the apostles received the holy Ghost;
For with cloven tongues of fire,
   They did preach God's boundless love,
For he did only them inspire
   With a commission from above.

9.
It was the gospel dispensation,
That was given unto each of them,
To preach unto all nations;
So they began at Jerusalem,
And they did all preach with power;
Peter and John did a miracle great,
Near the temple about the ninth hour,
On a man, at the Beautiful Gate.

10.
And those that did repent and believe,
In Jesus Christ that was crucified,
Sweet consolation they all did receive,
In their faith were well satisfied;
For the waters of life did arise,
Which did them with love inspire;

But all those that did despise,
Were tormented with internal fire.

11.

This fire was burning in wrath,
In all the ten persecutions;
For they put the apostles to death,
And believers in their commission;
Then a famine came in the land,
Neither of bread nor of water,
The true God they did not understand,
When the devils had made a great slaughter.

12.

Those devils were men of reason,
And true faith they did banish,
Then came that dark and dreary season,
When the elect was all famish'd;
In God's decreed time, two stars appear'd,
The wisdom of reason to confound,
Then true faith was again declar'd,
After seven anti-angels did sound.

13.

For Jesus Christ, who is God alone,
Gave the third commission
Unto John Reeve and Muggleton,
To tell the elect their blest condition;
If by faith they do believe;
This is the true worship of God,
Declar'd by Muggleton and Reeve,
In this third and last record.

14.

In this worship there is no preaching,
Nor prayers for external show;
For that's the way reason is teaching
The children of this world below;
We worship God in spirit and truth,
Without any external show;
We understand the forbidden fruit,
And the tree of life also.

15.

And whilst here on earth we live,
Let us sing praises to our king,

For all those blessings he does give,
Until we do feel death's sting;
For when grim death does come,
And our mortal souls does smite,
Then our race on earth will be run,
And we shall be put out of sight.

16.

And in the silent dust shall sleep,
Until our God does call;
Death then no longer can us keep,
We shall be freed from devils all;
All Adam's sons will then arise,
And unto heaven will ascend,
To live with God above the skies,
When this world is at an end.

JOHN BERRIDGE, 1829.

TWO HUNDRED AND TWENTY-THIRD SONG.
On 19th of July 1677, being the day the Prophet Muggleton was discharged out of Newgate.

THIS is the day God's holy Prophet came
Out of their hands, who are the seed of Cain;
Let us that are of Abel's seed then sing,
All praise and glory be to heaven's great king;
They spilt his blood, their cup for to fill,
As did their seed his fellow prophets kill;
But now there is no more for them to have,
Nor mercy left, their wretched souls to save;
But we that do our own salvation know,
Lift up our minds above these things below,
That by our spiritual worship we may bring
A savour sweet unto our heavenly king,
Who did for us his heavenly kingdom leave,
And to those serpents he his blood did give,
To be pour'd out, our souls for to redeem,
By death kept under by the seed of Cain,
Which these two prophets have to us made known,
That our eternal God calls us his own;
Then, let's rejoice, and let us merry make
Upon this day, for our great prophet's sake.

MARTHA JENKINS.

Divine Songs

TWO HUNDRED AND TWENTY-FOURTH SONG.
(TUNE, 'Oh! Wondrous great! amazing strange!')

To thee, my God, gratitude I owe,
Thou hast given me thyself to know,
By thy prophets in thy mission,
John Reeve and Lodowick Muggleton.
     By thy, &c.

2.
Thy mysteries they have made plain,
Though eat obtain'd by learned men;
Mercy and justice is all thine,
Thou'lt prove, I see, at end of time.
     Mercy and, &c.

3.
Light and darkness real substance be,
Distinct from all eternity;
Now God is light and life, I see,
In form of man eternally.
     Now God, &c.

4.
Death in darkness secretly lay,
Hid in the earth eternally;
Above this world in heaven high,
Distinct in root and fruit clearly.
     Above their, &c.

5.
God's person bright, his nature faith,
All power to create he hath;
Death without form in dark chaos lay,
Till God call'd him forth from that clay.
     Death without, &c.

6.
In man's form the angelic host,
Their nature's pure reason at most;
One angel brighter than the rest,
More Godlike wisdom manifest.
     One angel, &c.

7.
Created angels Resplendent all,

Swift as thought under a moral law;
A light that guides them God to know,
By which they pure obedience show.
  A light, &c.

      8.
Various creatures beside,
Their splendid forms a law doth guide;
All in sweet harmony they greet
Their God who made them so complete.
  All in, &c.

      9.
God had all things in heaven made,
This earth and water he survey'd;
Then fram'd this world and did create
Kinds like those in his blest estate.
  Then fram'd, &c.

      10.
The breath of life in Adam sown,
Immortal seed of God alone;
In Adam and Eve were replete,
God by his word made all complete.
  In Adam, &c.

      11.
That Godlike angel ho rebell'd,
When revelation, God withheld;
God and angels thought to destroy,
Almighty power he'd then enjoy.
  God and, &c.

      12.
Then God condemn'd, and cast him down,
Upon this earth to wear a crown;
Then those his thoughts he did fulfil,
When Christ and saints he here did kill.
  Then those, &c.

      13.
Goa gave to Adam a command,
'Harken not to that tree, now mind,
If thou dost, thou shall surely die,
His nature will thy life destroy.'
  If thou, &c.

14.
When the serpent appear'd to Eve,
In tempting her he did deceive,
His subtile counsel rais'd desire,
In her to embrace his subtile fire.
    His subtile, &c.

15.
In her womb himself he did sow,
Spiritual tares here below;
Adam beguil'd, then death did arrest
God's created immortal breath.
    Adam beguil'd, &c.

16.
All became mortal, death then reign'd,
Time and increase now took their range;
For Adam's sake God all things curst,
The serpent above all the rest.
    For Adam's, &c.

17.
God them a precious promise made,
'Again partake of life,' he said,
'My grace shall break the serpent's head;
For sin he'll bruise your life till dead.'
    My grace, &c.

18.
Cain is the angel god of death,
His brother he depriv'd of breath;
The tares and wheat together grow,
Love and strife in our souls doth show.
    The tares, &c.

19.
God's bright body became a son,
When he enter'd the virgin's womb,
In which did dwell the Godhead life,
The true altar and sacrifice.
    In which, &c.

20.
Eternal life was sacrific'd,
When Christ our God was crucified;
No other flesh, blood, or life's breath,

Could e'er conquer eternal death.
    No other, &c.

21.

Behold, our God he rose again,
See death and hell by him o'ercame;
All those that do this God despise,
Above this earth will never rise.
    All those, &c.

22.

It was eternal life, nought less,
Could redeem us from the jaws of death;
All you that see his wondrous ways,
With me praise the ancientest of days.

JOSEPH FROST, 1829.

TWO HUNDRED AND TWENTY-FIFTH SONG.
(TUNE, 'Believers now let us rejoice.')

OH! how my soul it doth rejoice,
  Now I my God can see;
To know of me he has made choice,
  A companion with him to be;
The more I view my happy state,
  With angels and saints to be,
And with our dear God so great,
  To all eternity.
    The more, &c.

2.

Our blessed prophets have declar'd,
  Such heavenly mysteries;
None but the elect are prepar'd,
  These glorious truths to see;
I see my God has died for me,
  This truth proud reason scorns;
But my dear God they'll never see,
  But on this earth will mourn.
    I see, &c.

3.

Their body's too heavy to ascend
  Into a kingdom that's so bright;

What sorrows will on them attend,
 It will be an endless night,
While we shall rise above the skies,
 Our glorious God to see;
The angels bright will us greet
 Into this great felicity.
  While we, &c.

    4.

Come then, my friends, and with me join,
 Our only God to praise,
Since he hath given us, here in time,
 A taste of those glorious rays,
Which we shall have with him above,
 New songs our souls delight;
The theme will be redeeming love,
 In that kingdom that's so bright.
  Which we &c.

      CHARLOTTE FROST, 1829.

TWO HUNDRED AND TWENTY-SIXTH SONG.

No more I despair...adieu to all grief,
What the prophets declare, I now truly believe
In the year ninety-five, I was cur'd of my blindness,
Though deaf, dumb and lame, now restor'd by their
   kindness.
  Though deaf, &c.

    2.

A land of thick darkness I left far behind,
Their chains or their fetters no longer could bind;
They're but cobwebs to faith, tho' stronger than iron,
The advantage we have who are come to Mount Zion.
  The advantage, &c.

    3.

I have got a new name which no man can read,
Wrote in a strange language, and few will believe;
I am a lamb of God's fold, with the sheep of his
   pasture,
Like the lunatic cloth'd at the feet of my master.
  Like the, &c.

    4.

I hear his sweet voice, no other can charm,

At the sound, I rejoice, and no danger alarm,
He's so mild and so patient, such sweet condescension,
Though my progress is small, he accepts my intention.
    Though my, &c.

5.

Oh may my heart be found upright before him,
Though late is my day, I but live to adore him;
But when I behold him in all his bright glory,
I shall sing a new song and repeat the glad story.
    I shall, &c.

6.

This is paradise sure, to be seal'd for heaven,
My peace is secure and my sins are forgiven;
Heaven's doors are wide open, the faith take the venture,
With the heirs of glory to make the grand enter.
    With the, &c.

ANN WARD.

TWO HUNDRED AND TWENTY-SEVENTH SONG.
(TUNE, 'When I spent all my money I gain'd in the wars.')

MY heart doth rejoice and I live now in peace,
  No longer in bondage I see;
The Father and Son I have found is but one,
  To my joy everlastingly.

2.

The spirit within was the Father alone,
  And the flesh that cloth'd, it was the Son,
'Tis prov'd so in the third record,
  By great Reeve and Muggleton.

3.

What mysteries they did declare,
  Than any before them did do;
But persecuted for the truth,
  As our Lord before them was too.

4.

When he told them of heavenly things,
  They despis'd and blasphem'd too,
And crucified him at the last,
  Blood and water from his side did flow.

5.

But at the third day our Lord did arise,
   Triumphant o'er death and the grave;
And gave his apostles commission
   To preach the Gentiles and save.

6.

But in this last confus'd age,
   Two prophets he did then inspire,
To fulfil the third and last record,
   The last until time be no more.

7.

Then at the word, 'come, ye blessed,' we shall rise
   In triumphs to soar up above,
To meet our king and redeemer,
   For ever to live in his love.

8.

Then in harmony we shall all join,
   In praises to him we shall sing;
Our tongues shall sound forth hallelujah,
   To Zion's most glorious king.

                         FREDERICK CATES.

TWO HUNDRED AND TWENTY-EIGHTH SONG.
(TUNE, 'The blue Bonnets over the border.')

LOVE! Love! sons of our only God,
Why, my dear friends, should we not love one another?
Love! love! sons of our only God,
Christ is our God, and we have no other;
   Darkness God overspread,
   When that his blood was shed,
Then did he enter, oh! death, thy dark border;
   But he rose from the dead,
   To break the serpent's head;
Blest be our God who hath done this in order.
      Love! love! &c.

2.

Now, now, great Reeve and Muggleton,
You are God's last prophets, we see it in order;
Now, now, great Reeve and Muggleton,

We will pass with you into death's border;
   God from death us will bring,
   Praises to him we'll sing,
When that we meet you in heavenly order;
   All saints will then arise,
   To reason's great surprise,
And leave them behind within this world's border.
      Now, now, &c.

3.

Come, come, king of Mount Zion, come,
We long to see thee according to thy order;
Come, come, king of Mount Zion, come,
We long to pass with thee from this world's border;
Sorrows with us will cease,
Thou will our joys increase,
When we are assembled before thee in order;
Reason on that day,
Will rue for the bloody fray,
When they caus'd thy soul to pass into death's border.
      Come, come, &c.

              JOSEPH AND ISAAC FROST, 1829.

𝔉inis.

B. BROWN, Printer, 26, St. John-street, Clerkenwell

www.ingramcontent.com/pod-product-compliance
Lightning Source LLC
Chambersburg PA
CBHW071435300426
44114CB00013B/1443